WITHDRAWN

Mental Health and Black Offenders

Mental Health and Black Offenders

Charles E. Owens
The University of Alabama

LexingtonBooks
D.C. Heath and Company
Lexington, Massachusetts
Toronto

To Bryant Holloway Owens,
my fun son, who has been
so very patient and understanding
throughout this project

Library of Congress Cataloging in Publication Data

Owens, Charles E
  Mental health and black offenders.

  Includes bibliographical references and index.
  1. Afro-American prisoners—Mental health services. 2. Criminal jus-
tice, Administration of—United States. 3. Prisons and race relations—
United States. 4. Racism—United States. 5. Mental health services—
United States. I. Title.
RC451.5.N4095   362.2   79-19588
ISBN 0-669-02645-X

Published simultaneously in Canada.

Printed in the United States of America.

International Standard Book Number: 0-669-02645-X

Library of Congress Catalog Card Number: 79-19588

Contents

Contents

List of Figures
and Tables

Figures

Tables

Foreword

One historical obstacle to heightened awareness and correction of racial discrimination in the mental-health professions has been the virtual absence of minority members. In the last few years, however, minority enrollment in mental-health graduate programs has slowly inched higher. Slowly rising numbers of minority students have been accompanied by even slower rises in the numbers of minority faculty. Still, these students and faculty together have developed the beginnings of a psychology and social work of minority Americans, particularly a psychology of blacks, studied by blacks and taught by blacks. This psychology of black Americans surfaces in specialized journals, in black-psychology and black-studies courses, and in studies of the particular problem areas of minorities. Thus, health and nutrition problems have been studied, education and employment problems have been investigated, and the problems of black citizens in conflict with the law and the legal system have begun to be delineated.

This book combines two areas of knowledge: mental-health concerns and legal conflicts. Mental-health professionals are attributed a great deal of power—much more than they attribute to themselves—in influencing the lives and futures of black offenders. Prison diagnosis and classification and psychotherapy are among several realms in which the lives of black clients may be influenced. Such influence has wide-reaching negative and harmful possibilities. However, a much more positive contribution is seen for mental-health professionals working with minorities in the schools, the family, and the community.

When a team of mental-health professionals gathers to evaluate a black offender, the discussion will most likely not include how accurately the evaluation methods apply to blacks. If one or more of the professionals is black, then it is possible that some racial bias of the procedure will be noted, but again little more is done. After all, what is expected is that the professional will act within the mainstream of contemporary social work or psychology, and no current of regularly applied knowledge specific to black offenders flows through that stream.

The issue of hidden racial biases within the evaluation or treatment should be raised at every stage at which offender decisions are made. However, the people who raise such issues quickly become frustrated at the extent to which nothing changes. For some who persist, an unfortunate and sad metamorphosis takes places; individuals who were idealistic, hopeful, and committed become bitter, derisive, and destructive.

In this book, Charles Owens offers an alternative both to diffuse indifference and to futile, pejorative attacks on biased practices with black offenders. While carefully and thoughtfully acknowledging the nature and limits of such bias, this book takes the next step; it presents serious, constructive, and realistic alternatives. Charles Owens is a person unusually well suited to encourage such constructive commitments. As a young man, he passed through Alabama when George Wallace was physically attempting to block admission of the first black student to the University of Alabama. Charles vowed that he would return and teach at that university someday—a vow he kept. His other work as well—in the schools and prisons and with families—has reflected the feasibility of what he preaches.

His constructive proposals include self-help models; that is, black offenders relying on and helping one another in personal growth and adjustment, not trusting or depending upon mental-health professions. One such effort, which is developed and expounded, is the Black Muslim movement in American prisons. The Black Muslims are seen as a cohesive philosophy and force that directs members toward respect for rules, other people, and positive ways of living. Loyalty toward one another and deep investment in a persuasive, religious code of ethical behaviors serve to bring out some of the best qualities in members.

Although scholarly writings are taking notice of minority issues, an imbalance is found when one examines discussions of black offenders and the mental health of blacks in criminology texts and journals. Such an examination reveals that blacks have been ignored or presented in limited ways. This book offers an important handhold in starting to redress that imbalance.

Stanley L. Brodsky
The University
of Alabama

Preface

Some years ago, a young, enthusiastic, soon-to-be director of a residential program for reintegrating ex-inmates into the community was discussing the scope of his program. He described the progressive program philosophy, the spacious facilities, and the liberal requirements for admission into the program. The program was located in an urban setting, and the population served was approximately 75 percent black males. The young man, rather proudly and matter-of-factly, mentioned that the staff included two psychologists who conducted therapy groups and that each ex-inmate was required to attend as part of his reintegration program.

I was surprised that therapy groups were required, and I asked him why he felt that psychologists were needed and why ex-inmates should be required to attend therapy groups. After a moment or two of reflection, he responded that therapy would be good for the ex-inmates, because many would have emotional problems, and group attendance was written into the grant that funded the program.

At a later date, a friend who had been working as a counselor with a similar program located in a southern urban area in a state with over a 60 percent black prison population asked for some input into the operation of his program. As we talked about the program, he described the services offered to the ex-inmates, including medical care, postprison employment assistance, a financial stipend, and temporary lodging. The geographical limits of the program restricted the clientele to ex-inmates from one county. Approximately 90 percent came from the major city in the county, and 85 percent of these were black.

In order to qualify for the program services it was mandatory that every inmate complete a personality inventory. However, in all the written material to the inmate about the program, there was no mention of this requirement. In fact, if the inmate refused to take the test, he would not be eligible for the program. I asked the counselor why inmates were required to take a personality test, and if he was aware of the questionable use and interpretation of personality inventories with blacks. He said that the tests were administered to all (regardless of whether their offenses were precipitated by emotional problems, or whether or not they had immaculate prison records) to determine if they had personality problems, so that some assurance could be given to employers that the client was emotionally stable. The test was deemed necessary to the survival of the program, and mandatory testing was written into the grant that funded the program.

In 1976, during the early phases of the court-mandated Alabama Prison Classification Project, a similar incident occurred while classifying a black inmate. One of the interviewers recommended that the inmate be referred for therapy. When asked to explain the rationale for the recommendation, in view of the fact that his behavior in prison had indicated that he was functioning at an acceptable emotional and social level, the interviewer explained that the personality test taken by the inmate some months earlier had indicated that he had some psychological problems. When queried further as to what she thought therapy could accomplish and what behavior the inmate should exhibit before he would be considered emotionally fit, the interviewer was unable to provide a satisfactory response.

There have been many similar conversations at different levels of criminal justice with different mental-health professionals. These conversations are perhaps the most pronounced and clearest examples of irregularities in the application of mental-health services to the black offender. The substance of these interactions indicates a lack of understanding of the proper role of the mental-health professional in the criminal-justice system and highlights some serious doubts about the relevance and appropriateness of mental-health services to the black offender. Issues of forced therapy, the use of inappropriate diagnostic instruments, biased test interpretation, and inappropriate labeling and referrals of blacks are just some of the issues that must be addressed by mental-health professionals as they interact with black offenders.

These situations and misunderstandings prompted the writing of this book, for if mental-health professionals are to fulfill their functions for all segments of society, they must not repeat or perpetuate the injustices and insensitivities to black clients that have been perpetrated in the past.

Acknowledgments

Most of all, I am indebted to my wife, Otis Holloway Owens, who has been a tremendous help in writing this book. Her contributions touch every page. Her keen insight, efficient organizational skills, and wealth of knowledge influenced the content from start to finish.

A number of other people have also been helpful: Jimmy Bell, Charles Crockrom, Anita Merriweather, Ruby Ryles, Vaughn Williams, Eileen Christi, Al Shaw, Christal Reed, and Harrell Roberts. They assisted in a number of ways, but most of all provided insight into the complex role of black mental-health professionals.

Many colleagues, students, and special friends provided research, encouragement, support, and inspiration. Stanley Brodsky, Jerry Rosenberg, Richard Tapscott, Jean and Marshall Garrett, Al Jackson, Barbara Critton, Charlotte Clark, and Gail Morgan were especially helpful. Mike Lindsey's contribution extends beyond the chapter he has written. Many of his ideas and concerns permeate the entire book. He has been a valuable resource.

A very special thanks is due the countless number of black offenders and ex-offenders across the country who have provided insight and understanding of their experiences and concerns with mental-health professionals and criminal-justice personnel. Mitchell Minor and Leon Kennedy (Akbar Ali) provided a wealth of information. I sincerely hope that in some way the publication of this book makes their lives a little bit easier and a little more meaningful.

Conferences of the National Association of Blacks in Criminal Justice and the National Association of Black Psychologists provided a rich learning environment for the accumulation of ideas and valuable information. Many conference individuals provided needed feedback and constructive criticism.

Several typists assisted in the initial and final drafts of the book: Dianne Wagner, Leona Johnson, Marilyn Matthews, Betty McGinley, and Brendal Brown. I am deeply thankful for their patience, time, and effort.

Introduction

It was inevitable that mental-health issues would eventually catch up to the prisons and the criminal-justice field. The prison riots that highlighted the inhumane conditions in prisons, pressure from concerned citizen groups for rehabilitation, and the intervention of the courts stimulated the entrance of mental health into the criminal-justice system.

The advent of the new mental-health thrust in corrections and criminal justice has provided access to offenders and employment to professionals in mental health. These professionals, individually and collectively, have been given license to fulfill the mandate of protecting the civil rights and mental health of offenders. Armed with ammunition from the courts and psychological concepts, mental-health professionals are finding a new and fertile frontier in criminal justice. Even prison guards are being converted into correctional counselors to assist in the mental-health effort.

The interface of criminal justice and mental health has instigated many philosophical arguments and debates regarding the proper role of the mental-health profession in such a system. Are the goals of the mental-health profession in conflict with the purposes of the criminal-justice system, which is designed to punish and control? To whom does the mental-health worker owe his allegiance—inmates or administration? Although these debates continue and will continue for many years, the fact remains that mental health has become entrenched in criminal justice, and from all indications the partnership will remain for quite a while.

Not so long ago, working in a criminal-justice setting—especially in institutions—was not very desirable employment for a mental-health professional. Many factors contributed to this negative image. Perhaps it was the location of the institutions; most large prisons are in rural settings. Perhaps it was the low salary or the lack of adequate space and facilities or the conflict of philosophies. Maybe it was the pervasive feelings of helplessness, powerlessness, and loneliness in trying to divert a system bent on punishing to one of concern for an individual's psychological development. There is no doubt, however, that the image of the criminal-justice setting is changing as many mental-health workers are now becoming involved with the criminal-justice system. More psychiatrists, psychologists, social workers, and counselors are beginning to find the criminal-justice field a lucrative area, and more criminal-justice agencies are reaching out for psychological assistance. The proliferation of mental-health-related criminal-justice organizations, periodicals, and programs in the last decade are a testimonial to this merger.

Not only is the number of mental-health professionals increasing, but the range of employment opportunities and services also reflects a noticeable shifting and expansion. The earlier role of the mental-health worker seemed to be primarily to ascertain the mental-health status of the individual at the bidding of the court. These determinations of mental-health status were then used by the court to determine the disposition of the individual offender. There were two critical points where the mental-health professional made his contributions. As an expert witness he shared information on some aspect of psychopathology that could assist the court in determining the extent of the influence of emotional factors in the commission of a crime. In the presentence investigation the mental-health professional accumulated data relevant to the offender's social, financial, and emotional background and made recommendations about a person's emotional and psychological potential for probation consideration.

The utilization of the mental-health worker in criminal justice now seems to be much more involved with the total experience of offenders, from beginning to end. In addition to therapy and assessment in general, some of the other possible services performed by professionals are as follows.

1. *Staff Services.* Mental-health professionals can train various staff members of the criminal-justice system to become sensitive to their own feelings and to become more attuned to the needs and lifestyles of those they come in contact with. This can include human-relations training for law-enforcement officers, correctional officers, residential-center personnel, probation and parole officers, and other staff personnel.

2. *Pre-release Services.* Ascertaining the mental-health status and emotional need level of the individual for suitability for reassignment to work-release centers, halfway houses, and the community are vital services performed by mental-health workers. Evaluating the home or other aftercare facilities for appropriate referral is also a needed service.

3. *Community Programs.* Various counseling, therapeutic, and testing services are provided in diversionary programs, postrelease programs, drug-abuse programs, and other community programs for offenders and ex-offenders.

4. *Consultant and Research Services.* Mental-health professionals are also utilized on an on-call basis to perform highly technical and special services, such as ascertaining the sanity of an offender, administering specialized testing, and assisting in research design and data collection.

Since mental-health professionals provide the same services to all offenders in the system, many have asked: Why write about black offenders and mental health? Why not write about all offenders? The most obvious reason is that the black man has been a central figure in both the criminal-justice system and mental health. Criminal justice has been criticized for its oversensitivity to blacks. Statistically, blacks in the criminal-justice system have always been represented in numbers disproportionate to their percentage in the population. Excessive police brutality and sentencing disparities have been cruel realities of the black experience. The highly emotional topics of crime in the streets and muggings have direct reference to blacks. In fact, it is difficult to talk about the crime problem at any level without reference to blacks.

Conversely, the mental-health profession has been severely criticized for its lack of sensitivity and responsiveness to the black population. Concerns have been expressed and issues raised about the relevance of psychological services and techniques, the level of sensitivity of mental-health workers, the tests and test interpretations, the standards by which the mental health of blacks have been judged, and the questionable effectiveness of mental-health workers with black nonprison populations. These concerns are sufficient reasons to ask if mental-health workers can be more effective with black offenders than with black nonoffenders. Is there something about blacks in the criminal-justice system that would make them more responsive to these services? What are some of the mistakes that mental-health professionals make with black nonoffenders that they should not make with black offenders?

Finally, the 1978 Task Panel of the President's Commission on Mental Health acknowledged that racism continues to be an insidious influence in the lives of blacks and in the delivery of mental-health services to them. They made the following recommendations for mental-health systems: (1) Racism must be clearly understood as a phenomenon in this country, with its socioeconomic and intrapsychic components. (2) One must then explore and understand how these phenomena can and do function as a stress factor for black people, as a force that results in adaptive and/or maladaptive behavior in black people, and as material that becomes part of the content of the symptomatology of various functional disorders. In addition, one must gain the ability to understand the difference. (3) Training programs must be designed in such a way as to help therapists develop the sensitivity to and understanding of these issues. (4) This sensitivity and understanding must then be a backdrop for the development of service-delivery models and the underpinning of the content/process of the various psychotherapies as they are used with black populations (p. 823).

This book is designed to address these issues and to enlighten those mental-health professionals who share some concern for the mental health of the black offender, for the criminal-justice system, and for the role of mental-health professionals in interacting with black offenders. It can be used as an aid to assist the mental-health professional in making the transition from the classroom to the prison, from the theoretical to the practical, and from the pleasant to the unpleasant. It provides an understanding of the very visible and overrepresented black population in the criminal-justice system.

The book comprises nine chapters. A review of the function criminal-justice system and the relationship between the criminal-justice system and the black population within that system is provided in chapter 1, "Victims of Justice." Research on causal factors of black crime and the role that mental-health professionals have played in criminal justice are also presented.

In chapter 2, "Black Offenders: Psychopathology and Mental Health," an evaluation and discussion of black mental health and mental illness are presented.

Chapter 3, "The Black Experience behind Bars" describes the nature of prison environments and prison relationships. The expectations of black inmates in reference to a mental-health professional are discussed.

An investigation of current classification programs is presented in chapter 4, "Classification and Assessment." The appropriateness of various diagnostic and testing methods is discussed.

Chapter 5, "Therapeutic Intervention," reviews relevant research on therapeutic models presently used in penal settings, and some of the problems associated with the use of therapy with blacks are addressed.

"Preventing Black Crime," chapter 6, focuses on the black family, community, and schools as vehicles for crime prevention. The role of the mental-health professional in crime prevention is discussed.

Chapter 7, "Mental-Heath Professionals as Agents of Change," presents strategies by which the mental-health professional can alter the criminal-justice system and reduce racial friction.

Chapter 8, "Black Mental-Health Professionals," is an overview of emotional stresses and strains peculiar to black mental-health professionals. Survival techniques for the black mental-health worker are delineated.

In chapter 9, "Moving Away From Dead Center: The Challenge," positive courses of action for mental-health professionals working with black offenders are presented.

This book is intended for mental-health professionals in criminal justice at all levels: psychiatrists, psychologists, social workers, counselors, and mental-health technicians. In addition, it is designed to serve as a resource book for undergraduate and graduate students in criminal-justice and mental-health programs.

1 Victims of Justice

There is a popular phrase that epitomizes the concerns that blacks have about the role that the helping professions are to assume in criminal-justice settings: "association brings assimilation." For blacks, in general, the criminal-justice system has been a negative experience and this linkage of the mental-health professional to the system has caused many blacks to distrust both the professional and the therapeutic process. The mental-health worker, therefore, is faced with the monumental challenge to maintain autonomy and integrity while being responsive to black offenders who hold a negative image of the criminal-justice system. Central to the development of a therapeutic relationship with black offenders is an understanding of the function of the criminal-justice system, the frame of reference of the black population, and the relationship between the two.

The Criminal-Justice System

The criminal-justice system is a legal system which derives its authority from the legislative, judicial, and executive branches of government. These same branches of government are charged with the responsibility of protecting the American society from those who offend against its laws, by providing the legal framework for the apprehension, adjudication, and incarceration of persons who commit crime. These protective functions are carried out by four separate agencies: the police, the courts, correctional instituions, and probation and parole officials. Conceptually these agencies are part of a network of ongoing relationships designed to process offenders throughout the criminal-justice system. In this process there are three basic stages—input, throughput, output—where critical decisions are made that effect the movement of the offender through the various agencies of the system (Coffey, Eldefonso, and Hartinger, 1974).

The Input Stage

The decisions made in the input stage determine which offenders will penetrate and be processed by the system. The initial actions of the police to apprehend an offender and the subsequent behavior of the officer with the offender are determining factors in the process. If the officer decides not to pursue or arrest or decides to release an individual, then the person will not become a part of the system at that point.

After apprehension of the accused, further determinations affecting entrance into the system are made by personnel in the legal structure composed of judges, district attorneys, and defense attorneys. The depth and scope of the input such as who will be prosecuted through the courts, the charges, guilt or innocence of the suspect, release on bail, length of sentence, probation, institutional assignment, pretrial diversion, and the countless decisions that affect how the person will enter the system are determined by this group.

A number of alternatives exist in the input stage, including diversion programs and alternate sentencing plans for youthful offenders, first offenders, victimless crime offenders, and non-violent crime offenders.

The Throughput Stage

Deciding what happens to a person after being legally designated an offender is a major decision to be made in the throughput stage. The type of programs and services available to the offender can influence the present behavior of the offender and preparation for reentry into society. Principal personnel in this stage are wardens, administrative staff, program personnel, and correctional officers.

Earlier practices of the throughput stage included isolation, penitence, and spiritual uplifting as the necessary elements to influence the offender's behavior. Later, hard labor, severe punishment, long sentences, and a regimented environment were deemed more appropriate. More recently, however, the notion of vocational and educational training programs, expanded inmate rights, contract release centers, adequate living and recreational space, and other more humane interactions at all levels have been advanced to assist in the humanizing of the institution in rehabilitation.

The Output Stage

After a required period of time in the throughput stage, the release of the inmate from the institutional setting to other environments becomes paramount, since all but 2 percent of those in prisons will eventually be returned to the community. Parole boards and parole officers render decisions that determine offenders' release date, follow-up supervision, conditions of release, community integration, and reentry into the system. Community programs such as halfway houses and alcoholic and drug treatment programs are important services in this stage.

These three stages need not be mutually exclusive. They could work together in a coordinated endeavor to accomplish their protective function and to assure an equitable and just system. Unfortunately, a coordinated and harmonious working relationship among components of the criminal-justice system's input-throughput-output stages has been cited as a major factor prohibiting the achievement of the mission of the criminal-justice system.

The uncoordinated and, at times, rocky relationship among the processing stages has prompted many to challenge whether the use of the term "system" is an appropriate and accurate description of the criminal-justice process. Consequently, it has been suggested that the use of the term "nonsystem" is more appropriate (Coffey et al., 1974). The word "system" implies a degree of organization, planning, and coordination between various segments working toward a common objective.

Contrary to most systems, however, there is no person or agency responsible for coordinating and controlling the entire criminal-justice system. Each agency is independent and autonomous, with separate budget and responsibility. The concerns and responsibilities of the police, for example, differ quite drastically from those of other segments of the system, such as the judge and the correctional administration. The net result in all too many cases has been the emergence of power struggles, communication gaps, and other negative factors which have hampered rather than facilitated an effective and smoothly operating justice system.

Each of the various components tends to point an accusing finger at the other agencies for the failings of the criminal-justice system. The police frequently mention the courts as being responsible for the rising crime rates because of their lenient sentencing policies which return the criminal to the streets. The courts, on the other hand, can point to the failures of police personnel who apprehend lawbreakers and who, in some cases, commit legal blunders even after capture that pave the way for the release of the accused on constitutional irregularities. Correctional officials, in their defense, have stated that they could do a better job of rehabilitation if a higher-quality criminal were sent to prison and if the communities could find jobs for the ex-offenders. These territorial defenses have contributed to conflict and disharmonious working relationships among the criminal-justice agencies.

Because of the lack of system coordination and other factors, a number of criticisms have been lodged against the criminal-justice process. Every aspect of the system has been attacked because of its failure to meet expectations of various segments of society. The rising crime rate, recidivism rates, the slowness of the courts, the inhumane and crowded living conditions of prisons, plea bargaining, the bail system, sentencing disparities, and inadequate parole and probation supervision have all been concerns expressed by different segments of society.

The Black Experience and Criminal Justice

The main objection of the system, however, especially by blacks and other minorities, has been the application of discretionary power throughout the criminal-justice process. This discretion in the system has been statistically reflected by the small number of arrests resulting in convictions, and even fewer convicted offenders subsequently incarcerated. For example, in 1965 1,780,000 people were arrested, 177,000 were convicted, and 63,000 went to prison (President's Commission, 1967).

It appears that decisions are being rendered which reduce the number of individuals trapped in the system but conversely increase the disproportionate percentage of low income and minority group members processed in the criminal-justice system. A number of studies have shown that blacks, when compared to their white counterparts, are more likely to be involved in the input stage, more likely to continue through the throughput stage and remain longer, more likely to be treated severely, less likely to get into the output stage, and less likely to be in positions to make crucial decisions in each of the three stages (Nagel, 1966; Overby, 1972; Wolfgang, 1958).

The discrepant treatment of blacks in the criminal-justice process is not a new phenomenon and is deeply rooted in American history. Beginning with the slave period, blacks were not considered equal to whites and thus the treatment of blacks was not equal. The early slave codes outlined the inferior position of the black man to the legal, social, and economic systems, and provided the center of gravity for the arbitrary and lopsided justice that has followed blacks well into the twentieth century. Specifically, the codes prevented blacks from having rights in the courts, owning property, and being witnesses against any white. The Constitution very directly declared that slaves were to be considered less than human beings, in fact, "three-fifths of a human," and the Dred Scott Decision at a later date reinforced this status by asserting that "no Negro has any rights which a white man need respect." During the pre-Civil War era, any justice administered to black slaves was generally at the discretion of the master of the plantation or by vigilante action.

The status of blacks in America did not change significantly as a result of the demise of the slave system. They were accorded a free man status as a result of the Civil War and the Emancipation Proclamation, but this did not mean an upgrading of equal treatment in the justice system. The devaluation of black life continued in America as recorded, most poignantly, in lynching statistics (see table 1-1). The startling realities of these facts reminded blacks that they were still vulnerable to the capricious justice of whites. In some instances the act that stimulated the lynchings was found to be little more than an insult of a white person (Williams, 1969).

Blacks have always been more easily absorbed into the criminal-justice system than whites during each of the processing stages. Further, blacks were

Table 1-1
Lynchings, Whites and Negroes, 1882–1962

Year	Whites	Negroes	Total
1882	64	49	113
1883	77	53	130
1884	160	51	211
1885	110	74	184
1886	64	74	138
1887	50	70	120
1888	68	69	137
1889	76	94	170
1890	11	85	96
1891	71	113	184
1892	69	161	230
1893	34	118	152
1894	58	134	192
1895	66	113	179
1896	45	78	123
1897	35	123	158
1898	19	101	120
1899	21	85	106
1900	9	106	115
1901	25	105	130
1902	7	85	92
1903	15	84	99
1904	7	76	83
1905	5	57	62
1906	3	62	65
1907	2	58	60
1908	8	89	97
1909	13	69	82
1910	9	67	76
1911	7	60	67
1912	2	61	63
1913	1	51	52
1914	4	51	55
1915	13	56	69
1916	4	50	54
1917	2	36	38
1918	4	60	64
1919	7	76	83
1920	8	53	61
1921	5	59	64
1922	6	51	57
1923	4	29	33
1924	0	16	16
1925	0	17	17
1926	7	23	30
1927	0	16	16
1928	1	10	11
1929	3	7	10
1930	1	20	21
1931	1	12	13
1932	2	6	8

Table 1-1 *Continued*

1933	4	24	28
1934	0	15	15
1935	2	18	20
1936	0	8	8
1937	0	8	8
1938	0	6	6
1939	1	2	3
1940	1	4	5
1941	0	4	4
1942	0	6	6
1943	0	3	3
1944	0	2	2
1945	0	1	1
1946	0	6	6
1947	0	1	1
1948	1	1	2
1949	0	3	3
1950	1	1	2
1951	0	1	1
1952	0	0	0
1953	0	0	0
1954	0	0	0
1955	0	3	3
1956	0	0	0
1957	1	0	1
1958	0	0	0
1959	0	1	1
1960	0	0	0
1961	0	1	1
1962	0	0	0
Total	1,294	3,442	4,736

Source: Daniel Williams, The Lynching Records at Tuskegee Institute.
Tuskagee Institute Archives, Tuskagee Institute, Alabama, 1969.

more likely to be singled out and to have felt the full brunt of the justice system.

Specifically, in the input stage investigations have generally shown that blacks were more likely to come into contact with the police than whites. The chance of a black citizen's getting caught or arrested on suspicion was much greater than for white citizens. Police were more prone to search out black offenders and to be patrolling black neighborhoods (Johnson, 1970; Barnes and Teeters, 1952; Halsted, 1967; Piliavin and Briar, 1964; Bayley and Mendelsohn, 1969). This aggressiveness toward blacks was also evidenced in arrest rates. Black crime arrest rates have been consistently high. The President's Crime Commission Report (1967), revealed that the 1965 arrest rate of blacks for the Federal Bureau of Investigation (FBI) Index Offenses was four times as great as that for whites; the black arrest rate for murder was almost ten times as high; and for burglary the rate was about three and one-half times as high. The arrest rates in the 1970s also mirrored a disproportionate number of blacks arrested.

Once arrested, blacks were more likely than whites to be put in jail and to be refused bail (Nagel, 1966). Being denied bail affected more than the person's freedom. The probability of being found innocent was found to be greater if the accused were released on bail. Therefore, not being free on bail increased the chances of being convicted on the charges. This meant that blacks were very likely to be found guilty because they were denied bail. In addition, even if they were later found innocent, there was a high probability that they would have remained in jail for a longer period of time than whites.

Because of their low income status, blacks were more prone to have received the services of a court-appointed attorney. Thus, in many cases, the defense of the black defendant has been inadequate, because attorneys for indigents generally did not have sufficient time or resources to adequately prepare the cases on behalf of their clients.

Sentencing of black defendants also has shown a pattern of differential treatment. In 1969 a study of the criminal-justice system by Wolfgang and Cohen (1969) revealed that not only are more blacks arrested, jailed, and convicted than whites, but they are also given more severe sentences. Nagel (1966) evaluated thousands of court cases and found that poor blacks were not likely to be granted probation or a suspended sentence.

In other studies, judges were found to administer two types of justice in sentencing. As late as 1971, an exhaustive study of sentencing practices of Philadelphia judges found that blacks were sentenced for longer periods of time than whites who committed similar crimes (Barlett and Steele, 1973).

Once in the throughput stage, blacks, already sentenced for longer periods, remain incarcerated longer than other groups. As a result, blacks typically comprise a significant percentage of the prison population. This percentage exceeds the estimated percentage of blacks in the general population (see table 1-2).

In some prisons, blacks have been found performing the most undesirable and lowest paying work assignments (McKay, 1972). They were also less likely to be enrolled in rehabilitation programs (Attica, 1972). In other words, they are least likely to be assigned to programs and services that prepare them for a smooth transition into society. However, the most glaring indication of disparity in the throughput stage has been reflected in the death penalty statistics. Blacks have comprised 53 percent of all prisoners legally executed in the United States. (see table 1-3).

In the output stage decisions about parole were influenced by the type of crime, length of sentence, the financial status of the offender, and the possibility for future employment. All these variables acted against the black offender and tended to restrict his chances for early release. Imprisoned for longer periods of time and located in distant rural areas where ties with their families and community were weakened, blacks were usually considered poor parole risks. In addition, their long imprisonment in an oppressive environment increased their

Table 1-2
Percentage of Blacks in Prisons and Percentage of Blacks in General Population, by State

State	Percentage of Blacks in State Prisons	Percentage of Blacks in General Population
Alabama	62	26
Arizona	21	3
Arkansas	48	18
California	32	7
Colorado	19	3
Delaware	60	14
D.C.	95	71
Florida	56	16
Georgia	64	26
Illinois	58	13
Indiana	41	7
Iowa	19	1
Kansas	32	5
Kentucky	27	7
Louisiana	71	30
Maryland	74	18
Massachusetts	33	3
Michigan	58	11
Minnesota	16	1
Mississippi	63	37
Missouri	49	10
Nebraska	30	3
Nevada	22	6
New Jersey	63	10
New Mexico	12	2
New York	58	12
North Carolina	54	22
Ohio	52	9
Oklahoma	25	7
Pennsylvania	61	9
Rhode Island	24	3
South Carolina	59	31
Tennessee	41	16
Texas	43	12
Virginia	49	18
Washington	17	2
West Virginia	15	4
Wisconsin	34	3

Source: Census of Prisoners in State Correctional Facilities, 1973, National Prisoner Statistics. Special Report, U.S. Department of Justice, Law Enforcement Assistance Administration. National Criminal Justice Information and Statistics Services, Dec. 1976.

Note: states with black prisoners less than 1 percent or blacks comprising less than 1 percent of the general population are not included.

chances of getting into trouble while in prison, which further decreased the possibility of early parole.

Many black inmates who were released left the institutions without educational and vocational training that could have prepared them for gainful employment. In a society where it has always been difficult for blacks to obtain a job, this problem was compounded for the black person who was also labeled an ex-convict.

Generally, black inmates are poor when they enter prison and their financial status does not improve significantly as a result of being incarcerated. Lenihan (1975) reviewed the wages paid to inmates at all state prisons and found that only nine states paid inmates more than $1 a day. Typically, the only men with savings were those who were long termers or those who spent some time on work release or work furlough, a number Lenihan estimated to be only about 2 percent of the prison population. He cited one study of prisoners released during a one-year period from an eastern state prison which paid inmates up to $1 a day that showed that 56 percent had less than $50 in savings; about 75 percent had $100 or less; and only 8 percent had over $400.

In spite of low prison wages, most states provide less than $60 gate money to released inmates (Lenihan, 1975). As a result of these and other factors, many black ex-offenders are confronted with overwhelming adjustment obstacles and many found themselves back in the institution. It is not surprising that the recidivism rate of the black inmate is high.

The consistently high percentage of blacks in the criminal-justice system year after year has prompted many to hypothesize that qualities endemic to blacks predispose them to be more criminal in their behavior than their white counterpart.

Factors cited as the basis for criminal behavior overlap. Numerous explanations have been proffered. However, most themes can be categorized, although not succinctly, into one of the following three schools of thought; criminal behavior is the function of either individual responsibility, systems responsibility, or a combination of the two.

Individual Responsibility

Those who see the causes of criminal acts as the result of an individual or personal deficiency, shortcoming, or failure would subscribe to the individual responsibility model. According to this position, the individual's deviant acts are not related to the society or to the culture of which he is a part, but to some internal trait or factor present or absent in the individual.

Biological theories best represent the individual responsibility model. These theories suggest that biological differences between a criminal and a noncriminal

Table 1-3
Prisoners Executed under Civil Authority in the United States, by Race, Offense, and Year, 1930-72

Year	Total	White	Black	Other
		All Offenses		
All years	3,859		2,066	42
Percent	100.0		53.5	1.1
1930[a]	155	90	65	0
1931	153	77	72	4
1932	140	62	75	3
1933	160	77	81	2
1934	168	65	102	1
1935	199	119	77	3
1936	195	92	101	2
1937	147	69	74	4
1938	190	96	92	2
1939	160	80	77	3
1940	124	49	75	0
1941	123	59	63	1
1942	147	67	80	0
1943	131	54	74	3
1944	120	47	70	3
1945	117	41	75	1
1946	131	46	84	1
1947	153	42	111	0
1948	119	35	82	2
1949	119	50	67	2
1950	82	40	42	0
1951	105	57	47	1
1952	83	36	47	0
1953	62	30	31	1
1954	81	38	42	1
1955	76	44	32	0
1956	65	21	43	1
1957	65	34	31	0
1958	49	20	28	1
1959	49	16	33	0
1960	56	21	35	0
1961	42	20	22	0
1962	47	28	19	0
1963	21	13	8	0
1964	15	8	7	0
1965	7	6	1	0
1966	1	1	0	0
1967	2	1	1	0
1968	0	0	0	0
1969	0	0	0	0
1970	0	0	0	0
1971	0	0	0	0
1972	0	0	0	0

Source: U.S. Sourcebook, Department of Justice, Washington, D.C. (1976).

[a]For years 1930-1959 Alaska and Hawaii are excluded, except for three federal executions in Alaska in 1939, 1948, and 1950.

influence whether a person will commit crime and that physiological, morphological, or genetic differences in criminals account for criminal behaviors. Chief proponents of biological differences are the following: body type and physical features (Lombroso, 1912; Hooten, 1931; Sheldon, 1942; Kretschmer, 1925); heredity defects (Goring, 1913; Lange, 1939); endocrine imbalance (Berman, 1938); intelligence differences (Goddard, 1914), and the extra Y chromosome (Owen, 1972).

The biological determinism theories appear especially appropriate to explain black behavior because of the obvious color difference and other accompanying racial traits. In most of the earlier investigations of black crime after the Civil Rights Act, it almost appears that the objective was to prove that blacks were inherently criminal. However, while there may be lingering traces of these biological explanations, a person's race, biological structure, or physiological makeup alone has not been empirically demonstrated to be an acceptable explanation of crime.

The psychoanalytic explanation of crime likewise focuses on individual responsibility. The source of the problem is considered resident in the individual rather than in the environment, with the individual being the target for treatment rather than the external environment. The criminal acts are allegedly committed in response to some psychological imbalances, conflicts, or unmet needs within the individual. The criminal behavior is regarded as symptomatic of deeper, underlying, unresolved conflicts (Abrahamsen, 1973).

Psychoanalytic concepts have frequently and freely been used to explain black criminal behavior. Terms such as displaced aggression, low self-concept, and self-hatred regularly appear in the literature as possible answers to black criminal behavior. Black on black crimes have been explained as unconscious expressions of pent-up hostility. Striking out at a safe object (another black person) allowed the black man to vent his anger and frustration that was unconsciously directed at the white man. Even some acts of criminal behavior which resulted in capture and indicated that the black offender could have escaped have been explained in a psychoanalytic framework as a symbolic attempt by blacks to be caught and punished.

The psychoanalytic approach, while academically seductive, has been criticized for a number of shortcomings. First and foremost is that the influence of the unconscious is not empirically demonstrable in either offenders or nonoffenders. Second, it minimizes or does not account for the influence of the environment. This oversight is a major one since many feel that it is not possible to adequately describe black behavior without noting the effect of the environment.

More recently, Yochelson and Samenow (1976) added fuel to the individual responsibility model by suggesting from their research that as criminals develop they form value systems that are different from those of noncriminals. While there has been a flurry of interest, other investigators have neither confirmed nor denied their position.

Systems Responsibility

This model is at the extreme from individual responsibility. Through a systems responsibility model the individual offender is absolved of any responsibility for the crime. Accordingly, the nature and structure of society and social systems are considered the critical determinants of crime. The individual essentially has no control over his environment and is merely reacting to environmental conditions.

Most sociological explanations tend to emphasize the importance of the offenders' environment in criminal behavior. Generally, there is some conflict or pronounced schism between the group to which the individual belongs and other segments of society (Dahrendorf, 1958; Turk, 1966), including cultural conflicts between socioeconomic classes (Miller, 1958; Bainfield, 1968) and a lack of access to legitimate means of success and goals attainment (Cloward and Ohlin, 1960; Merton, 1957).

The pervasive theme of dissatisfaction and frustration engendered by the environment has been advanced by many writers as a catalyst for criminal acts. Marx and Engels (1965), for example, have pointed out that the structure of economic systems can breed discontentment wthin segments of the population which can lead to crime. Dollard and his colleague's (1965) frustration-aggression hypothesis emphasizes the influence of the environment on the individual's behavior. According to them a frustrating environment, typified by the blocking of goals, can provoke aggressive and criminal behavior.

In the same vein, Sutherland's (1968) differential association theory accentuates the importance of environmental rewards, punishment, and role models in the commission of criminal acts. According to Sutherland and other behaviorists who view crime as learned behavior, criminal behavior is learned in the same way that noncriminal behavior is learned. They maintain that criminal behavior, like noncriminal behavior, is a function of environmental consequences.

The systems responsibility model is appealing because most of the blacks caught up in the system represent a single group of people—low income. Therefore, it would seem that the system or the way a society is structured is very much responsible for singling out a particular group of people to include in the criminal-justice system. Perhaps, the argument goes, if society were restructured or if goods and services were redistributed, poor people would no longer have a cause to commit crime.

While the systems responsibility model may appear cogent, the major shortcoming is that this perspective fails to account for the fact that there are so many others in the same environment, exposed to the same structural differences, who do not become criminal.

It seems evident that the causes of crime do not fit neatly into either the individual or systems categories. As an alternative, many suggest that the causes of crime lie somewhere between these two extremes, where both the individual and the system are responsible for the behavior.

Individual and Systems Responsibility

This view maintains that both the individual and external environmental factors share culpability for the criminal behavior. Central to this position is the emphasis on the individual's association and interaction with the social environment as a critical determinant of future criminal acts. Within this context, the offender is seen neither as a helpless reactor to his environment nor as having total control of his behavior.

Containment theory (Reckless, 1967) attributes criminal behavior to the interaction of an "outer containment system" and an "inner containment system." Included in the "outer" system are external motivating factors such as unemployment, education, and group membership. The "inner containment system" incorporates motivations such as self-control and an adequate self-concept. The unique balance of the external and internal system will influence the person to become criminal or noncriminal.

An interesting view is presented by Letkeman (1973), who proposes that many people commit crimes for the same reasons that people work at other jobs. In other words, crime is a job. Crime is committed in lieu of regular noncriminal jobs. Offenders, by choice, prefer to engage in crime rather than the more traditional and sanctioned jobs of society. While the environment may be limiting and oppressive, Letkeman emphasized that crime can become a satisfying and rewarding endeavor.

The position of shared responsibility is much more palatable to a greater segment of the population because while it is impractical to blame society for all the crimes committed by blacks, the legacy of unequal treatment of blacks in our society cannot be totally ignored as a contributing factor in black crime.

Black Definitions of the Causes of Black Crime

A review of the literature for an explanation of the causes of crimes committed by blacks reveals two rather obvious conditions. First, even though blacks have been overrepresented in the crime statistics, explanations by blacks for crimes committed by blacks have been noticeably absent from the literature. This means that not only has the criminal-justice system been administered by whites, but definitions and theories of the causes of crime, and the interpretations of research conducted on black offenders, have also reflected a white perspective, leaving a lopsided explanation of black crime.

Second, the limited perspectives available by black investigators show no consensus on the etiology of black criminal behavior. The individual blame model, however, is generally rejected as a viable explanation. The primary focus tends to be on the interaction of the individual with the social, economic, and political institutions and systems in America. This was evidenced as early as 1904, when blacks convened at a conference in Atlanta, Georgia, to investigate the causes of Negro crime (Dubois, 1904). Their published conclusions stated that black crime was a complex phenomenon that included environmental racism, victimless crime laws, unequal justice through the courts, all-white systems of control, the social climate, method of punishment, and the unique makeup of the individual.

There is a pervasive belief among blacks that economic inequalities and employment disparities, as exemplified by the large representation of blacks in the low income groups and unemployment statistics, are the root of much black crime. A contemporary study by Davis (1975) of black males in the Los Angeles area demonstrated this point. A sample of black males responded to questions about what they perceived to be the causes of black crime in America. There was most agreement that unequal access to institutions and other opportunities was a critical factor. Davis suggested that certain antecedent conditions existed that predisposed blacks to criminal behavior: (1) a feeling of being discriminated against because of color, resulting in poverty; (2) a feeling that there was no meaningful redress within the legal system; and (3) being willing to accept the consequences for criminal acts.

While the research of Grier and Cobbs (1968) does not specifically focus on black criminal behavior, it does provide some insight into possible motives for black crime. They attribute a greater responsibility to the racial attitudes of society for black criminality than do traditional psychoanalysts. Their research, based on case studies, led them to conclude that as a result of historical racial injustices, blacks tend to harbor angry feelings. Using a basic psychoanalytic reference, they explained that blacks unconsciously act out their anger in symbolic ways, and much of their behavior represents the internal frustration of being dehumanized in a predominantly white society. Using their model, it would seem that some of the criminal acts of blacks are also symbolic acts. For example, mugging white victims may be behavior that allows blacks to vent their anger toward white society rather than behavior performed for financial gain, and raping white women may be a way of getting revenge on the white male for subjugating blacks, rather than satisfying a sexual need.

Frantz Fanon (1965) employed a political and economic model to articulate the causes of black crime. He suggested that the decisions that are made by those in power are political in that they are ultimately designed to maintain the status quo. The majority culture, in their efforts to maintain the power equation, will oppress those who are in the minority and are powerless. In this context there will continue to be cultural and class conflict because efforts by the minority and oppressed to equalize the distribution of power will be countered with resistance from those in power. Even the definition of crime and the administration of the criminal-justice structure will be controlled by the powerful, according to Fanon. This is reflected by the fact that the poor who break the law are more likely to go to prison than the rich who "misappropriate funds."

The concept of blacks as political prisoners was extended and amplified by both Angela Davis (1971), and Robert Chrisman (1971). They consider blacks to be political prisoners because blacks lack political clout to influence and determine critical decisions that affect their lives and, therefore, are victims of a political system into which they have no input.

The overrepresentation of black offenders in the system is viewed by many blacks as the result of built-in covert biases in the system, rather than blacks' being more criminal than whites. The policeman who is biased against minorities will arrest minorities and release nonminorities. Judges, because of their biases, may more often deny bail and probation to minorities. Because blacks are more often sent to prison, and for longer periods of time, they have more difficulty finding jobs than do white ex-offenders.

The inflation of statistics and misleading interpretations of statistics has been identified as another source of a subtle bias that distorts the criminal behavior of minorities. Gilbert Geis (1970) supports the previous assertion in the following statement on the misleading nature of crime statistics:

> Present statistics which pretend to report the criminal behavior of minority ethnic and racial groups both reflect and perpetrate a large number of errors and myths, which can be, in their most innocent forms, misleading and, in their least innocent, both vicious and malevolent. . . . At the same time, it is traditional for the mass media, as well as other agencies and commentators, to ignore the patent inadequacies of such numerical data, to publicize the released figures, to moralize about their presumed meaning, and then act upon them as if they were reliable.

Thus the fact that the etiology of black crime is not easy to explain and that no theory explains all black criminal behavior seems evident. The causes of black crime are as diverse and as complex as the number of offenders. In every black offender there probably exists some partial validation for each theory of the causes of crime, but there is no comprehensive theory to explain *all* black crime. Johnson (1970) concluded that

> the position of the Negro in American Society, with all that this means in terms of subordination, frustration, economic insecurity, and incomplete participation, enters significantly into almost every possible aspect of Negro crime causation. The administration of justice itself is from beginning to end so much a part of the whole system of Negro-White social relations that it must be viewed not only as a process which discriminates against Negroes and thus biases the statistics of crime, but also as a direct and indirect causative factor in the production of Negro crime.

Mental-Health Professionals and Criminal Justice

The role played by the mental-health profession in broadening our understanding of the behavior of black offenders has been both limited and questionable.

For example, the research conducted by mental-health professionals has been rather narrow and restrictive in scope. An analysis of the *Psychological Abstracts* revealed that sixty-five studies were conducted specifically on black offenders and listed in the *Abstracts* over the fifty-year period from 1926 to 1976. These studies were centered on two noticeable themes, intelligence and personality.

During the time span from 1926 to 1945, a significant number of studies focused specifically on the intelligence of the black offender. The implication of this line of research was that a relationship existed between black crime and intelligence. Using culturally biased measuring instruments, some rather ludicrous findings emerged. For example, Franklin (1945) found that only 19 percent of the total black institutionalized population tested with the Wechsler-Bellevue Scales placed in the normal range. The remaining 81 percent were classified as below normal. Watts (1941) compared test results of a delinquent black male population with those of a nondelinquent black population and concluded that both populations were retarded. In spite of concerted and repeated research efforts, studies have not provided consistent and convincing data to corroborate a relationship between black intelligence and criminality.

The other theme, prominent after 1946, focused on various aspects of the black personality to explain black criminality. Using various psychological tests, black attitudes and emotions were dissected and evaluated. Black psychological profiles and family relationships were constructed and examined. The results, similar to the findings from the intelligence research, did not support the assertion that a consistent relationship existed between black personality and criminal behavior.

There are two general conclusions that can be made about the research on black offenders. First of all, black behavior and responses were evaluated by white standards. Utilizing a deficiency hypothesis which emphasizes white behavior as the norm, blacks were generally found to be deficient on practically every personality variable investigated, especially when compared with white subjects. Many studies revealed a clear lack of understanding of black behavior and culture. The most glaring example was the result of an investigation by Yaker (1962) comparing Black Muslim inmates, black inmates who were not Muslims, and white inmates. One of his conclusions was that the projection of the devil into human form by Muslims seemed to serve as a "defense against unconscious, latent homosexual drives." The investigator did not realize that Black Muslims were taught that whites were "blue-eyed devils" as part of their belief system.

Second, the mental-health professional community has not accumulated a knowledge base on black offender behavior that can be used reliably by its membership to guide its interaction with black offenders. Further, it is questionable whether mental-health professionals have amassed any new and relevant material about blacks or if distorted evaluations of black behavior have been eliminated.

Unfortunately, the knowledge obtained by mental-health professionals from years of working with blacks in general may not be the beacon in the darkness that can assist their colleagues. There has been and continues to be serious doubt about the effectiveness of mental-health professionals with black clients. And far from being viewed as assets and vital to black survival they have been seen as appendages of an already existing oppressive and unresponsive system. In fact, many mental-health professionals have simply reflected the social and economic climate of the times. As a result, the treatment of blacks has been simply tailored to the perceived socioeconomic and cultural realities of the day. For example, Malcolm X was told early in his education by a mental-health professional that he should downgrade his occupational aspirations, not so much because of his academic progress as because of his race. Being an attorney was not considered a realistic goal for him because he was black (Haley, 1966).

We cannot begin to accurately assess the number of blacks who have been dissuaded from high aspirations, from achievement, and from positive self-concepts by mental-health professionals who were allegedly trying to help them to have a realistic view of their chances for success. Ironically, it is probably true that many of these professionals honestly felt that they were acting in the best interests of the black person by preventing the failure and rejection that might have resulted from high aspirations in a racist society.

In all too many cases, they have been no better trained to understand black psychological concerns and social problems than any other discipline or institution in America. In addition, the mental-health profession has not seen its role as a societal change agent. In general, the orientation has been toward maintaining the status quo and searching for the cause of black criminality in the psyche of the black offenders. Consequently, they have directed their efforts on individual rather than environmental change. Even today, highly charged emotional debates continue about the proper role of the therapist in resolving a client's problems—whether to work exclusively with the client or to intervene in the environmental stresses that may be aggravating the client's condition.

Judge Bazelon, who was instrumental in the decision on the Durham Test of Insanity and other major judicial decisions, succinctly outlined the scope of the problem mental health professionals are faced with in criminal justice (Brodsky, 1973). Obviously distressed by the questionable and contradictory leadership provided by the mental-health profession to criminal justice personnel, he posed a number of penetrating questions to psychologists. These questions may be paraphrased as follows: Are psychologists in criminal-justice settings doing what they have been trained to do and do best? Are we asking too much from mental-health professionals when we ask them to solve criminal-justice problems that have existed for years? The question that may have added significance for blacks was: How effective can psychologists be when they utilize a mental-illness model to treat offenders who might be in prison because they are poor and not mentally ill? Finally, he asked, are mental health professionals in criminal justice part of the problem or are they part of the solution?

The absence of data prevents an early determination of whether mental-health professionals in criminal justice are part of the problem or solution. However, there is mounting evidence that black offenders have been abused under the guise of mental-health services. In some instances, the mental-health worker has legitimized the mistreatment and other aversive circumstances in which blacks have found themselves. For example, at least three of the court decisions that demonstrated irregularities by mental-health professionals and subsequently have influenced the treatment of offenders diagnosed as mentally ill were initiated by black men, Charles Rouse, Edward McNeil, and Johnnie Baxstrom. *Rouse* v. *Cameron* (1966) stimulated interest in the right to treatment and the prediction of dangerousness; *Edward L. McNeil* v. *Director of Patuxent Institution* (1971) opened up the discussion of the right to refuse treatment; and *Baxstrom* v. *Herold* (1966) concerned due process of mentally ill offenders, and the issue of dangerousness.

Conclusion

The combination of the criminal-justice system, which is ultimately designed to control and restrain and to view offenders with suspicion, and the mental-health profession, which purports to stimulate individuality, personal freedom, and adequate emotional coping skills, is a delicate mixture.

Since mental-health professionals must dispense services in criminal justice settings and within the restraints imposed by criminal justice agencies, it is imperative that they have an understanding of the functioning of the criminal justice system. The criminal-justice system continues to be criticized by groups for its apparent failure in administering justice in an unbiased manner.

It is important to note that at least 40 percent of the population flowing through the system will be black, and in order to work with these offenders it is critical to understand the unique relationship that has existed between the system and blacks. Over the years many stereotypes, half-truths, and myths have been generated about black offenders and their criminal propensities. It is clear, however, that there is not a single theory that explains black crime. Mental-health practitioners have typically not carried out the type of research that has contributed positively to our knowledge of black offenders.

The mental-health professional is faced with the unenviable challenge of applying psychological principles of mental health that encourage free will, independence, and self-expression in an environment that is by nature designed to punish and encourage obedience from the same population. However, the greatest challenge of all is ministering to the mental-health needs of the black population in a system that has traditionally and consistently demonstrated irregular, negative, and discriminatory responses to blacks.

2

Black Offenders: Psychopathology and Mental Health

The continuing concerns of mental-health professionals are the types of psychopathology and the extent of these disorders existing among the offender population. Brodsky (1973) reviewed a number of studies reporting on the extent of mental disturbance among prisoners. His findings revealed that most studies showed that approximately 20 percent of the prison population had been diagnosed as mentally ill. However, only between 1 and 2 percent of the population was found to be psychotic.

Unfortunately, most studies have said very little about black psychopathology and consequently many questions about emotional problems among black offenders remain unanswered. What type of psychopathological behavior can psychologists expect to see manifested in black offenders? Are blacks more likely than whites to be mentally disturbed? Are they more prone to be suicidal? Are they more likely than whites to be excused from criminal proceedings because of insanity?

Historically, blacks have been characterized as both more criminal and more psychologically deviant than whites. This stereotype has been reinforced by their disproportionate overrepresentation in the two major societal institutions designed to control deviant behavior—prisons and mental institutions.

A comparison of blacks admitted to state mental and correctional institutions shows that while blacks disproportionately populate both institutions, the disparity is greater in prisons (see table 2-1). Blacks account for about 40 percent of the national prison population but they comprise only 22 percent of inpatient admissions to public mental hospitals (Task Panel Report, 1978). This basic pattern seems to exist in every state. Blacks tend to consistently comprise a higher percentage of the total number of state prisoners than of the total number of state mental patients (see figure 2-1).

While no definitive conclusions can be drawn from this comparison, there are a number of possibilities to explain this pattern. Blacks as a group may deal with their emotional problems in ways that do not bring them to the attention of mental-health professionals as much as whites; they may not have as many serious emotional problems that require hospitalization; they may act out their problems in a criminal manner which qualifies them for the criminal-justice system rather than the mental-health system; or in situations where the black offender's criminal and emotionally disturbed behavior are equally obvious, the criminal justice system will win out.

The latter two statements are of particular interest to mental-health

Table 2-1

Comparison of Black Male Residents in State Mental Hospitals and State Prisons
(approximate percentages)

	Percentage of Black Males in State Prisons[a]	*Percentage of Black Males in State Mental Hospitals*[b]
Alabama	62	44
Arizona	21	9
Arkansas	48	20
California	32	10
Colorado	19	6
Delaware	60	25
D.C.	95	60
Florida	56	31
Georgia	64	33
Illinois	58	18
Indiana	41	10
Iowa	19	3
Kansas	32	10
Kentucky	27	10
Louisiana	71	39
Maryland	74	26
Massachusetts	33	4
Michigan	58	18
Minnesota	16	2
Mississippi	63	34
Missouri	49	12
Nebraska	30	7
Nevada	22	8
New Jersey	63	16
New Mexico	12	3
New York	58	19
North Carolina	54	31
Ohio	52	16
Oklahoma	25	10
Pennsylvania	61	13
Rhode Island	24	6
South Carolina	59	37
Tennessee	41	15
Texas	43	17
Virginia	59	39
Washington	17	6
West Virginia	15	5
Wisconsin	34	3

Note: States with black prisoners or black mental hospitals residents less than one percent are not included.

[a]Census of Prisoners in State Correctional Facilities, 1973, National Prisoner Statistics Special Report, U.S. Department of Justice, Law Enforcement Assistance Administration. National Criminal Justice Information and Statistics Service, Dec. 1976.

[b]U.S. Census, 1971.

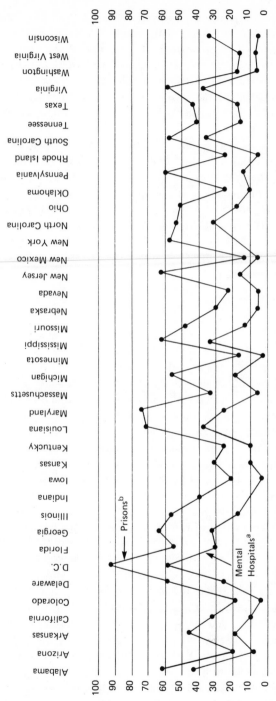

Note: states with black prisoners or black mental hospital residents of less than 1 percent are not included.

[a]U.S. Census, 1970

[b]Census of Prisoners in State Correctional Facilities, 1973, National Prisoner Statistics Special Report, U.S. Department of Justice, Law Enforcement Assistance Administration. National Criminal Justice Information and Statistics Service, Dec. 1976.

Figure 2-1. Comparison of Black Male Residents in State Mental Hospitals and State Prisons, in Percentages

professionals in the criminal-justice system because they suggest that there may be a large number of black offenders with severe emotional problems who should have been diverted to mental-health systems and/or who attempted to solve their problems by using temporary antisocial and criminal behavior. It would seem then that blacks with emotional problems may be routinely routed through criminal justice settings rather than mental-health settings and as a result a higher percentage of blacks in prison should be in need of intensive mental-health intervention.

Undoubtedly the position that there is a high degree of psychopathology among black offenders is not a popular one as many believe that most blacks are in prison primarily because they are black and poor. In other words, the main reason for their incarceration is not directly related to psychological problems. Their problems are that they are poor, lack equal access to goods and services, and consequently commit criminal acts. Therefore, there should be a very small percentage of black offenders with serious mental problems. Given these opposing views, what are mental-health professionals to believe about black offender psychopathology?

Black Psychopathology

The black offender is typically young, urban, uneducated, and a product of the lower socioeconomic level of society. Being from the lower strata predisposes one to a variety of stressful conditions that others who are from different backgrounds do not experience. These conditions are financial strains and tension, lack of adequate education, overcrowding, inadequate goods and services, and limited employment opportunities. Moreover, accompanying these poverty conditions are feelings of alienation, inferiority, helplessness, marginality, and hopelessness that affect both the person's perception of the world and his psychological coping skills (Lewis, 1961; 1966).

Studies have generally shown that persons in the lower socioeconomic class are disproportionately represented in mental hospitals and there is a correlation between the type of psychopathology the person is likely to exhibit and his social class. In an extensive study of the Midtown Manhattan population, it was concluded that there was an inverse relationship between schizophrenia and social class. The authors found that the lower the social class, the higher the prevalence of schizophrenia (Srole et al., 1962). Similar findings were recorded from a study of social class and mental illness in New Haven, Connecticut (Hollingshead and Redlich, 1958). Since blacks form a large percentage of the poor population it is not surprising that they would be overrepresented in admission statistics to mental institutions.

However, studies comparing black and white admissions to mental hospitals have yielded contradictory results. Consequently, doubt has been raised about whether the incidence of serious mental illness is higher in the general black population (Fisher, 1969). For example, some investigators have found that the schizophrenic admission rate for blacks was higher than for whites (Malzberg, 1963; Wilson and Lantz, 1963). Others have recorded that the admission rates were not higher among blacks (McLean, 1963; Pasamanick, 1963). The most consistent finding from earlier studies on black mental illness was that depression was rarely found among blacks (Prange and Vitols, 1962; Wilson and Lantz, 1963).

There is, however, a danger in using data from epidemiology studies to make sweeping generalizations about the mental-health status of blacks. Thomas and Sillen (1972) suggest that admission rates of blacks to public hospitals are influenced by a number of factors, including racism, inaccessibility of private hospitals to blacks and the unreliability of psychiatric diagnosis. Consequently, admission rates to mental hospitals may not provide an accurate assessment of the extent or degree of black psychopathology.

The literature seems to be consistent with their observations. Research results indicate that as compared to their white counterparts, blacks are more likely to receive the more severe psychiatric diagnosis with the less favorable prognosis; more likely to be treated by interns and to receive the most physical type of therapy, such as chemotherapy; more likely to be responded to on the basis of their most bizarre symptoms; and more likely to be referred by institutional representatives to mental-health facilities for mental illness rather than being self-referred (Fried, 1969; Terry, 1962; Singer, 1967; Gross et al., 1969). These factors influence not only admissions to mental institutions, but also the length of time spent in the mental hospitals.

Although both black offenders and black-poor nonoffenders share common environments it may be fallacious to assume that they manifest similar psychopathological behaviors. In fact, in contrast to the rather contradictory picture of black psychopathology in the general black popultion, most studies comparing black and white offenders on mental-illness dimensions suggest that there is less mental illness among black inmates than white inmates. For example, Wholey (1937) concluded from his prison study of psychopaths that white inmates tended to be more psychopathic than black inmates. Bromberg and Thompson (1937) reported on approximately 10,000 convicted criminals seen in the psychiatry clinic in New York, finding that the majority of the population was psychiatrically normal. Approximately 18 percent were suffering from some form of psychopathology. There was no indication of any significant racial differences in the group manifesting mental disorders. Black offenders, however, were mentioned in the group that did not manifest psychopathological behavior. Most of the black offenders were classified in a "shiftless category." This label was meant to describe pleasure seekers whose main ambition was to satisfy their pleasures. Black offenders were also categorized as "primitive." This designation described those who were naive, as most of them had just made the transition from the rural to the urban area.

A later study by Silverman (1946), who investigated 500 psychotic federal inmates over a four-year period, found that blacks constituted almost 20 percent of the federal prisoners but only 12 percent of all the psychotic prisoners. His conclusion was that there was less mental illness among black prisoners than among white inmates. However, he did note that blacks had a higher incidence of paranoid conditions than the general population.

London and Myers (1961) studied eighty-five black and white male offenders, aged sixteen to twenty-six, confined in the New Haven County Jail for ten days or more. Forty-one percent of these inmates were black. They reported no significant psychological differences between blacks and whites, although whites manifested more psychiatric disorders than blacks. Only 30 percent of the jail population was considered mentally healthy, and this group was predominantly black. Schleifer and Derbyshire (1966) used a sample of fifty white inmates and fifty black inmates and found that black inmates did not have higher admission rates to mental hospitals than whites.

Black Suicide in Prison

Suicide rates are another indicator of emotional distress among inmates. Past research has indicated that black offenders were not typically suicidal. When Johnson (1976) reviewed the prison suicide rate, he found that relatively few blacks injure themselves or attempt suicide while in confinement. "We have noted that black men who injure themselves in confinement are unrepresentative of black prisoners; some ghetto blacks seem resilient to the stress of prison" (p. 92).

However, other findings tend to suggest that self-inflicted deaths by black offenders are increasing (Thornton, 1977). Suicide for incarcerated black males is approximately twice the rate of that for the general black male population, according to a report by Wooden (1976). In the Wayne County, Michigan, jail, during the period from 1967 through 1970, six out of ten inmates who committed suicide were black (Danto, 1973).

It appears, therefore, that although suicide rates may be increasing among blacks, black offenders do not demonstrate more severe psychopathology than whites while they are incarcerated. Are blacks more likely to show up in greater numbers in the group of those classified as "not guilty by reason of insanity" or those in an "incompetency to stand trial" status?

Not Guilty by Reason of Insanity

From all indications blacks do not constitute a sizable percentage of those entering not guilty by reason of insanity pleas (NGRI) or those categorized as criminally insane. Steadman and Cocozza (1979) noted from their research on the personal characteristics of the criminally insane that few studies identified the race of the population. Those studies where race of the criminally insane was specified did not indicate that blacks were overrepresented. The majority of those labeled as criminally insane tended to be white, in their mid-thirties, and not married. They concluded from their review of the literature that "we currently know very little about those people we so facilely call criminally insane."

Little may be known about the criminally insane, but there are strong cultural and social reasons to discourage blacks from entering an NGRI plea which may disguise the real extent of black offenders who are psychologically disturbed.

The quality of the legal representation is a prime consideration. Black defendants are typically poor at the time they are arrested, and indigent defendants are usually defended by public defenders or court-appointed lawyers. There is ample reason to believe that attorneys for poor clients may not be as diligent, persistent, and thorough in preparing and researching the client's case as they might be if the client were paying a substantial fee. With poor clients, lawyers seek a speedy and uncomplicated disposition of the case. Plea bargaining is the preferred method of closure since it is more expedient than a trial, whether or not there is a question about the person's guilt or innocence.

Insanity plea cases require the retention and cost of the services of one or more psychiatrists and extra demands on the attorney's time. The probability of being successful with an NGRI plea is extremely low, which might probably account for the insanity defense's being used in less than 2 percent of all criminal trials (Simon, 1967).

Another reason concerns the perceived quality of the sentence by the public. To the general public, sending an offender to a mental institution in lieu of prison is equivalent to being exonerated for the criminal behavior. It means that the appropriate punishment has not been administered for the acts the individual committed. Generally, the more vicious, heinous, and repulsive the acts, the more the public will feel cheated if the person is not sent to prison and the punishment has not matched the crime. When Charles Berkowitz, the "Son of Sam Killer," was found incompetent to stand trial, the relatives of Berkowtiz's victims felt that a terrible injustice had been done to them. Many felt that he should have been executed for the atrocious crimes he committed (Carpozi, 1977).

However, it appears that when race is a variable in the equation, the punitive value of a sentence may far outweigh the concern for the mental status of an offender, especially when the offender is black. In an experiment studying the effects of race and sex on insanity pleas, it was found that race and sex do influence NGRI pleas (McGlynn, Megas, and Benson, 1976). Using white undergraduate college students as jurors in a hypothetical murder case, black males received the NGRI verdict less often than white males, white females, and black females. In other words, black males were held more criminally responsible for their maladaptive behavior than any of the other groups, even though the actual case description was the same except for race and sex.

Similarly, race may have been the critical consideration in a case involving a mentally retarded black male convicted of raping a white woman (*Alabama* v. *Tommy L. Hines*, 1978). The traditional white attitude toward a black man raping a white woman has historically resulted in severe consequences for blacks. Black males have accounted for 89 percent of all legal executions for rape in the United States (U.S. Department of Justice, 1976). Tommy L. Hines, a twenty-six-year old black male, was charged with raping and robbing three white women in Cullman, Alabama. Earlier in his life he attended a school for the mentally retarded. His IQ was assessed at about 35, which is equivalent to an intellectual capacity less than that of a seven-year-old child. In spite of his acknowledged mentally retarded status, he was found competent to stand trial, found guilty of rape by an all-white jury, and sentenced to thirty years in prison.

The Tommy L. Hines case may not be an isolated incident. The extensive media coverage has certainly heightened public awareness of this singular event. However, the extent to which other blacks who might have been mentally retarded or mentally disordered and were channeled into prison rather than appropriate mental health facilities because those institutions were not punitive enough will never be known. It is interesting to note that the governor of Alabama intervened in this much-publicized case, and based on his recommendation, Tommy Hines was reevaluated. Mr. Hines was diagnosed as a catatonic schizophrenic and committed to Bryce Hospital, a mental institution in Alabama.

Finally, as has been pointed out in a number of cases, the person who is diverted from the criminal process into the therapeutic process might possibly spend more time incarcerated than if he had gone through the criminal process. Because of that many attorneys may feel inclined to persuade their poor clients to plea bargain and go through the regular criminal process rather than plead NGRI, even if there is some question about their mental status. These are very powerful inducements for a poor black defendant to not enter an NGRI plea when he assesses the reality of the possible consequences. We can, therefore, expect to find a very small number of blacks who enter NGRI pleas or constitute the criminally insane offender population. Halleck (1967, pp. 216–217) brings all of this into focus by the following observation:

> In many jurisdictions, for example, it would be unlikely that an uneducated Negro offender would plead insanity, and even more unlikely that he would be found not guilty by reason of insanity. . . . Obviously, factors other than the degree of emotional disturbance preceeding the criminal act must operate in the selection of those who plead insanity. It seems that this selection is just as likely to be based upon factors

such as the economic status of the offender, the type of crime he commits, his race, the attitudes of local psychiatrists, the type of negotiated plea which is made with the district attorney or the whim of the community.

Incompetency to Stand Trial

Competency evaluation is a procedure reserved for individuals accused of a criminal act when there is some doubt as to whether they are mentally competent to either understand the trial proceedings or to participate in their own defense. Prior to the trial the individual is remanded to a mental institution to determine if he is competent or incompetent to stand trial. Although the intended purpose of this procedure is to assess the mental status of an individual, many now feel that the use of the process has been expanded to accommodate other needs of those involved in the adversarial process. In some cases, incompetency to stand trial (IST) has been used as a standard procedure employed to delay trials; to suppress controversial and potentially damaging political or social information; and to confine certain undesirable individuals indefinitely without benefit of due process (Szasz, 1963; Leavy, 1973; Stone, 1975).

Those individuals declared incompetent to stand trial form a significant percentage of those confined in mental hospitals. Steadman and Cocozza (1979) estimate that about 40 percent of those in mental institutions are confined for competency clarification and evaluations. The number of blacks confined for incompetency to stand trial is unclear. See (1975) reviewed over 2,200 state mental-hospital admissions records in Florida during 1969 and concluded that blacks were not adjudicated incompetent more frequently than whites. However, Stone (1975), citing Taube's unpublished results of admissions to state and county mental hospitals in the United States, reported that blacks had a higher incidence rate for detainment in mental institutions for incompetency to stand trial than did whites.

Irrespective of contradictions, knowing the number of blacks in an IST status is not especially helpful in broadening our understanding of the scope and depth of mental illness in black offenders. First of all, Cooke et al. (1974) compared blacks and whites committed for competency evaluations and found a tendency for assessors to clinically overstate the degree of psychopathology in blacks. This would tend to inflate the number of blacks involved in the competency process.

Second, it must be understood that incompetency to stand trial is not a desirable status. Other than the opportunity for lawyers to gain time to prepare the defense, there are minimal advantages to an individual adjudged incompetent to stand trial or being evaluated for competency. IST merely places an alleged offender on a "hold" or "frozen" status, and the time spent in confinement in the mental institution may not accumulate to good time that can be applied to any subsequent prison sentence. The person must still be tried for the alleged offenses. In a sense then, the person is a victim of the worst of both worlds; he is treated as criminal and mentally ill. He is automatically denied bail and incarcerated in a mental institution for an indeterminate period of time until his "hold" status is removed.

Therefore it would seem that the data reflecting the total number of blacks in an IST status is not an accurate statement of black psychopathology but more of a reflection cf the manipulation of the IST process by various components of the criminal justice system.

Alcohol Use and Black Offenders

The major implication from research seems to be that the types of behavior black offenders typically display are those revolving around the difficult task of coping as a poor black in an economically and racially unbalanced society. These behaviors are very similar to what Thomas Szasz (1976) described as "problems of living" in a complex society. Most studies, in fact, tend to indicate that the maladaptive behaviors of most black offenders reflect those conditions that most specifically relate to being black, poor, and powerless in American society. The most consistent themes that emerged from a review of studies on black offenders in the *Psychological Abstracts* from 1926 to 1976 were that black offenders more often than white offenders felt powerless, helpless, pessimistic about the future, and subject to feelings of external control. Typical of these studies are the following: black inmates revealed greater expectancy of control being external (Lefcourt and Ladwig, 1966); blacks were more external and had shorter time perspectives (Cross and Tracy, 1971); blacks had more hostility toward police and more feelings of powerlessness (Woodburg, 1973); and black inmates reported more aspiration-reality conflict, feelings of separation, resentment, and pessimism about the future (Costello, 1973).

The use of alcohol is one way that blacks express their frustration and sense of helplessness. In fact, alcoholism is one of the two most prevalent psychiatric diagnoses for both black males and black females admitted to mental institutions (National Institute of Mental Health, 1978). Moreover, blacks are more than eight times as likely to become institutionalized for drug addiction than are whites (Staples, 1976).

The results of a study by Guze (1976) showed that sociopathy, alcoholism, and drug dependence are the psychiatric disorders characteristically associated with serious crime. These areas (especially alcoholism and drug usage) weigh very heavily in blacks coming into contact with the criminal-justice system. In 1975, almost 97,000 blacks were arrested for violation of drug laws and over 220,000 were detained for public drunkeness (U.S. Department of Justice, 1975). Harper (1976, p. 16) showed a strong relationship between alcohol-related crimes and blacks in his review of the literature on alcohol and crime.

He reported that alcohol appears to be a factor in almost half of all criminal deaths in the black community and in a larger percentage of nonfatal crimes. He concluded:

> Alcohol brings out the frustration, anger and courage that lead to homicides and assaults. The etiological factors of heavy weekend drinking, high accessibility to liquor stores and dealers in the Black community, values for heavy drinking in urban America, and the use of alcohol to cope with racial and economic stress are several major reasons that contribute to alcohol related offenses and crimes in the Black community.

It is obvious that black offenders do manifest maladaptive behavior, but there does not seem to be research supporting the view that they are more psychologically disturbed than white offenders. However, restricting our view of black offenders to only black psychopathological behavior is myopic and does not provide mental-health professionals with a comprehensive profile. An evaluation of mental health rather than mental illness may be more enlightening. Since black offenders have not been shown to have more mental illness than whites, do they enjoy better mental health?

Black Mental Health

As defined by the *Psychiatric Dictionary* (Hinsie and Campbell, 1970), mental health is "psychological well being or adequate adjustment, particularly as such adjustment conforms to the community-accepted standards of what human relations should be. Some of the characteristics of mental health are: reasonable independence; self-reliance; self-direction; ability to do a job; reliability; persistence; ability to work under authority, rules and difficulties; ability to show friendliness and love; tolerance of others and of frustrations; and a sense of humor. . ." (p. 338).

The American Psychiatric Association defines mental health as "a state of being, relative rather than absolute, in which a person has effected a reasonably satisfactory integration of his instinctual drives. His integration is acceptable to himself and to his social milieu as reflected in his achievement, his flexibility, and the level of maturity he has attained" (Erlich and Abraham-Magdome, 1975, p. 23).

These definitions are based on criteria that are essentially value oriented. For example, adequate, acceptable, and satisfactory are all defined according to a value system rather than being empirically based. In addition, the definition relies on social relationships and interaction and community acceptance, which implies that a sameness exists among all communities. Erlich and Abraham-Magdome (p. 23) noted this in their critique of the APA definition, which, incidentally, is equally relevant to the *Psychiatric Dictionary*.

The definition places heavy emphasis on social adjustment and is therefore inconsistent with the definition of mental illness. That is, mental
health is defined in a relativistic way as whatever is acceptable to other
people; this will obviously be different at different times and in different places, but mental illness (schizophrenia, paranoia, etc.) is treated
as though, like fever and irregular heartbeat, it had some existence
separate from particular social systems.

Obviously a viable, clear, comprehensive, and universally accepted definition of mental health does not exist. While it is difficult to define mental health
in general, it is much more difficult to apply a functional definition of mental
health to blacks for two reasons. First, judging black behaviors by the criteria
of white standards may be an inaccurate measure of black mental health. Second, only recently has it been acknowledged that racial self-acceptance and
identity are vital components in black mental health.

Standards for Black Behavior

The traditional method for judging black mental health has been to compare
blacks to the majority white culture and to use white standards as the norm of
acceptance. This has inevitably resulted in blacks' being found deficient and
inferior. A study of all research in psychological journals comparing blacks and
whites over a six-month period revealed that almost all interpretations of black
deviations were considered signs of inferiority (Caplan and Nelson, 1973). No
matter what the variable under investigation, any divergence by blacks was
considered a sign of pathology. Although the differences were quantitative,
they were interpreted qualitatively. From these comparisons a mentally healthy
black has been characterized as the one who most approximates white behaviors.
In other words, the more a black embraces the attitudes and values and norms of
white society, the more mentally healthy he is adjudged. For many blacks this
definition of mental health is totally inappropriate.

The black citizen typically grows up in an environment where blacks have
been considered second-class citizens; where race has traditionally determined
status; having been denied opportunities or being aware that others have been
denied opportunities because of color; and living in a subculture that may still
harbor values different from those of the majority culture.

Because of their racial and social status, their access to those conditions and
opportunities that help assure maximum satisfaction in life and positive mental
health has been almost automatically limited and defined at birth. As a result,
the advancements and achievements by blacks have not been as pronounced as
those of their white counterparts. It is very difficult to imagine black people
(who are considered second-class citizens, who are unemployed, and whose
values and behaviors may not be accepted by the larger culture) being satisfied

with life or being adjudged mentally healthy by either of the above definitions of mental health.

Racial Self-Acceptance as a Measure of Black Mental Health

Living under racially defined conditions has been and continues to be a concern to blacks. They constantly redefine their relationship in a society where race is still very much an issue. Contemporary events such as the filming of *Roots,* school desegregation conflicts, and KKK marches not only open up old racial scars but further aggravate the problem as they serve to remind that being black continues to mean being something different.

This concern with being black can influence a black person in very subtle ways. Years ago, before being black was considered fashionable, the story is told of a young black student who always sat in the back of a predominantly white class. It was later discovered that the reason he sat in the back of the class was because he was worried that white people would stare at his hair. Whenever he sat in the front of the class, he found it difficult to concentrate on the subject matter because he was so concerned about what they might be thinking about his hair.

For each black person, the responses to racial conditions and events may be different, but there is one thing that is certain—every black person has at some level and at some time had to face up to his or her relationship as a black person to today's society. This process is inescapable for blacks must come into contact with the major institutions (economic, educational, and political) that are controlled by the majority culture and that dictate the values and standards that blacks are judged and evaluated by.

Blacks who have had early positive experiences, both in terms of racial identity and positive interactions with the majority culture and educational institutions, are more likely to develop racial coping skills and attitudes that allow them to function satisfactorily in both black and white cultures. Accepting themselves in spite of temporary or permanent racial irregularities and discrepancies in their environment frees their psychic energy from the compulsion to achieve acceptance by the larger white society.

Blacks who grow up with negative racial experiences such as being rejected because they are black or feeling that they have received inferior education and services because of their color, may refuse to accept themselves as black because black is perceived as being negative. In still other situations, because of growing up with rewarding situations that reinforce separatist behaviors, individuals may so completely accept themselves as black that they reject any interactions that are nonblack.

There are many different manifestations and gradations of racial self-acceptance. It is probably safe to say that there is a continuum from high acceptance of one's race to low acceptance. If a person does not accept himself or herself as black, he or she will have a tendency to be overly sensitive to racial situations, to feel inferior in interactions with whites, and to interpret all racial stimuli as being negative toward him as a black person. The person tends also to be sensitive to racial stimuli if they overidentify with being black, and is much more likely to feel attacked by racial remarks, to become aggressive and hostile toward whites, or to avoid contact with whites.

These reactions are similar to what Pettigrew (1964) described when he explained how blacks react to and interact with the larger white society, which he designated as the aggressor. He identified blacks who joined nonmilitant black organizations as "moving away from the aggressor"; blacks who joined integrated organizations as "moving toward the aggressor"; and blacks who joined militant all-black organizations as "moving against the aggressor."

Grier and Cobbs (1968) strongly believe that it is necessary for blacks to develop a part of their personality, called the "black norm," to maintain psychological balance in society. According to them, this black norm is a procedure to survive in a predominantly white society and consists of adaptive behaviors developed in response to a hostile racial environment. Thus, blacks are often paranoid in their relationships with whites.

Other black investigators have linked positive mental health with the successful resolution of racial disparity and the acceptance of one's color. Thomas (1970; 1971) and Hall, Cross, and Freedle (1972) independently identified stages of black development in defining their relationship to the larger white society. Thomas's model consists of five stages: (1) *self-hate*—a stage characterized by low self-esteem, hostility and fear, and a disallowment of blackness; (2) *self-pity*—a period of self-denial, self-indulgence, and lingering in one's sorrows and misfortunes; (3) *self-examination*—a stage of exploration of black heritage and more involvement with positive black experiences; one tries out new and different roles and images; (4) *self-knowledge*—a period typified by more involvement with positive black experiences; the black experience becomes more individualized and fewer negative and irrational patterns are exhibited; (5) *self-esteem*—a stage where blacks have realized their own identity as blacks and feel optimistic about being black; they have feelings of worth, confidence, pride, and optimism; they have discovered how they are part of society; they have worked through their racial concerns and have learned to deal with them.

Hall, Cross, and Freedle (1972) observed four stages of black development: (1) *preencounter*—a time when a black person is programmed to view and perceive the world in terms of nonblack, antiblack terms; (2) *encounter*—a stage where the person begins to view himself as black and to understand what being black in America means; he begins to encounter and challenge his preencounter beliefs about himself; (3) *immersion*—a period in which everything of value must be relevant to blackness; the person involved in black culture attempts to integrate the total philosophy of being black into his life; (4) *internalization*—the level where the person focuses on things other than himself and his own interest or racial group; the person has inner security and satisfaction and can have love and compassion for all people.

Hall et al., and Thomas identify the mentally healthy stage as the final stage where the black man comes to grip with his blackness and only then develops feelings of confidence and inner security. When the black man reaches that stage where he can accept his color, then, and only then, is he able to relate to others in a positive manner. His psychological energies are no longer diverted toward manufactured racial inadequacies.

Blacks in a higher socioeconomic level and those who are successful in manipulating the academic challenge have an opportunity to evaluate and clarify their relationship to the larger society. As compared to blacks on a lower socioeconomic level, they have more success experiences, feel much more a part of the mainstream of society, and therefore can resolve their racial dissonance. However, blacks at the lower level of society have much less opportunity to properly resolve their racial conflicts. Many of these are the ones who will populate the prisons, and not surprisingly they are the ones who will feel the full brunt of racism, discrimination, unemployment, lack of education, and insecurity. As such, their perceptions of being black will not be congruent with those who have had a much more satisfying relationship with society.

There are limited constructive mechanisms by which this segment of society can develop its racial component. The feelings of alienation, hopelessness, and marginality fostered by unemployment and lack of achievement continue. In many respects, the commission of a criminal act can become a means of acting out the frustration and humiliation one feels at being black. It can even become a symbol of achievement and serve as a way of becoming somebody. A crime can sometimes be seen as a solution to an emotional conflict. If a person kills his wife, who is causing stress, his emotional stress is removed. In the same vein, for those who feel trapped in a world of unemployment, abuse, racism, and competition, a criminal act removes that source of stress and conflict. It also is a way of striking back at the system.

However, going through the criminal-justice system does not generally facilitate the chances of the black offender coming to grips with his black status. In fact, the prison experience may actually aggravate the feelings of racial friction and distance that cause many offenders in the prison setting (and even after release from prison) to continue to act out their racial frustrations.

There have been inmates, however, who entered prison labeled as antisocial, irresponsible, directionless, hard-core, and deficient in self-pride. These same inmates left the institution with commitment, a sense of responsibility, black pride, and feelings of self-worth. Their manner of dress, their interactions with others, and overall attitude seemed to say, "I am somebody." Black inmates exhibiting these behaviors were likely touched by the Black Muslim philosophy. The process that many inmates went through to become a Muslim is captured in the following letter from an inmate.

1978

Salaam,

Dr. Owens,

My birthing into the Alabama prison was one of my most shocking and horrifying experiences. Even though I'd been well versed on the expectations there, what I experienced was far beyond my expectations.

Within the back of my mind already was that deeply embedded fear, that every man takes to prison with him. He may fear other people, he may fear the environment, he may fear himself; then he may fear the unknown.

The fear I carried was one of myself. One which was self-induced, a feeling of inadequacy, insecurity. Unsure, I felt I wasn't capable of dealing with this environment from an intelligent perspective.

My first entrance into the dungeon-like filthy, wastely environment, was one of disbelief and shock. The environment shocked me, the people shocked me and I found it all to seem unreal.

During these times, older, well-seasoned cons, awaited the entry of the younger ones into the society. They would try to sense fear, instill fear and cominate [sic] through fear, for whatever sadistic whims and desires they had. Even though I knew this, my fears were not of this, but of myself.

My entree into prison brought me face to face with the reality of myself, and I found that what I related to as myself was not a concept strong enough to stand in an environment of the nature I was in. I found myself without any type of positive self-identity or self-concept I could depend upon. Out of this I developed a sense of abandonness, loss or disorientness. During this time I began to read a great deal in the field of psychology to try to bring my situation into some type of undeterstandable perspective.

I didn't want any part of the prison environment; I became totally involved in myself, my books. I thought any day I would go mad, completely. (I thought I already was.)

I seemed for 24 hours inwardly to be wracked with fear. I slowly felt myself losing contact.

I felt at the time so distant from my family, that I didn't write them, and explain my situation. I didn't have any real friends in the prison environment I could turn to either.

All my dreams, hopes, future and aspirations seemed to have dissolved into nothing.

All of this took place during my first five months of incarceration in prison.

Along this time a relationship began to develop between myself and a Muslim inmate. He began teaching me Islam.

I began to become more interested in these strong teachings of Islam and subconsciously hoping it would be a saving force in my life. So I began romping at the heels of the Muslims, seeking knowledge. My personality, intelligence and conversation enabled me to be accepted in their circles, so far as outsiders could.

These were my people, they created an atmosphere I needed to thrive in. The prison environment is a cold, harsh, isolated one. My gregariousness was out of perspective here, and without being able to move to people in the manner I would like stifled me. But these Muslims were all smiles and wisdom. They took me as a part of the family, and for the first time in prison, I slept contentedly.

Within the walls of the prison the Muslims are very powerful in their attracting force. Their principles, conduct and their belief made an entirely different society in the walls, from the confined inmates and free officials.

They were looked upon in mixed emotions of awe, fear, respect and hatred. If they could be avoided they were, and by the same token they were sought after for their perspectives and views on various situations.

In this environment I began to slowly develop a sense of self-concepts which I found to be positive and productive to this day. I consider myself one of the few fortunate individuals, who have been exposed to such a unique experience, and gained the wealth of knowledge available without becoming subject to the debilitating influence that exists there.

Will be glad when this is over.

Hope to hear from you soon.

Respectfully yours,

Omar

Figure 2-2. Letter from an Inmate

There has been some recognition of the national impact that Black Muslims have had on the legal and religious areas of the prison experience. However, even with the apparent success that the Muslims have had with black inmates in terms of raising their sense of worth and instilling black pride, there has been little attempt to study the techniques and process by which they influenced the positive mental-health status of black inmates. Since the Muslims during the 1960s and early 1970s advocated a strong problack, antiwhite, and anti-Christian position, their techniques may not have been seriously considered as a legitimate area of study. Consequently, mental-health professionals have been denied exposure and access to an understanding of procedures that seemed to have been effective in impacting the mental health of blacks in prison.

The Black Muslims prison program was similar in format to Synanon, Daytop, Therapeutic Communities, and other therapeutic approaches that utilized a confrontative process. The goals of the Muslims were to educate the inmate and make him more aware of his environment while concurrently raising his self-concept level. The assumption was that before the inmate's incarceration he was not aware of the external forces that contributed to his present conditions and therefore could not have prevented what happened to him. However, with new information, positive guidelines to follow, and a strong support group, he could hopefully view himself and others differently and adopt a new lifestyle and a new attitude toward himself as a black man. He would no longer look at being black as negative—as he had been taught by the larger white society. He was told that society was sick and oppressive, that life had been rough for blacks, and that it was difficult for the black man to survive in society. Being black and living in an oppressive environment had contributed to his incarceration.

Although Muslims articulated that society was the main reason that black inmates were in prison, they placed most of the responsibility for change on the inmate. They further emphasized that society was not going to change while the inmate was in prison and that he might have to change his lifestyle in order to exist in society. It was stressed to the inmate that even though he was in prison and may have hit rock bottom and had nothing, he could make a choice of whether to continue in life as a loser, or change his lifestyle and become a winner. Akbar Ali, former Minister of Muslims in a southern institution, describes part of the training process as follows:

> We would systematically break him down mentally. Three or four brothers would sit around and would start to talk about our brother until he started to cry. It is almost like brainwashing. We would attack the man's identity. If he was a bank robber, we would all get in a closed session and we would learn all about him. "Tell us about what you did." He would say, "I was from Birmingham you know, man, and I pimped whores and I rolled Cadillacs and I robbed banks." We made him tell it all, and when he finished we would jump him. We would destroy him. We would give him reasons why this behavior was jive and why this was negative. We would explain how he was a disgrace to black people and he had a welfare mentality, how lazy and stupid he was; how he had been made ignorant by the white man by not being allowed access to a better education or facilities,but, at the same time, he was responsible for himself and didn't take advantage of the opportunity to improve. Then we told him we would give him an opportunity to do something for himself. We told him that he has the time to do it, he has got five to ten years so he can do anything he wants to do. We told him that he has seven and a half ounces of brain that moves and that thought travels at 24 billion miles per second. We have a list of facts that we give

him, and after he learns these, we test him daily. We do not give him time to relax or to regress into unacceptable behavior.

Unacceptable behavior, according to Islamic teachings, was called the six. This was behavior a person had learned through television, books, or other man-made influences in society. Anything that a person did, such as selling dope, robbing, and stealing, was behavior that was taught by society. The sixth consciousness level was compared historically to the 6,000 years that the Caucasians ruled the world. The six was called the white man's number. The seventh consciousness level was the God level, and this was achieved when man had mastered himself and his emotions. Seven was called God's number, the black man's number.

One of the first principles of Islam presented to the new member was that *God is a man.* This gave the inmate an initial focal point and provided him with hope that he could become God-like. It exposed him to a concrete concept. This information was then interfaced with Islam (I, Self, Lord and Master). Then systematically he was told that he had control of his life and could do anything he wanted to do. By bombarding and saturating the inmate with messages that he was superior, that he was God-like, and that he could succeed, an attempt was made to undo years of programmed self-doubts, self-hatred, inferiority feelings, and fears of failure. This information was complemented with basic education skills training, the teaching of current world events, and interpreting the relationship of this information to him as a person and as part of the larger society.

Interspersed with increasing skills, techniques that were designed to maintain a state of internal and external harmony were supplied. The basis of these techniques was the set of rules of conduct Muslims were to follow (see figure 2-3).

These rules were basic standards of behavior, and if the inmate adhered to them they would help him to exist within the prison setting in a state of peace and harmony with himself and his environment. They also helped him to become a responsible person. These rules dictated individual conduct in various situations. For example, aggressiveness in word or other acts toward anyone was forbidden. Therefore, if a guard came to an inmate and said, "All right, goddamn nigger, move!" the inmate would try to resist aggressive behavior. This helped the inmate to live in prison without responding to situations that may have brought him in conflict with prison officials.

What the Black Muslims accomplished that others had not was that black inmates were allowed to develop the racial component of their personality. They were able to come to grips with being blacks, being on the bottom rung of society's ladder, and to realize what the effects of racism and a hostile white environment were.

By helping black offenders to develop their racial component, they helped

1. A Muslim must show the greatest intelligence at all times.
2. Never be the aggressor by word or action, but in the event you are attacked, stick together and battle as a solid wall.
3. Obey the Laws of the land or government you must live under, for if you cannot keep those laws, how can you obey the Laws of Allah (God)? But if those Laws conflict with the Laws of Allah, then fear Allah, and Allah alone must you fear.
4. What is the Duty of the Captain and Lieutenant? The Captain.s duty is to give the order to the Lieutenants, and the Lieutenant's duty is to teach the private soldiers and train them.
5. A Muslim's word is Bond and Bond is life, I will give my Life before my word shall fail.
6. A Muslim must always keep purity of Mind and cleanliness of body.
7. A Muslim does not give to the use of oath.
8. A Muslim acknowledges and recognizes that he is a member of the Creator's Nation and acts accordingly to this in the Name of Allah, as a Muslin we must set an example for the Lost-Found. This requires action and Deeds, not words and lip service.
9. We must recognize the necessity for unit and group operation.
10. Stop needless criticisms of your brother; we must remember that jealousy destroys from within.
11. The Law of Islam says that if one brother has a bowl of soup, the other brother has half of that bowl; his success is your success.
12. Be patient in matters where others are involved; remember that there were times when we that know, knew not.
13. Do not take the bad side of a thing that appears to us as bad, as there is always a good side, it is better to take that side.
14. Actions are judged by intentions, actions may appear wrong, but motives bring rewards.
15. Seek not to find fault in your brother; this does not mean to make unnecessary excuses for wrong doing.
16. Only by true repentance and reform can we escape the consequences.
17. If you should see your brother in error then correct him in the strictest privacy.
18. There should be at least two witnesses in order to bring a charge against a brother.
19. Do not pray as Muslims and act like Christians.
20. Muslims should not participate in activities leading from Allah.
21. A true Muslim should act justly not only to other Muslims, but also non-Muslims and even to those who are enemies of Islam.

22. Islam prohibits many things, but they are divided into grades and classes:
   a. Some being unlawful
   b. Others being forbidden
   c. Unlawful things have a great and direct bearing on the moral and spiritual development of man, but this is not true of the forbidden things.

Source: Notes from a Muslim inmate, 1976.

Figure 2-3. Rules of Conduct

turn blacks who come to prison into self-respecting, responsible, proud individuals. Very simply, they gave blacks the opportunity to develop positive racial coping skills in American society. With this resolved, black offenders were ready to move toward positive mental health.

What the Muslims did for blacks can be implemented by other mental-health professionals. In fact, many of the more directive types of therapies, such as reality therapy, transactional analysis, and gestalt therapy, tend to use the same type of format. The basic difference is that Muslims realized the importance of one's racial feeling and racial position in the lives of black offenders and consequently their mental health.

Today there are an estimated 12,000 Muslims in prison. It has been suggested that for every 1,000 blacks in prison at least 200 will be Muslims (Butler, 1978). Not only has the number of Muslims increased, but it also appears that many prison officials are finally beginning to recognize the positive influence that Muslims have had and can have on black inmates. There is more communication between prison officials and Muslim leaders. In fact, at least two prisons have hired Muslim chaplains. Part of this popularity is perhaps attributed to the fact that the Muslims no longer advocate an antiwhite philosophy and are seen much more as a religious rather than a militant force in prison. Whether or not this new image will effect the basic technique used to help blacks cope in a predominantly white environment remains to be seen.

Another approach that recognizes the importance of the development of the racial component of black personality is systemic counseling, developed by Gunnings (1972; 1977). Systemic counseling is a structured counseling program designed specifically for urban youth. It evolved out of a need to provide counseling services to inner-city black youth when it was felt that traditional counseling techniques were ineffective with this population.

One of the central features of systemic counseling is that it does not sidestep the issues of race, racism, and poverty. It allows for an early analysis of the client's relationship with his racial environment at the beginning of the process. By doing this, it gives the individual an opportunity to develop his racial component and reach a state of positive mental health. The process focuses on the system as the source of the problem, not the black youth. The person is told that the system is why the person is having problems. After the youth has had an opportunity to examine himself in this perspective, then the systemic counseling process begins to help him to accept responsibility for resolving the problem through systematic problem solving techniques.

Because mental-health workers have not had to understand or generally be aware of culturally different populations, they may be unaware of what growing up black in America means. Therefore, black behavior can be misinterpreted by middle class oriented mental-health professionals, and determining the presence and severity of psychopathology can be difficult until blacks are seen as a culturally distinct group with unique values and coping mechanisms.

In many cases, however, mental-health professionals are either unprepared or choose not to help blacks to develop this very necessary component, in essence, to help blacks attain positive mental health. Eldridge Cleaver, in *Soul on Ice,* articulated this position when he described how he had been indoctrinated to value white women as more beautiful and desirable than black women. He was sent to prison for raping white women, and the fact that he had been conditioned to believe that white women were more desirable sickened him. This was painful to Cleaver, and his inner turmoil and hatred for white people precipitated a "nervous breakdown" while in prison, which led to a referral to the prison psychiatrist. Cleaver's (1968) description of the session with the psychiatrist was as follows:

> I had several sessions with a psychiatrist. His conclusion was that I hated my mother. How he arrived at this conclusion I'll never know, because he knew nothing about my mother and when he'd ask me questions, I would answer with absurd lies. What revolted me about him was that he heard me denouncing the whites, yet each time he interviewed me, he deliberately guided the conversation back to my family life, to my childhood. That in itself was all right, but he deliberately blocked all my attempts to bring out the racial question, and he made it clear that he was not interested in my attitude toward whites. This was a Pandora's box he did not care to open. After I ceased my diatribes against the whites, I was let out of the hospital, back into the general inmate population just as if nothing had happened.

It is clear that any serious attempt at developing the positive mental health of the black offender must address this issue of the racial awareness and acceptance of the black offender.

Conclusion

Black mental illness is indeed a complex phenomenon, and an understanding of it becomes even more clouded when the behavior is crime related. The insidious influence of racism has prevented an accurate assessment and definition of black aberrant behavior. Historically, black maladaptive behavior has been defined by white standards of behavior. In some cases this has meant that racially adaptive behaviors utilized by blacks have been labeled as maladaptive behaviors.

There is obviously much more to positive black mental health than simply accepting one's blackness. However, it is not possible to realistically talk about black mental health without including racial acknowledgment and acceptance. Racial acceptance helps blacks to complete the "gestalt" that Frederick Perls deemed essential to adequate psychological functioning. Black Muslims were perhaps the first group in correctional settings to reach out to blacks to help them complete their gestalt.

3

The Black Experience Behind Bars

Working in correctional settings poses the greatest challenge to those in mental-health fields because the very existence of these environments signifies the failure of a free society to socialize and control the behavior of a segment of society. Prisons are emblematic of the ultimate and final restriction of basic human freedoms. These institutions produce ghetto environments where defeatist attitudes prevail, and the overwhelming majority of those imprisoned come from the bottom of the social and economic ladder. They provide a conduit for the discharge of sadistic, aggressive, and hostile urges and the erosion of the basic human helping relationships. Prisons, by their very nature, isolate the individual both physically and psychologically from his natural community. To exist the individual is encouraged to restructure his view of what is real and normal.

Mental-health practitioners in these settings are charged with the responsibility to administer programs and services that obviate many of the negative practices and policies of the prison environment. In addition, they are expected to interpret and predict human behavior. Given the history of prisons and the manner in which blacks have been treated in prisons, this is no easy task. In order to effectively work with black offenders, mental-health professionals should have an awareness of the prison environment and its effect on the psychological functioning of black offenders. They should be able to distinguish reality from the myths and stereotypes that have been a part of the folklore about black offenders. They should understand how black inmates survive in correctional settings.

Correctional Institutions as Conflict Environments

Correctional institutions have been deeply embedded in American society since the construction of the Walnut Street Jail and the Auburn Prison in the nineteenth century. There are three major types of correctional institutions: maximum security, medium security, and minimum security. Each classification represents the amount of security and surveillance inmates are subjected to while in the particular prison.

Maximum security prisons house the offenders who have committed the most serious crimes, are considered the most dangerous, and are perceived to be the biggest escape risks. In these prisons maximum use is made of surveillance, control, and supervision. A high percentage of black inmates will generally be found in this type of prison. The minimum security prisons are generally the least restrictive and contain the offenders not considered to be dangerous or escape risks. More freedom of movement and other inmate privileges are available in these settings than in either the maximum or medium security institutions. The medium security prisons fall between the maximum and minimum security prisons. Inmates who have committed crimes that are not serious enough to warrant them a dangerous category would be housed in the medium security institutions.

The classification of the prison is important because of the potential effect on the type of program that a mental-health practitioner is able to administer. The degree of security needed for a particular group of offenders determines the accessibility of the offenders to the mental-health professional and the nature and content of the services offered. Mental-health professionals will be able to offer a wider variety of programs and services in those settings where offenders have more freedom of movement, where sentences are shorter, and where less of the guard's time is required in providing security for inmates.

The early emphasis on isolating the criminal from society influenced the construction of most major institutions in rural settings. As a result, prison guards and support staff have typically been elderly residents of the rural prison community. In contrast to the predominantly white, elderly, and rural guard population, the offender population is typically young, minority and urban. The contrasting age and cultural experiences have contributed to strained relations between guards and inmates.

Fear seems to permeate most prisons and to maintain a natural conflict environment. Those confined in correctional institutions are aligned with either the kept or the keepers. There is no middle-of-the-road position. It is a climate of "us or them."

Inmates have their own general informal social norms and code of ethics that serve to unify and solidify the inmate population as a group and to separate them from the guards. The proverbial advice from the 3 monkeys, hear no evil, see no evil, and speak no evil, certainly seems to undergird these codes. Sykes and Messinger (1971) suggested that the inmates' code could be roughly grouped around five major themes: (1) caution: do not interfere with inmate interest; never rat on a con; do not be nosey; (2) refrain from arguing with other inmates: do not lose your head; play it cool and do your own time; (3) do not take advantage of other inmates: do not break your word; do not steal from cons; do not welsh on debts; (4) maintain self: do not weaken; do not cop out; do not whine; be tough; be a man; (5) forbid prestige or respect to the custodians or the world for which they stand: do not be a sucker. Guards are hacks or screws and are to be treated with constant suspicion and distrust.

Guards also have stereotypic views of inmates and their own code of operation. Generally they perceive most inmates as trying to manipulate them, out to

get them, and not trustworthy. The code of conduct that governs their interactions with inmates dictates that they maintain social distance from the inmates. Getting too close to inmates is dangerous. Touching inmates, shaking
hands, and, in some cases, calling an inmate "Mister" are forbidden acts. The
following letter by inmates (Figure 3-1) describes the tension between inmates
and guards.

To try to understand a prison guard is like trying to understand a
man who is speaking German, when the only language you speak and
understand is English—no communication. The guards have been programmed to think that a prisoner has no rights, therefore, anything
goes. Most of the prison guards take on a beastly and sadistic type
attitude toward the prisoners. Most prison guards are semi-illiterate and
hate and despise more so the intellectual type prisoners than the other
prisoners because the intellectual prisoner asks him questions he can't
answer because it is not in his handbook. The intellectual prisoner
frustrates and angers the guards because he embarrasses his illiteracy
openly so it is apparent to everyone.

These types of prisoners are branded as agitators and are targets of
constant harassment. . .

If a prisoner grumbles about finding a roach in his food, he is an
agitator. If a prisoner grumbles about the shower water being ice cold,
he is an agitator. If a prisoner grumbles about the unsanitation of his
living quarters, he is an agitator. Any time a prisoner grumbles or speaks
out against inhumane and wretched conditions he is compelled to live
in, he is labelled as an agitator. And he is constantly being watched by
the prison guards, waiting for him to make any little slip, so they can
tag him with a disciplinary. On many occasions he is provoked into
committing an infraction.

Most Alabama prison guards only have an average third grade education which is all that is required, standard criteria. Therefore, how is
it possible for these semi-illiterate men to consel us toward rehabilitation (whatever that is), when they themselves need counseling? In
reality they are only qualified to teach us how to dip snuff or chew
tobacco, for we see these semi-illiterate, unsanitary pigs spitting on the
floor daily, not to mention pissing on the side of the building, when all
they have to do is walk about 50 to 60 feet to a toilet.

How can these semi-illiterate share-croppers teach us better standards of life when the prisoners have more moral principles than they
[guards] do?

In order to improve the relationship between prisoners and prison
guards, the standard criteria for hiring prison guards must be raised,

people with humane interests toward prison reform should be placed in positions of wardens, deputy wardens, etc., instead of ex–police chiefs, state investigators, etc.

People who have for years used brutality to handle all situations, people who are anxious to see another Attica, people who thrive off busting a head, or macing and tear gassing someone.

These are the type of people who cause Atticas, San Quentins and the like. To prevent another Attica in the state of Alabama, the concerned public must hear our protest and support our cause.

The prisoners are human. We are your loved ones, product of your society. Help us make our home away from home more human and liveable for human dwelling.

Concerned Prisoners

Source: Open Letter to the Concerned Community, from the *House of Horrors* (Atmore Prison), Concerned Prisoners, 1976.

Figure 3-1. Open Letter to the Concerned Community from the "House of Horrors" (Atmore Prison): On Prison Guards

The divisive nature of an oppressive environment fosters this adversarial posture between the haves and have nots and encourages individuals to adopt such prescribed rules. This was aptly demonstrated by the Stanford Prison Experiment (Zimbardo et al., 1971). This experiment was a simulated prison experiment conducted at Stanford University using male college students as subjects. Students who volunteered for the experiment were randomly assigned to be either guards or inmates. The basement of a building—on the campus—was set up to simulate a real prison.

In order to duplicate the atmosphere of humiliation, emasculation, and loss of individuality that exists in prisons, the students who were the prisoners were required to wear stocking caps, a dress with no underpants, and chains on their legs, and they were referred to by a prison number. Guards wore khaki uniforms and reflecting sun glasses, and carried billy clubs and whistles. The ease with which both groups assumed their roles was amazing. The guards became very authoritative, coercive, and punishing. The inmates, after a brief show of solidarity, soon began to act in stereotypic conforming behavior. So intense and so real was this experience that two inmates had to be released because of severe emotional reactions. The experiment had to be canceled before the scheduled two weeks.

Even the experimenters themselves became so involved in control and punishment that they lost all perspective of their original purpose for conducting the experiment. When Zimbardo, a social psychologist and primary author of the experiment, was told by one of the student guards that he suspected that the student inmates were going to attempt an escape, he reacted as a prison adminis- trator, instead of a behavioral scientist. He commented on his behavior when a colleague came by and inquired about the experiment:

> I described only briefly what we were up to because I was anxious to get rid of him since I thought the intrusion would erupt at any mo- ment. He then asked me a very simple question. Say, what's the inde- pendent variable in this study? To my surprise, I got really angry at him. Here I had a prison break on my hands. The security of my men and the stability of my prison was at stake and here I have to be bother- ed with this bleeding heart, liberal, academic, effete ding-dong whose only concern was for a ridiculous thing like an independent variable. The next thing he would be asking me about was rehabilitation pro- grams. The dummy!

Prison riots in most of the major penal institutions during the late 1960s and early 1970s dramatized the dehumanizing environment of prisons. The grievances and demands generated by the inmates generally focused on their rights to be treated as human beings and requests for improved living condi- tions, medical attention, and more humane treatment in all aspects of prison life. The Attica prison riot was one of the bloodiest prisoner-guard confronta- tions and, perhaps more than other riots, accentuated the oppressive nature of prisons and the conflict between the "kept and the keepers."

Court Decisions on Prison Conditions

While the riots and protests by inmates opened the door to improved prison conditions, more productive results were obtained when inmates changed their tactics. They channeled their grievances through the federal courts, using class action suits. As a result, a number of state correctional systems and individual prisons and jails have been required to upgrade facilities, programs, and services to offenders.

Correctional systems in the south, which annually contain a high percen- tage of black offenders, were the first to be reprimanded as a result of the successful application of class action suits by inmates. The states of Arkansas, Mississippi, and Louisiana were the first three states to have their entire prison systems declared unconstitutional by the federal courts (Gettinger, 1977). It is not surprising that these state systems, with a high percentage of black of- fenders, a low percentage of black correctional employees, and a history of slavery, should be the first states cited for abusive treatment.

There were some common themes of negligence and abuse that surfaced in all these institutions: overcrowding, inmate control, lack of adequate facilities and programs, and cruel and excessive punishment.

Overcrowding was evident because inmates were cramped into institutions that were originally constructed for a much smaller population. But, in addition, the effect of overcrowded conditions led to tension and aggression among the inmates themselves. In these environments, violence was rampant. A physician who examined Alabama prison inmates as part of a court mandated investigation found that out of 2,000 inmates, approximately 1,600 required medical attention for a rape or stabbing (*Pugh* v. *Locke,* 1976). One investigator found that offenders were as likely or more likely to be homicide victims as were nonoffenders. Nacci (1978) recorded the homicide rate in federal prison as 5.43 per 10,000 inmates and 7.44 homicides per 10,000 inmates in state prison. These rates exceeded the homicide rates for the general population. In 1972 there were 8.9 victims of murder for every 100,000 inhabitants in the nation (U.S. Department of Justice, 1972).

Overcrowding diminished the amount of control and surveillance guards and administrators could exert on inmates. In some institutions this led to compromises with certain factions of the inmate population. These groups of inmates were allowed to run the institution and controlled their fellow inmates in return for certain freedoms and liberties. The treatment meted out by inmates who had nothing to lose by aggressive acts against other inmates was considered equal to or worse than the treatment of even the most sadistic guards.

The condition of the physical plant and the quality of the services were added burdens the inmates had to contend with. The broken and leaky toilet facilities; the shabby furniture; the peeling paint; the nonnutritional and unsanitary food; the inadequate or ineffective medical facilities services, equipment and personnel; the lack of educational and vocational programs; and the lack of mental-health professionals were all testimonials to the reality of the low status inmates occupied in the scheme of prison life.

Examples of cruel and excessive punishment abounded. Inmates were physically abused by the guards, and were placed in various forms of isolation facilities referred to at different institutions by names, such as "the hole," "the pit," "the sweatbox." All referred to almost identical oppressive conditions which consisted of separating inmates from the rest of the population for a period of time and then exposing them to a number of severe deprivations and abuses.

All of these conditions, individually and collectively, served to maintain environments of violence, despair, frustration, fear, and inhumane conditions. The common denominator in almost all prisons was that offenders were treated like animals, forced to live like animals, and consequently acted like animals. The basic abuses of inmates were most often expressed through the courts as violations of the Eighth Amendment of the Constitution—Cruel and Unusual Punishment.

The court decision on prison conditions that served as a prototype for other states was issued by Federal Judge Frank M. Johnson in Alabama (*Pugh* v. *Locke,* 1976). In the Alabama prison system approximately 62 percent of the offenders were black. The credit for the initiation of the suit was given to an eighty-one-year-old black inmate named Worley James, who had spent much of his adult life incarcerated. It was said that he sent a handwritten note to Federal Judge Johnson, complaining of the lack of treatment available in the Alabama prison system. His complaint was subsequently combined with other allegations about the inhumane prison conditions and emerged in the form of a class-action suit.

Judge Johnson's ruling was based on an investigation of the Alabama penal system which revealed that many of the same abuses and discrepancies rampant in Arkansas, Louisiana, and Mississippi were present in Alabama. Moreover, it was found that an inordinate amount of idleness among the inmates existed and no rational classification system was available. Judge Johnson concluded that not only were there no effective treatment programs available to rehabilitate inmates, but the total barbaric and inhumane prison environment made debilitation inevitable.

Most prison environments are poverty-stricken environments. They are by all standards as much ghettos and slums as those in many inner city areas, where money and goods are scarce. In prisons resources are limited and offenders are forced, and sometimes encouraged, to prey upon each other for goods, money, and services. They are predatory environments where strong inmates prosper and gain access to certain advantages at the expense of weaker inmates.

Conceptually, the functioning of those poverty settings can be understood by using Maslow's hierarchy of needs model (Maslow, 1968). According to this model, individuals are motivated by a set of needs of differing levels. The needs, arranged in a pyramid fashion, are dependent upon the fulfillment of the needs at each preceding level before the person moves to the next higher need level. The most basic survival needs (food, water, sex, and others) comprise the bottom level of the pyramid, followed by safety and security needs, love and belonging, self-esteem, and the highest level, self-actualization. After a person satisfies his basic physiological needs and is assured of some order and stability in his environment, he then will be able to attend to higher and more abstract needs, such as love and belonging, self-esteem, and, finally, a self-actualized state.

The prison environment, however, does not encourage movement up Maslow's hierarchy of needs scale. Quite the contrary. In the prison environment, where poverty conditions abound, heterosexual sex is denied, fear is nourished, privacy is nonexistent, and individual needs are largely ignored, individuals are forced to be concerned about their day to day existence. Consequently, offenders are primarily concerned with basic survival and safety needs. And in these settings where the quest for one's survival is paramount, staff members, including mental health workers, are perceived by many as only an avenue to assure their survival in an oppressive environment.

In prison there is a tendency to relegate offenders to a childlike status. They are treated as though they are not capable of independent thought and action. Dependency is encouraged and strict obedience is enforced. Autonomy and independent decision-making are discouraged. In fact, inmates are not required or even motivated to make important decisions that affect their lives. Almost all decisions are made for them. They are directed when to eat, sleep, read, work, shower, go to classes, and sometimes even when to use the bathroom.

Lack of Psychological and Emotional Reinforcers

Because of the nature of the prison environment and the lack of quality interactions, very few opportunities exist for the inmate to receive positive psychological support or emotional boosters. Lacking reinforcement or environmental input can prevent inmates from feeling emotionally fulfilled as worthwhile individuals and reinforce negative self-concepts. The countless opportunities, however, for psychological pain and emotional stress are available from a number of sources within the immediate environment, including the guards, other offenders, and instructors.

Even those close to the inmate outside of prison can inadvertently trigger unpleasant emotional states. Parents, wives, and friends can aggravate an inmate in a number of ways. Most of the frustration and aggravation has to do with the quantity and quality of communication. Since prisons are generally located in rural areas, visits can become a burden. Some may visit the offender regularly at first, but these visits become more infrequent as time progresses. In a similar vein, commitments and promises are not kept.

Moreover, relatives and friends, though corresponding with good intentions, may do a disservice to those confined. They may not realize that letters bearing sad, disappointing, or frustrating news can be very painful to those incarcerated, who have very little power over the forces that control their lives or their relatives' lives. Letters that contain themes of debts owed, wives leaving, kids getting into trouble, unemployment and poverty, not being able to visit, accidents, sickness and death, and fights and arguments do not help the inmate feel good. In these cases, no news may truly be good news.

Undoubtedly, a number of methods are utilized by black inmates to survive in an environment where they have little control over their lives, one that does not value human life, is oppressive, is monotonous and boring, encourages homosexual interactions, and isolates them from meaningful relationships.

Inmates who have been abandoned by society, friends, and relatives soon assume their lives to be worthless, but they discover that their bodies can be used to procure certain privileges, protection, and/or monetary rewards. Some offer their bodies for sexual purposes, and others allow their bodies to be used for medical research. For biomedical experimentation it is estimated that inmate subjects receive an average payment of $2 per day. At least ten states reported in 1975 that drug research was still being conducted on their prison populations (Jonsen, Parker, Carlson, and Emmot, 1975).

The unnatural sexual makeup of the prison environment makes homosexuality a major form of sexual release. Although the American Psychiatric Association no longer considers homosexuality between consenting parties a mental disorder, there is sufficient cause for alarm about this behavior in prison, as there is concern that the act is committed involuntarily on unsuspecting new inmates.

The extent of homosexuality existing among prison populations has been the subject of much research. Wicks (1974) reviewed a number of studies on the percentage of inmates who had participated in homosexual activities while in prison. He reported that these investigations revealed that around 30 percent of the offender population had engaged in homosexual relations, and one study showed a rate as high as 80 percent. However, he also found that 30 percent of a sample of inmates released from one federal institution had been propositioned for sex by other inmates; and over one-half the homicides in another federal institution were related to homosexual activity.

The issue of homosexual activity within correctional settings is especially important because of the racial implications. Research has shown that the typical aggressor is black and the victims are white. In a study jointly conducted in Philadelphia by the district attorney's office and the police department, 156 sexual assaults were documented over a twenty-six-month period. Black on white sexual assault accounted for 56 percent of the reported incidences. Interracial aggression accounted for the remaining 44 percent, and there were no accounts of white on black sexual aggressive acts (Davis, 1968). The results of a study conducted at the Eastern Correctional Institution in Rhode Island showed that approximately 75 percent of the recorded rapes involved black aggressors and white victims (Carroll, 1974). The main reason offered for the overwhelming black on white assault is that blacks are symbolically acting out their revenge against a white society by humbling the white inmates to a degrading homosexual experience.

While this might appear to be a cogent explanation for black on white sexual attacks, there are less complex reasons that reflect simply the need of the black inmate to survive both in prison and after release. One of the most pragmatic reasons not to attack another black inmate is that a large percentage of black inmates are in prison because of violent crimes, which increases the possibility of retaliation by the black inmate in prison. Another reason is that a large percentage of black inmates will come from the same or from neighboring geographical inner-city neighborhoods. This means that black inmates' chances of running into other black inmates after release from prison is greater than for white inmates.

There may be some black inmates who harbor racially unfulfilled feelings that might lead them to seek out white inmates rather than black inmates for sexual favors. There are perhaps others who consider the white inmate a weaker and therefore safer victim.

Psychological Survival of Black Offenders

Why is it that more offenders do not become psychologically unbalanced in the prison environment of violence, stress, abuse, and poverty? Frankl (1962), based on his experiences as a prisoner in Nazi concentration camps, strongly believed that individuals can endure the most oppressive conditions without psychological damage. During his incarceration he noticed that some of the other prisoners, no matter how horrible the treatment administered by the Nazis, seemed to remain psychologically intact. Other prisoners displayed many of the behaviors and symptoms we now label as mentally disordered behaviors. Frankl's evaluation of individuals who maintained psychological integrity was that they had come to feel that there was a purpose for their suffering, that the ordeal was not meaningless, and that they were in contact with a force that transcended the physical beings that controlled their destiny. In other words, they had found meaning in their lives and could relate the pain to a spiritual life.

Similar to Frankl's analysis of psychological survival in oppressive conditions, some inmates make religion an important aspect of their life. The Black Muslims, for example, were able to attract large numbers of black inmates because they presented logical reasons to explain the suffering blacks were subjected to and also gave them a method for improving their present life.

Directing one's energies into constructive pursuits is another technique. Keeping busy fills a vacuum for many offenders and reduces the time one has to face up to the reality of one's status in life. Reading, arts and crafts, lifting weights, and writing are all activities that can distract one from self-pity, guilt, anger, and other ruminations and channel energies into worthwhile pursuits.

There is a price that some offenders pay to survive psychologically in the prison environment. Many defense mechanisms, such as denial, projection, rationalization, and displacement, help them to deal with any guilt associated with the criminal act and to distort the realities of their existence to make their environment acceptable. It helps them to accept and even to participate in abnormal behaviors. In fact, much of the behavior which seems to be abnormal to those outside prisons is accepted and adaptive behavior in the institution. The behavior is adaptive behavior because of its survival value in an abnormal environment.

Some offenders cope by withdrawing all emotional feelings from the environment. The person in essence is not dependent on those in his environment for emotional support and gratification. There are no expectations from others.

There is no excitement about promises and commitments from others. Communication from loved ones is not anticipated. This allows the offender to cope with disappointments and reduces the odds of psychological hurt by others. If relatives say they are coming to visit and do not, or if the classification team promises placement in an education program and does not the inmate may not express psychological pain and anger because there was no emotional investment. The inmate did not build up hope that these things would actually occur.

This emotional isolation contributes to the advice given to young convicts to "do one day at a time." Once emotional energies are withdrawn from the outside world and loved ones, they are able to maintain a strong present time orientation. Other than general plans to get out and do something (that is, go straight; not get caught next time; not beat up my wife), they do not make or dwell on long-range plans.

In the most extreme form of this condition there are no highs and no lows—no peaks and no valleys. Emotions are not shown, since emotions are generally considered to be signs of weakness. The inmate demonstrates the same consistent, nonchalant, bland, blank look. Overt signs that suggest emotions are avoided and/or omitted, such as eye contact, laughing, and touching of others. The individual takes on a zombielike appearance.

Carter and Jordan (1972) suggest that the emotionally insulated behavior of blacks confined in white-dominated institutional settings may be adaptive:

> The black patient frequently behaves in learned stereotyped roles of feigned stupidity, withdrawal, patronizing attitudes, superficial conformity—never letting real problems, true behavior, genuine feelings, come through in front of white staff.

Prison as a Way of Life for Black Offenders

As an explanation for the high recidivism rate of blacks and their seemingly resilient tendency to resist psychological decompensation while in prison, some have speculated that a symbiotic relationship exists between blacks and prisons. In other words, there are psychological needs resident in black offenders that are satisfied by being incarcerated. This position suggests that prisons serve a very useful function for poor black citizens and that being incarcerated is not as painful to them as we are led to believe. For example, the channels open to poor blacks for recognition and achievement are limited. Therefore, even prisons, with their inconveniences, can afford inmates status and recognition that might evade them in their own communities. Attorneys, guards, teachers, classification specialists, chaplains, counselors, recreation leaders, and others are all part of the cadre of workers who are attentive to inmates while incarcerated. Moreover, being incarcerated removes a black offender from a competitive, white-controlled environment. Thus, he does not have to be concerned with failure.

Finding a job, being unemployed, or fulfilling the role of husband, father, or chief provider are no longer real or potentially frustrating situations for the black offender.

This line of thinking parallels the concept advanced by Braginsky and Ring (1969) described as a "flight to mental health." Their research with mental patients in mental hospitals led them to conclude that many mental patients, in order to escape the pressures of society, choose to stay in the mental hospitals. One study, for example, demonstrated that those patients who had been in the mental institution for a long period of time purposefully changed their behavior to coincide with the criteria necessary to insure their continued stay in the mental hospital.

As proof to strengthen this position some will allude to case studies showing that some blacks have committed crimes in such a careless and obvious manner that their capture and ultimate incarceration are almost guaranteed. There are even some examples of blacks who were eligible for release from an institution purposefully getting into trouble and consequently having to extend their stay in prison. Still others point to the short periods of time between release and return to the prison system for some black inmates.

There are those who contend that since blacks have been poor and have been accustomed to discrimination they have a higher threshold for prison conditions. It is much easier for a poor black person to adjust to the poverty-stricken environment of prison than someone who has had an abundance of material possessions. In other words, the higher the socioeconomic level and the more power and worldly possessions one has to relinquish, the more aversive prison will seem. What rights and power does one who feels disenfranchised from society and at the bottom of life's ladder relinquish by being incarcerated? Does he cherish the right to vote, to hold public office, to serve on juries, to obtain a license for certain occupations? What worldly possessions do such individuals surrender—their homes, boats, or airplanes?

The similarities of environment are said to facilitate the transition from one poverty situation to another. This perspective is reflected by the joke that is told of a defense attorney for a black client in court. He says to the judge, "Your honor, my client grew up in a squalid, barbaric and inhumane environment. He has been poor all his life and has had the worst of everything!" The judge replies, "Good, he'll feel right at home in prison!" Some may truly believe that it might not be too difficult to sleep in a dormitory environment if one is from a large family and accustomed to sleeping with others in one's bedroom. It may not be distasteful to eat institutional food if one does not eat regularly or if one's meals are not tasty. It may not be too aversive to remain idle in prison if one is accustomed to being unemployed and "standing on the corner."

While this line of thinking is provocative, these types of unsubstantiated generalizations about blacks must be viewed with caution and suspicion. It is true that some blacks do adapt to the aversive conditions of prison, but some blacks have always adapted to oppressive conditions—even slavery. It is probably true that just as there were slaves who eventually felt that slavery was a satisfactory lifestyle, so too will some black offenders learn to tolerate and perhaps even find incarceration a more acceptable existence than being in a non-institutional environment where they may feel that they may fail because of discrimination.

However, it is not plausible to assume that either an early acceptance of prison life or a high recidivism rate is indicative solely of emotional need satisfaction for the vast majority of black offenders. The fact that blacks can become institutionalized to oppressive conditions speaks even more to the urgency with which mental-health practitioners must assure the implementation of programs that provide opportunities for success experiences and community contact throughout an offender's stay in prison.

Survival for Mental-Health Professionals

Prisons are places where people hurt and hurt others, where the sides are divided into the haves and the have nots, and where mental-health professionals and their programs will be viewed with suspicion and apprehension by both sides.

It would, perhaps, be an ideal situation for psychologists, social workers, and counselors if they could be untouched by the conflicts and abrasive conditions that exist in prisons and attend to their areas of interest, such as testing, classification, and therapy. But in such closed, violent, and sometimes racially tense environments it is almost impossible to remain neutral and to be untouched by the conditions. A number of critical questions must be addressed by professionals in these settings. Where do mental-health practitioners fit in an environment of "us versus them?" How can they maintain neutrality and objectivity in a combative setting? Who should they align themselves with? What should their responses be to ethnic minorities? How can they be effective in settings where survival is the name of the game for both the correctional staff and the inmates?

Mental-health professionals must realize that simply going into correctional settings with good intentions may not be enough to equip them to cope with the divisive and sometimes desperate forces in these environments. And as unattractive as it may seem to many professionals, in order to implement and carry out programs in correctional institutions and to maintain professional integrity, they may have to construct their own survival code. This code should include as a minimum, the following:

1. Be honest and know one's limits. Honesty is generally respected in prison. A concerted effort should be made to tell the truth and keep all commitments to inmates. The level of honesty in relationships with inmates will determine how one is labeled and can influence relationships with other inmates.

Mental-health workers should have a realistic understanding of what their limit are in the prison setting. If inmates request services that cannot be provide or that will not be provided, they should be told. One black ex-inmate in a Alabama prison tells of the importance of honesty and knowing the limits o one's power:

> Like there was a counselor in a college program that came in and told the inmates all the things he could do and what he was going to do for black people. And what happened was that he could not pull any of these things off. When the administration got down on him, he couldn't bring the books he said he was going to bring in, he couldn't get the entertainment, or the different people he said he was going to bring in. Then within a month's time he had lost all of his rapport with the black inmates because he had come in promising too much and he could not do it.

2. Be aware of decision making processes. A mental-health professional should understand who makes important decisions and how these decisions are made. This includes knowing both the obvious formal power structure, such as the warden and other staff, and the informal power relationships among guards and inmates. In some prisons, certain inmates or inmate groups may be more helpful to the success of a program than the administrative staff.

3. Expect to be tested on racial issues. It is important to black inmates to know the racial feeling of staff members, and they will attempt to find out what they are. An understanding of the needs and senstivities of the various cultural groups and the racial frictions that exist is critical.

4. Be consistent. Establish a consistent philosophy and policy for inter-acting with all inmates and staff. To be discovered doing more or less for one inmate or a group of inmates will severely damage one's credibility. In all rela-tionships, make sure that the ground rules are the same.

5. Avoid the temptation to accept favors from inmates. Some inmates will try to maneuver the staff into a compromising position. For example, they may do little favors, whether solicited or not, such as geting coffee, the paper, bringing news from the grapevine, and so on. At some later date they may ask a small favor in return.

6. Avoid showing fear. It is a natural reaction to be afraid of inmates. However, working in an environment where showing fear is seen as a sign of weakness can only hinder a professional's interactions with offenders.

Conclusion

The mental-health professional has a monumental task in administering programs and services in a correctional setting. Prisons are generally environments where goods and possessions are limited; where people prey on each other for goods and services; where the sides are clearly divided into the kept and the keepers; where abnormality is accepted as normality; where inmates become masters at deception and manipulation; and where the mental health person becomes analogous to a meal ticket or a pass or ticket for freedom. Prisons breed an atmosphere where any positive emotional gain made by an inmate can be eroded in seconds by an insensitive guard.

In these constricted environments the reputation of the mental-health professional is important. Black offenders will be concerned at some level about racial injustices and programs that relate to them as black individuals. It is imperative that mental health professionals be responsive to these needs.

4 Classification and Assessment

A critical service that almost every mental-health professional in criminal justice will be required to perform is that of assessing and making decisions about the behaviors and/or mental functioning of black offenders. Psychiatrists and psychologists are frequently called upon to evaluate competency to stand trial and mental responsibility at the time a crime was committed; social workers are invoked to appraise and summarize social and psychological histories for pretrial investigations; and a variety of other mental-health professionals are asked to provide various assessments of black offenders during their stay in correctional institutions.

While a select group of offenders may receive psychological evaluations prior to or during their trial, the larger assessment process that effects all black offenders is the classification process administered during the early phases of their incarceration. During this initial evaluation black offenders generally receive personality, intelligence, and skills assessments.

Although assessment and subsequent classification occur routinely in almost every correctional system, a number of concerns have been voiced about both the assessors and their assessment instruments, particularly as they relate to black offenders. These doubts about the classification process and the assessors are sufficient reason to cause mental-health professionals to be cautious and sensitive to any evaluation and classification of black offenders.

Classification Systems

The first state prison classification program was initiated in New Jersey in 1918 (Barnes and Teeters, 1952). The Federal Bureau of Prisons established its classification system in 1929. From these early systems classification programs have become integrated into every state and federal correctional program.

The purpose of a prison classification system is twofold. The first mission is concerned with the safety of those around the inmate and society at large. Therefore, a major determination to be made is the amount of security and supervision an offender will require to protect others. The security classification an offender receives determines how he will spend his time in prison and the services that will be available to him. The number of passes and furloughs, the type of institutional job, work and study release, and participation in other programs are influenced by the amount of supervision needed for him. The higher the security classification, the more restrictive the opportunities.

59

The second purpose focuses on the needs and deficiencies of individual inmates. The underlying assumption here seems to be that inmates commit crimes because of basic deficiencies in education, employment skills, or unmet psychological needs. Through the classification process these areas can be identified and treatment programs provided to reduce or eliminate these problem areas. Once these deficiencies no longer exist, the need for further criminal acts is eliminated.

An ideal classification system should utilize as much information as possible on an offender, such as his social, educational, employment, and emotional history and any other relevant information. With this data, decisions can be made about him with respect to his present and future relationship with the criminal justice system. In order to get an accurate assessment, input from a variety of disciplines is usually represented in the decision-making process.

Some classification programs, however, have not evolved into the workable systems that they were designed to be. This was clearly demonstrated as late as 1976 when Federal Judge Frank Johnson noted in *Pugh* v. *Locke* (Alabama, 1976) that a viable classification system did not exist in the Alabama Correctional System. Judge Johnson, in requiring the state to institute a satisfactory classification scheme, highlighted several deficiences of the system: there was no viable process to identify and separate the dangerous inmates from the non-dangerous inmates, which encourages inmate abuse by the dangerous inmates; mentally retarded and mentally ill inmates were not identified and therefore did not receive appropriate treatment; too many inmates were assigned to the maximum security category without benefits of a regular review of dangerousness status; and inmates were not given the opportunity to upgrade employment and educational skills, which has been linked to rehabilitation.

One glaring shortcoming of the classification system was the implication that the process was arbitrary and capricious. Offenders were not classified and assigned on an objective, sound, and consistent basis but rather on subjective and "gut level" feelings. In other words, the appearance of the inmate, how he looked, his demeanor, and his race very much influenced how he was classified. Being black tended to be a disadvantage in classification. In Alabama, for example, the honor camps and minimum security institutions were generally over-represented by whites, while the most restrictive prisons, containing the most dangerous offenders, tended to be overpopulated by blacks.

While the Alabama prison system was spotlighted as having inadequate classification, other states have displayed similar shortcomings. Classification irregularities were cited in the Atttica riots as being one of many grievances voiced by the inmates. For example, black and Chicano inmates were generally assigned the worst jobs and the lower paying jobs (Wicks, 1974). In 1978 the state of Tennessee's prison classification system was declared totally inadequate and unconstitutional (*Trigg* v. *Blanton,* Chancery Court for Davidson County, Tennessee, 1978).

Mental-health professionals have been involved in classification in a number of ways. One direct way has been the creation of classification schemes that separate offenders along psychological dimensions and thereafter into treatment modalities. Three prominent classification schemes have been developed thus far, and all have been directed toward youthful offenders.

Quay's system provides for the classification of offenders into four categories: inadequate-immature, neurotic-conflicted, unsocialized-aggressive, or subcultural. Based on these categories and other test data, the individual is then matched with a particular therapy and program that is tailored to his particular needs (Warren, 1970; Quay and Parsons, 1970).

Interpersonal maturity classification (I-Level) is another system that facilitates differential treatment (California Youth Authority, 1968; Peoples, 1975). This process classifies individuals into one of seven levels of interpersonal maturity levels ranging from the least mature to an idea level of social maturity. These individuals, once classified, are then matched with appropriate treatments and settings.

Megargee et al., (1979) developed a computer-based classification system for offenders based on MMPI profiles. On the basis of an inmate's responses he is assigned to one of ten groups. The authors choose not to label the groups with traditional psychological terms such as schizophrenic, neurotic, sociopathic, but selected more neutral terms for groups names such as able, baker, delta, and jupiter.

Most generally, however, mental-health workers assist in the classification process by providing specific services that assist in determining security, classification, and identifying deficiencies. These services are testing, test interpretation, and the assessment of behavior, which includes diagnosing abnormal behavior and predicting dangerousness.

Administration of Testing Programs

Various assessment instruments have been utilized with prisoners ever since the entrance of psychologists into criminal justice. Tests of intelligence have been used with prisoners as early as the first quarter of the twentieth century, soon after the Stanford-Binet Intelligence Test was introduced in this country. The primary justification for early intelligence testing with offenders was based on a presumed relationship between crime and low intelligence. The early results from these tests indicated that at least 70 percent of most prison populations could be considered feebleminded (Goddard, 1914). More intensive research revealed that prisoners were not any more or less intelligent than the general population, and the notion that intelligence was a primary causal agent in criminality was generally abandoned by the early 1930s (Vold, 1958). Efforts to identify personality variables that clearly and unmistakably distinguished the criminal from the noncriminal has likewise been unsuccessful.

However, the use of personality and intelligence tests with offenders continued. In fact, testing programs exist in almost every state and federal correctional system. A national survey of correctional institutions revealed that with the exception of one system, every state in the sample routinely gathered information on levels of intellectual functioning, achievement, and psychological functioning. In many cases, diagnosis was based primarily on objective psychological tests such as the Minnesota Multiphasic Personality Inventory, the California Personality Inventory, and the 16 Personality Factors Test (Center for Correctional Psychology, 1972, p. 23).

While the federal correctional system shows some uniformity in testing instruments and procedures, most state correctional systems do not. Each state has selected its own test and developed its own testing programs. Consequently, little consistency exists among states in the particular tests administered or the types of tests used. For example, the Wisconsin correctional system administers an aptitude test battery to its offenders while some states such as Alabama and Mississippi do not.

While there may be inconsistencies among states with regard to the particular tests used, there seems to be a standard procedure emerging. Many state correctional systems now administer personality and intelligence instruments to every offender as a regular part of their intake procedures. These tests are given to offenders where intelligence is not an issue (high school and college graduates) and where abnormality is not really a serious concern (income tax evasion, embezzlement, robbery).

Routinely administering intelligence and personality tests to offenders sets them apart from most groups. Rarely can one find any training program or educational program that requires the administration of intelligence or personality tests to a population strictly on the basis of their participation and without relevance to their expected performance.

The only comparable groups routinely screened with psychological tests are those that are admitted to mental hospitals and institutions for the retarded. The admission procedure generally requires a battery of tests, including personality and intelligence. But in these instances there is a relationship between testing and behavior. Individuals are institutionalized because of some question or concern about their psychological and intellectual functioning. Testing is indeed relevant to their diagnosis and subsequent treatment.

This is not the case with offenders. Except for the small percentage of inmates evaluated for mental illness and retardation early in the criminal-justice process, most inmates are not sentenced to prison because there is a question about their intelligence and emotional behavior. The existing policy of administering personality and intelligence tests to offenders, especially on a routine nonvoluntary basis, where inmates are not given a choice to refuse, needs to be critically examined. Not only is the motivation to take the test a factor that must be weighed in the results, but there is the unspoken assumption that a link exists between intelligence, personality and crime. And even if it was suspected that as many as 15 percent of the prison population could be classified as mentally retarded and/or seriously disturbed, requiring everyone to take the tests would mean that approximately 85 percent of the prison population would have their privacy intruded upon by taking personality and IQ tests.

The most commonly used contemporary justification for testing of offenders in general is that the test results are beneficial in classifying offenders by identifying individual strength and weaknesses and that test scores allow for individual and group comparisons. According to this logic, information can be obtained from tests in a variety of areas such as intelligence, reading, arithmetic, and specific skills that can help to channel offenders into various academic and vocational programs. Offenders with special psychological and biological disabilities and problems such as brain damage or severe mental disorders can be identified through testing. Pre- and posttest comparisons can be made that can provide an evaluation of both the individual's progress and the program's effectiveness.

While these reasons may appear to be legitimate, there is a need to be skeptical about the administration of any tests to blacks, whether they are offenders or nonoffenders. Testing has generally been a negative experience for a large percentage of blacks. Historically, blacks have been found to be deficient on most standardized tests whenever they were compared with whites—no matter what type of test it was. By the time blacks become adult offenders, many will have received their share of negative test evaluations. In fact, their poor academic performance and low test scores, with the accompanying problems, may have been a contributing factor in their involvement with delinquency and criminality.

There have been two basic and prominent issues in testing black populations with any standardized test. The first concerns test construction and the resulting criteria by which blacks are compared and evaluated. Many of the frequently used standardized tests were constructed without taking into account the unique behavioral patterns necessitated by the black experience in a racially conscious environment. The original Stanford-Binet Intelligence Test, for example, was standardized on an all-white population, and yet it was used to evaluate and label the intelligence of blacks (*Larry P.* v. *Wilson Riles,* 1979). Only four blacks were included in the original sample used to standardize the MMPI, and yet judgments about black mental health have been made based on the results of this instrument (Elion and Megargee, 1972). Many other tests have been standardized on predominantly white middle-class populations and used to evaluate low-income blacks. Collectively, these standardized tests have formed the foundation for the basic assumptions that have been made about the nature of black intelligence and personality. As a result, blacks have generally been denied access to educational, social, and cultural experiences similar to those for whites because they were judged by white standards.

Many contended that cultural experiences are critical ingredients that affect the score an individual makes on tests that are culturally slanted. In order to demonstrate this test bias, two tests, the Dove Counter-Balance General Intelligence Test and the Black Intelligence Test of Cultural Homogeneity, were constructed with items on the tests culturally weighted toward the black experience (Samuda, 1975; Williams, 1970). Black subjects inevitably scored higher on both these instruments.

The second issue focuses on the use of the test and the interpretation of the test results. While tests may discriminate against blacks and other minorities by virtue of their construction and cultural exclusiveness, many contend that tests can still yield useful information for diagnostic purposes. They claim that it is not the tests but what they are used for and how they are interpreted that is most damaging to blacks. For example, to deny blacks access to opportunities based on test scores without being aware of cultural factors contributing to a depressed score or to use a test as the determining factor in making critical decisions about blacks is the real problem.

There is an abundance of evidence to at least partially support the position that tests have been used in a discriminatory fashion. The scores from intelligence tests have been used to eliminate and restrict blacks from various educational, occupational, and other kinds of benefits and services. It was not until 1968 that the practice of using intelligence tests to qualify jurors in jury trials was considered illegal (*People* v. *Craig,* 1968). In 1971 the Otis Quick Scoring Mental Test used by the Mississippi State Highway Patrol was considered discriminatory (*Morrow* v. *Chrysler,* 1971). Mercer (1972) concluded from her study that intelligence tests were used to disproportionately place blacks and Spanish-speaking children in special education classes.

Griggs v. *Duke Power Company* (1971), was a landmark case in which the Duke Power Light Company, a conglomerate in Durham, North Carolina, denied employment to Mr. Willie Griggs as a coal handler because he did not have a high school diploma and did not pass a battery of psychological and sociological tests administered to him. The Supreme Court ruled among other things that if tests are administered as screening devices, they should only test attributes essential to that particular job performance. In other words, it must be clearly demonstrated that the tests used are not arbitrary and are relevant to the performance of a particular job. In a similar case in Massachusetts (Castro v. *Beecher,* 1971), state civil service tests administered to applicants to the Boston Police Department were ruled discriminatory.

Intelligence tests have caused the most heated debates, as their use has been especially harmful to blacks. Studies have shown that as a group blacks score at least one standard deviation or fifteen points below the average for whites on intelligence tests (Coleman, 1970). While most researchers have tended to explain these differences in terms of environmental factors, some have overlooked these factors and have concentrated on the notion that blacks are genetically inferior (Jensen, 1969; Samuda, 1975).

IQ scores have been used even though there is still not consensus on the definition of intelligence. However, it is now generally acknowledged that intelligence comprises much more than what is revealed by an IQ score. Unfortunately, the IQ score has continued to be interpreted in many situations as being equivalent to one's innate intellectual ability.

Being labeled as having a low IQ affects a person's self-concept and influences access to educational programs and employment. Rosenthal and Jacobson's study (1968) raised the possibility that teachers' expectations and subsequent treatment of students could be swayed by the label a child received prior to class, whether or not the labels were accurate. Teachers tended to treat children exactly as they were labeled. Children tended to act out the label ascribed to them.

Personality testing has also tended to picture blacks in a negative image. Gynther, Erdberg, and Fowler (1971) found that most blacks in a small rural southern community scored in the severely maladjusted category on the MMPI, although they were reported to be well adjusted and functioning well in their community. Gynther (1972) conducted a review of the literature with the MMPI, specifically with reference to black and white performance on the MMPI. He found that consistently blacks seem to score higher on the schizophrenic and hypomania scales. Gynther concluded, on the basis of all factors, that the differences between white and black subjects reflected a cultural difference rather than racial psychopathology. He noted how the results had been interpreted in such a way as to eliminate blacks from consideration for jobs which require good judgment and good mental health.

While the problem of testing affects all inmates, no matter what their race, the problem is exacerbated for black offenders. It cannot be assumed that conditions have changed that would offset the historical abusive testing with blacks. If the same basic culture-specific IQ and personality tests are being used, and the same criteria to judge black mental health exists, we can expect similar results.

At least one state is beginning to take affirmative action against the use of standardized intelligence tests. Chief U.S. District Judge Peckham in California ruled that the use of standardized IQ tests to place youngsters in special classes violated state and federal constitutions. He ordered the state to receive court approval before administering standardized IQ tests (*Larry P.* v. *Wilson Riles*, 1979).

In spite of this positive step, however, there is some early evidence that standardized intelligence testing is still being used and interpreted in very much the same fashion in criminal justice as it was used in academic settings. The tests merely serve to compare black and white offenders and to label them. For example, Wooden (1976) reviewed the IQ scores by race in six state juvenile institutions (Tennessee, Louisiana, Arkansas, Texas, Nebraska, and Michigan) and found white IQs higher on the average from seven to eighteen points. Santamour and West (1977) reviewed the published findings of studies identifying the mentally retarded adult offenders. They found that consistently over half, and as high as 70 percent, of those classified as mentally retarded on the basis of the IQ test score were black.

Ironically, while important decisions are being made about black offenders based on their test results, many of them may not be even taking the test seriously. The following statement by a black inmate in one prison describes how he and other offenders viewed the test and its relevance to their lives:

> The guards told us that they were giving an IQ test or personality test and at first everybody was kind of really psyched up about the tests. And then everybody, on the night of the test, turned it into a real plaything. Like we said, if they find out you're a crazy man, they are going to send you to a hospital. That's how we went in to take the test. Nobody wanted to be caught writing so everybody would be doing it real fast and then drop their pencil on the page so everybody could see that they were finished. That's how everybody proved to each other how fast their minds were, by how quick they finished. Nobody really took it serious. You have to take the tests. They give you a "stop up" and put it on the board and then your name is on there, so if you don't show up then that's a disciplinary, that's how they go with that. So everybody had to be there, and everybody was. And, of course, a "stop up" means no work, so that's good. So everybody's kind of happy to see their name on the "stop up" list.

In those situations where testing is so deeply engrained in the political and financial structure of the institution that testing will continue regardless of its impact on blacks, mental-health professionals have attempted to counteract and reduce the effects of test discrimination by employing various remedies. On intelligence test scores some have routinely added an additional ten or fifteen points to the test scores of blacks. In cases where test profiles indicated mental retardation or severe psychopathology blacks are questioned about specific items and responses they made that might have contributed to such results. Others have simply ignored the test results.

There is no doubt that assessment instruments can be beneficial in criminal justice settings. When used properly with the population it was designed for, useful and valuable information about black offenders can be obtained. The administration of reading and math tests is an appropriate and relevant endeavor because educational programs can improve reading and math skills. Further, these screening devices allow for the identification of those offenders who may be academically and mentally retarded. Those that have academic difficulties will score low and in some cases be unable to complete forms properly and even follow written directions.

Offenders who have serious emotional problems will generally manifest their inappropriate behaviors in the interview, in their social and learning environments, or through their past history. Those individuals displaying some suspected emotional pathology or learning difficulty can be singled out and a more extensive and more individualized assessment can be made.

When tests are used properly they are used for the purpose for which they were constructed, they are not used coercively, and the ones who take the tests will derive some service from their use. This does not include routinely administering intelligence and personality tests to a person simply because he is an offender. The *Griggs* v. *Duke* decision seems to be somewhat pertinent unless correctional administrators are testing attributes that are essential to the performance of a particular job or program in prison.

Assessment

In assessing black behavior in both interview and noninterview settings, an understanding of black behavior and language is critical. This will help to insure that assessors are not simply responding to racial myths and stereotypes and therefore failing to accurately assess black behavior.

Whitehurst (1973) suggests that there are three personal shortcomings that assessors must overcome before they can become good evaluators of black behaviors: (1) the handicap of inadequate knowledge and experience, (2) handicap of preconceived notions, and (3) resistance to change. In order to overcome these deficiences he recommended that the assessor rid himself of faulty generalizations about blacks; be prepared to change diagnosis if new data warrants a change; and most of all, he says: "If we would become good assessors for black clients, or any other clients, one of the best strategies is to learn more and more about them and ourselves—not just about superficial features or demographic data but about their hopes,their fears, their aspirations, their motives and their coping strategies as well." (p. 34).

Based on past irregularities in the assessment of blacks by assessors, Whitehurst's recommendations certainly seem appropriate and timely. Research has demonstrated that assessors without an understanding of black behavior and culture have tended to present distorted evaluations of blacks. For example, it has been shown that compared with their white counterparts, blacks are more likely to receive the most severe psychiatric diagnoses with the least favorable prognosis and more likely to be responded to on the basis of their most bizarre symptoms (Thomas and Sillen, 1972; Gross et al., 1969; Singer, 1967). As a result, they tend to appear more psychologically disturbed than whites with parallel symptoms.

The same concerns that have been voiced about the assessment of blacks in general must now be raised about the assessment of black offenders. The following actual evaluation of a black offender by a white female mental health professional highlights these concerns:

Mr. X is a rather tall, slender, dark-complected, black male who smiled somewhat inappropriately and required a good deal of prompting and encouraging before he would attempt to complete certain test items. Additionally, he would often say that he could not recall certain information. Although single, he has fathered one child; when asked if he planned to marry the mother of the baby, he said, "no." He has never known his father. According to him, his mother married for the first time in the 1960s. He reports a total of 10 half and whole brothers and sisters. He says that he gets along just fine with family members. He attended public schools through the 9th grade. He then joined the Job Corps and stayed for some two months. He said, "I got homesick. I did not stay there long enough to take up nothing." His longest period of employment seems to be 3 months. He denies experiencing any serious medical problems. Mentally, he denies having ever sought mental health treatment. When asked if he had ever felt that he needed treatment for a mental problem, he said, "Yes, sometimes I get real nervous and start shaking." He was originally sentenced in 1975 to 40 years for second degree murder. He admitted to the offense for which he is currently incarcerated. Of the victim, he said, "He was trying to hurt me with a pistol." He also had one conviction in 1973 for burglary and grand larceny and was placed on 13 months probation.

Dull normal intellectual functioning is suggested by his performance on the Revised BETA examination. It is felt that he is somewhat brighter than his dull normal performance on the BETA. According to his performance on the Wide Range Achievement Test–Level 2 Reading, he is reading at the 6.0 reading grade placement. This is felt to be a rather accurate estimate of his current reading level. His personality structure was assessed with the use of an MMPI Profile, the Critical Items Scale of the MMPI, the Bender-Gestalt Design Test, the MCFP Sentence Completion Test (Geil), selected cards of the TAT, and a diagnostic interview. A diagnosis of chronic undifferentiated schizophrenic reaction is being given. Though he is not openly psychotic at this time, a persistent prepsychotic state appears to be present in his test data and his social-legal history. He is characterized by inappropriate affect, worry, depression, nervousness, tension, poor work adjustment, inadequate feelings, dependency and hostility.

Despite worry and tension, he is likely to be resistant about obtaining help for his problem to head off the possibility of a complete psychotic breakdown and to prevent further withdrawal from his social environment. His behavior should be monitored closely, and he should be encouraged to participate in programs and/or activities within his environment. Needless to say, professional assistance will go a long way toward helping him to deal with his day-to-day life situational problems.

There are a number of questions and criticisms that this evaluation should evoke. The most obvious concern is: what clinical significance is the fact that the black inmate is "dark-complected"? Does this information contribute to an overall understanding of him as an individual? Second, there is no discussion of environmental conditions that may have contributed to his behaviors. For example, the black inmate may have "smiled inappropriately" and "required a good deal of prompting" because the interviewer was white and female which might pose a problem for a black inmate. Moreover there is no explanation of the assessor's behaviors that might contribute to the inmate's responses. Did the examiner feel insecure, uptight, or nervous in the interview? Without this information there is the implicit assumption that the assessor was blameless for any of the inmate's behavior. The responsibility for the behavior labeled as inappropriate by the assessor is placed on the shoulders of the black offender. Third, there is no attempt to analyze the inmate's test responses for possible misunderstanding or cultural differences. Fourth, labeling the inmate with such a lethal title such as schizophrenic and suggesting that he be watched carries with it the implication of dangerousness. In addition, the evaluation seems to be permanent, timeless, and indefinite, with no provision built in for a reassessment and possible removal of the label.

For many assessors the task of assessing normal from abnormal behavior may be difficult in most situations, but it is even more complex when acts of violence and other criminal acts must be considered in the evaluation. Then the additional responsibility is to identify the dangerous black offender and to predict levels of dangerousness, which has recently become a controversial topic.

The case of *Rouse* v. *Cameron* (1966) highlights the potential abuse involved in predicting black dangerous behavior. Charles Rouse, a black man in Washington, D.C., was arrested for carrying a deadly weapon, an offense that carried a maximum penalty of one year. However, he was acquitted by reason of insanity and sent to a mental hospital with a diagnosis of "antisocial reaction." He remain there four years, three years longer than he would have stayed in a regular institution. One of the main reasons that he was confined for such an extended period was because his assigned psychiatrist recommended that he not be released based on his analysis and diagnosis of Rouse's mental status. He summarized Rouse as a person who displayed poor judgment and had a lack of insight. The analysis was based mainly on Rouse's abrupt termination of group therapy and his reluctance to become involved with other patients. These acts and others reaffirmed the psychiatrist's belief that he was antisocial. Although his only history of mental illness was an evaluation as a youngster, the psychiatrist concluded that Rouse was a danger to himself and predicted that if he were released he would be inclined to shoot someone. Although other psychiatrists did not concur with the diagnosis of dangerousness, Rouse was not released (Ridgeway, 1967).

Davison and Neale (1974) reviewed this case and concluded that once a person is labeled as mentally ill, almost any behavior of the person can be perceived as indicative of the presumed mental illness and any unorthodox behavior or behavior not understood by those assessing behavior can be regarded as evidence of a dangerous mental disorder. If their analysis and observations are at all accurate, a black person may find himself in an unfortunate dilemma when he goes to see a therapist; if he is on time he might be described as compulsive; if he is a little early he might be labeled as anxious; and if he is late he could be accused of resisting. With this much diagnostic latitude given to clinicians who do not understand blacks, who fear them, or who are racist, the chances are increased that blacks will be categorized negatively in the assessment. In fact, any unfavorable recommendations concerning a black offender can be justified on the basis of his presumed dangerousness.

In spite of the problems associated with white assessors diagnosing black behaviors, mental-health practitioners are being given more responsibility throughout the criminal-justice process for the prediction of violent and danger-ous behavior. Judges, probation and parole officers, and others in criminal justice use this information to make crucial decisions about offenders. A number of recent studies, however, have suggested that mental-health professionals are not as accurate at predicting violent behavior as they might like to believe (Monahan, 1976). Wenk, Robinson, and Smith (1972) conducted three separate studies using a number of predictors that mental-health professionals use to assess and predict violence, including extensive background investigation, psy-chological test batteries, psychiatric diagnosis, number of prior commitments, history of violence, and commitment offense. Follow-up of actual behavior from each study revealed that none of the predictors, individually or collectively, proved effectively to forecast violent behavior. They found, for example, from one study that for every correct identification of a "potentially aggressive" person, there were 326 incorrect ones.

Kozol, Boucher, and Garofalo (1972; 1973) followed up offenders con-victed of violent crimes, clinically examined by psychiatrists, psychologists, and released from the Massachusetts Center for the Diagnosis and Treatment of Dangerous Persons. Of those still considered to be dangerous when released, only 35 percent committed a violent act, while 65 percent did not, which meant that they erred in two out of three predictions.

In a similar study involving the release of offenders identified by mental-health professionals as dangerous and potentially violent offenders into the community, parallel results were obtained (*Baxstrom* v. *Herold*, 1966). Johnnie Baxstrom, a black resident of an institution for the criminally insane, was judged to have been denied equal protection of the law by being detained longer than the maximum sentence in the criminally insane institution without benefit of a new hearing to determine his current dangerousness level. This ruling by the U.S. Supreme Court resulted in the transfer of almost 1,000 persons judged to be dangerous from criminally insane hospitals to civil mental hospitals, or the direct release into the community. Subsequent follow-ups revealed that the over-whelming majority of released patients did not live up to the label of dangerous that had been bestowed on them. During a four-year span, only 3 percent were considered dangerous enough to be returned to a hospital for the criminally insane (Steadman and Cocozza, 1979).

The research on the prediction of dangerousness has shown that mental-health professionals tend to overpredict dangerousness. This is understandable since it is much safer to predict that a person will commit a violent act than it is to predict that the person will not commit a subsequent violent act.

However, the ability or inability to accurately predict the potential violent behavior of offenders has serious implications for black offenders. A number of studies have indicated that one's race and socioeconomic status are important variables in the prediction of dangerousness. Those who are black and poor are the most vulnerable recipients of this label (Magargee, 1976; Monahan, 1976; Levinson and York, 1974).

Because most clinicians have not generally been required to understand black culture and therefore have not had a clear understanding of black behavior in general, it is not surprising that there is an inclination to consider blacks more dangerous than they really are.

Part of the reason that professionals are not able to accurately identify the potentially dangerous black offender is because much of the evidence used to classify black offenders as dangerous has been influenced by and predicated on the negative image of blacks, which started during slavery and which continues today. During the slave period dangerous black behavior was not defined solely by the act but in terms of black aggression against whites and the perceived impact of their behavior on the status quo. Thereafter, almost any type of assertive or aggressive behavior by blacks, especially males, was met with swift and severe retaliation. In fact, at least eighty-seven black lynchings resulted from nothing more serious than blacks insulting whites (Williams, 1969).

This historical legacy has led to a distorted image of black dangerousness and has contributed to blacks as a group being seen as more potentially violent and dangerous, which has prompted many whites to overpredict blacks as potentially dangerous. It is not surprising that blacks have been unequal recipeints of the death penalty.

Nash (1975) brought this point into focus from his research. He compiled three books of those individuals he considered to be the most notorious and dangerous criminals in America, including Billy the Kid, Jesse James, Machine Gun Kelly, Al Capone, and Charles Manson. There are two noticeable aspects of this research. The first is the absence of any identifiable black criminals in this directory of infamous characters. The absence of black offenders leads to the conclusion that even though blacks received the death penalty disproportionately, they were not as dangerous as white criminals and their crimes were not as serious.

The second aspect is that those white offenders who received the death penalty had clearly committed crimes of a vicious nature. For example, Richard

Speck killed eight student nurses in Chicago in 1966; Winnie Ruth Judd killed and dismembered two women in Phoenix, Arizona, in 1932; Melvin D. Rees, "The Sex Beast," killed nine people and raped at least four of the women; Harvey Glatman, sex maniac and murder, sadistically killed three women; and Charles Starkweather, the mass murderer, killed at least ten people.

The behavior considered most dangerous in blacks and punished most severely and disproportionately was rape. Although the act of rape is very serious, the gravity of the act was increased when the victim was a white female. Of all death sentences for rape, 89 percent were administered to blacks (U.S. Department of Justice, 1972). In some cases, such as the Scottsboro rape case, there was reason to doubt the validity of the evidence and consequently the appropriateness of the death sentence (Carter, 1973).

There are, of course, other indicators that would lead officials to believe that blacks, as a group, are prone to be dangerous and to exhibit aggressive behavior. Blacks comprised about 25 percent of all arrests in 1976, however, they accounted for a much larger percentage of those arrested for crimes of violence. Approximately 54 percent of those arrested for murder and nonnegligent manslaughter were black; 46 percent of forcible rape arrests were black; 59 percent of robbery arrests were black; and 41 percent of aggravated assault arrests were black. Blacks have been charged with killing police officers in 48 percent of all those charged with this offense from 1972–1976. (U.S. Department of Justice, 1978). In a very recent episode, a black ex-offender with a history of offenses, including attempted rape, carrying a concealed weapon, and disorderly conduct charges, fatally wounded a staff psychiatrist at a mental-health center (Stoffels and Fauber, 1979).

However, even when all these factors are taken into account, much of the evaluation of black behavior is still questionable. Assessments have been and continue to be colored by the legacy of racism, fear, and misunderstandings from the past, and have not been based on empirical data. The social and economic position of blacks makes it easier and more convenient to overpredict dangerousness. Blacks are typically poor and powerless, and there are fewer repercussions if one inaccurately labels a black as potentially violent. After all, most blacks will possess many of the predictors almost endemic to urban low-income communities commonly used to diagnose dangerous behavior. Consequently, this makes all of them potentially dangerous.

Factors such as poverty, unemployment, broken homes, single parent families, child abuse, delinquent peer group, low IQ scores, and poor educational background are considered part of the hazards of being born black and poor. These same criteria are conditions that many blacks atuomatically inherit and experience as a result of being born black. And many blacks with this background do not come into contact with criminal-justice agencies.

However, these factors contribute significantly to blacks' being labeled by mental-health professionals as dangerous, high risk, and untreatable. The result of this labeling has resulted in harsher sanctions and more inconveniences for blacks throughout the criminal-justice process than might have been warranted. For years a member of a poor minority was more than likely to be denied bail and released on his own recognizance (ROR) in the courts. Denial of bail and ROR suggests that the magistrate believes that the person will not be present for his hearing and/or is dangerous. Two monumental and successful projects (Manhattan Bail Project and the Des Moines, Iowa, Bail Project), involving hundreds of indigent subjects, demonstrated that there was not a significant increase in the number of runaways or additional crimes during release. Only then did most judges consider release on one's own recognizance and bail as viable alternatives for those suspects who were poor and black.

The labeling process is very likely to begin in childhood. Stone (1975) looked at the research on the placement of black and white youth in voluntary child care agencies by the Family Court or Bureau of Child Welfare in New York and found that whites were disproportionately placed in these facilities. His review indicated that white delinquents were generally considered more treatable and more rehabilitatable. Whites had an acceptance rate as high as 78 percent, as compared to a 27 percent acceptance rate for minorities. He summarized: "As one reviews the data, what emerges is that these agencies use traditional diagnostic criteria and indices of treatability. The latter include such variables as intelligence, literacy, intact family, lack of dangerous acting out, etc. The result of these criteria generated by the traditional approach is a failure to accept youths of minority background."

The frequent outcome is that blacks and other minorities receive a label of dangerousness and untreatability that follows them throughout their lives. Because of the label they may be denied services and programs that might be of benefit to them and are routed through institutions and programs for the most dangerous. Stone further noted that almost 91 percent of the black delinquent boys and only 20 percent of the white delinquent boys were sent to last resort training schools.

Some seriously question whether blacks are really more dangerous than whites and contend that the most plausible explanation for the propensity to label blacks as potentially more dangerous is based on racism. As a result, the excessive treatment they receive is only incidentally concerned with their presumed dangerousness. In other words, they are treated more harshly primarily as a general deterrent—to frighten other blacks from similar acts and to maintain the status quo rather than because they are dangerous. The severe punishment serves as a reminder to other blacks as to their unique place in the social order. There is no doubt that this possibility must be considered in any discussion of dangerousness.

On the other hand, some suggest that if assessors really believed that the criteria for predicting dangerous behavior were valid indexes separating the dangerous offenders from the nondangerous, then the biased decisions made concerning black offenders were made because the black offenders were actually considered more dangerous, more of a threat to society, and less rehabilitative than whites who might have committed the same acts. In other words, while concerns with deterring other blacks from committing similar acts and maintaining the status quo may have been a consideration, harsh sentences were administered for specific deterrence—to punish and restrain the individual.

Unfortunately, it is not possible to isolate or even identify the various ingredients that form the basis for each individual diagnostic decision resulting from interactions between blacks and whites. The interaction of race and diagnosis is so intertwined and so subtle that any type of diagnosis may result.

Most typically the literature shows that black offenders tend to receive a label of dangerousness rather than the opposite. However, some assessors may not label black behavior as dangerous for a number of reasons related to race, including trying to convince either themselves or others that they are not prejudiced.

The murder trial of Roxanne Gay is an interesting case that raises some question about the possible relationship between race and assessment. Roxanne Gay killed her husband, Blenda Gay, while he slept. What made this case particularly noteworthy was that Blenda Gay was black and played professional football for the Philadelphia Eagles. Roxanne claimed that she killed her husband in self-defense because he frequently battered her as a result of pressures from playing football. A psychiatrist examined her and attested that she was sane at the time of the stabbing. During the evaluation there was no evidence produced to substantiate her allegations. There was no body injury or witnesses that the husband had ever abused her. By the end of the trial, however, there was agreement among all the psychiatrists (including the psychiatrist who had originally judged her sane) that she was insane when she stabbed her husband. She was diagnosed as a paranoid schizophrenic (Wallace, 1978).

How could Roxanne Gay be considered sane by a psychiatrist? Why would it be believable that a black football player would physically assault his wife, in the absence of any type of evidence? A professional explanation is that paranoid schizophrenics have a way of sounding believable, and once one accepts the basic premise of their delusional system, the rest sounds rational. However, others might question whether subtle racial factors might have influenced the diagnosis. For example, it would be much easier to accept Roxanne Gay's explanation if one believed that abusing family members is common behavior for black males. Once this basic principle about black males is accepted, an absence of evidence does not alter the belief. While this is certainly not an attractive explanation for mental-health professionals, the possible influence of race in assessment of black behavior must be questioned.

Racial factors can play a part in both the assessment process and black behavior, in general. In fact, it is quite possible that the most potentially dangerous offender is the one who, in addition to possessing many of the characteristics commonly assumed to be associated with dangerousness, is disliked and rejected by others and learns to hate himself as an individual and as a black person. The person has nothing to live for and has not respect for the lives of others, black or white. In a sense, he becomes a man without roots and without a country. Without a commitment to others, the person truly becomes dangerous.

What is surprising about predicting black dangerousness is that even though racism has been an important aspect of the black experience, how blacks feel about being black and their reaction to whites has seemingly not been taken seriously in the prediction of dangerous or violent behavior. For example, of all the predictors listed for dangerous behavior, racial hostility and feelings about being black are not among them. And yet, much of the behavior that has been labeled as dangerous or violent black behavior has been a result or a reaction to racism or racial conflicts. Nat Turner's revolt, in which black slaves murdered whites, was a result of slavery conditions; the Black Panther party was a direct outgrowth of blatant police abuse of the black community and the urban riots in Watts, Cleveland, New Jersey, Detroit, and other major urban areas have all been aggressive and violent reactions to being black in America. The "Zebra" killings in California in which black assailants purposely murdered and robbed only white victims were racially motivated. Many of the black-on-black attacks have been viewed as a form of displacement of the hostility and anger that blacks have felt towards whites.

In fact, a number of other potentially violent acts have been clearly associated with the racial positions occupied by blacks. Two hostage-holding incidents by blacks exemplify this position. In 1977 a couple invaded a Salvation Army home for unwed mothers in Cincinnati and held eight hostages in an attempt to locate and reclaim the son they had given up for adoption some twenty years earlier. The desire to reunite with their son was allegedly inspired by the television miniseries "Roots," which emphasizes black heritage (*Washington Post*, February 12, 1977). Cory Moore sequestered a police officer and a female clerk as hostages for forty-five hours in Warrensville, Ohio, as a protest against the treatment of blacks in America. He put a curse on white people and demanded that white people leave the planet (*Cincinnati Enquirer*, March 8, 1977).

Conclusion

Assessing black behavior is an extremely important responsibility of mental-health professionals. The validity of evaluations obtained on many blacks has been questionable. Obtaining a valid evaluation has been difficult because of the negative stereotypes that have been imposed on blacks, the utilization of biased assessment instruments, and the attitudes of the assessors themselves. With these factors as backdrops, assessments have tended to portray blacks in an unfavorable posture. These evaluations ultimately affect the classification of black offenders in the criminal-justice system.

It is now generally acknowledged that mental-health professionals cannot predict future violent behavior with a high degree of accuracy. This means that the propensity to label blacks as more violence-prone than whites has resulted in unfairly labeling blacks as potentially dangerous. Because of this a great many blacks have been inconvenienced and denied opportunities and received harsher sanctions throughout the criminal-justice system.

It is imperative that assessors reevaluate themselves, their tools, and the basic assumption used to measure and classify black offender behavior if they are to provide useful and relevant assessments.

5 Therapeutic Intervention

Michael Lindsey

Each day all over the country thousands of blacks, including black offenders, are referred for therapy to therapists who more than likely are white. In these interactions it is assumed that the therapist is qualified and capable of understanding the black client, will use methods that are effective in changing behavior, and that both the client and therapist are able to set aside racial differences that might interfere with a successful resolution of the client's problems. However, as often as this referral process takes place and in spite of the faith put in therapy, we actually know very little about what therapy really is and what is effective therapeutic intervention.

Therapy is generally considered to be a process whereby human behavior is changed in a direction that is consistent with the needs of society and sometimes the needs of the individual. In all too many situations, therapy is seen as the final answer to most of the behavior considered inappropriate and objectionable.

However, since Eysenck (1952) published his results from a review of studies measuring the outcome of therapy, the effectiveness of therapy in influencing behavior change has been seriously questioned. He found that approximately 2/3 of all neurotics recovered or improved within two years whether they participated in therapy or not. Some have challenged Eysenck's findings, but therapeutic effectiveness remains questionable. The efficacy of therapy is an especially critical issue because there is evidence that suggests that the therapeutic process is influenced by race and socioeconomic status, and is less successful with black low-income clients.

Blacks and Therapy

There is an abundance of research that indicates that traditional therapy does not work well with blacks, especially when the therapist is white (Miller and Dreger, 1973). In addition, blacks seem to prefer black counselors (Banks, Carkhuff, and Berenson, 1967) and to make better progress in the therapeutic process with black counselors (Carkhuff and Pierce, 1967).

Black offenders are generally from low socioeconomic backgrounds and research seems to indicate that one's socioeconomic status does affect the type of treatment they are exposed to. There has been a noticeable trend to subject low-income patients to the physical types of therapy such as chemotherapy

(Hollingshead and Redlich, 1974). Studies have shown that therapists generally appear to prefer and are more comfortable with middle- and upper-class clients, that is, clients who are more similar to themselves. The YAVIS (Young, Attractive, Verbal, Intelligent, and Successful) syndrome has been mentioned frequently as the prototype of the preferred client (Monahan, 1975). Psychologists tend to blame the lower-class clients for failure to make therapeutic gains and to ascribe more negative traits to this population. In a study by Brill and Sorrow (1960), low social class, as viewed by psychologists, was found to be significantly related to estimation of low intelligence, a tendency to view the problem as physical rather than emotional, a desire for symptomatic relief, lack of understanding of the psychotherapeutic process, and a lack of desire for psychotherapy. In addition, intake interviewers had less positive feelings for lower-class patients and saw them as less treatable by means of psychotherapy.

Most studies suggest that black clients tend to remain in therapy for shorter periods. In a study of 366 cases at Yale Medical School, only 25 percent of those patients who were from the low socioeconomic levels returned after their initial appointment. Seventy-four percent of those who remained in therapy for more than six months were from the upper socioeconomic levels (Jones, 1975).

It seems then that therapy as traditionally practiced is not meeting the needs of blacks who are commonly from low income levels. In essence, when we refer to therapy in general we seem to be referring to an average phenomenon at best, that has not been shown to be highly effective even with the clientele that it caters most often, and even less successful with those from low socioeconomic backgrounds who are forced to participate in the process.

Therapy in Correctional Settings

Therapy in correctional settings has not fared much better. Bailey (1975) evaluated the results of 100 studies of correctional treatment between 1940 and 1959 and his analysis led him to the following conclusion (p. 738):

> Therefore it seems quite clear that, on the basis of this sample of outcome reports with all its limitations, evidence supporting the efficacy of correctional treatment is slight, inconsistent, and of questionable reliability.

Even at Patuxent, an institution administered and staffed by mental-health personnel, impressive therapeutic results have not been demonstrated (Schwitzgebel, 1975; Rothman, 1976). Prettyman (1974) offered this evaluation:

> Treatment is a myth, and vocational training is a fraud. For various reasons ranging from inadequacy of staffs to the difficulty of therapy

in a maximum security atmosphere, inmates are neither treated, trained, nor rehabilitated. Claims of therapy simply cloak banishment to institutions devoid of treatment process.

Further, some therapeutic abuses have surfaced. For example, one prison psychologist, under the pretense of using therapeutically sound techniques to change the behavior of inmates at Walla Walla State Prison in Washington, had inmates wear diapers, carry baby bottles, and crawl on the floor. Some were chained and handcuffed to beds. This treatment was designed to make inmates act grown up and mature (*Corrections Digest*, 1976).

It would seem then that therapy should be abandoned. However, it is naive to think that since therapeutic intervention has not been shown to be successful in correctional settings that it cannot work, or that it should or will be abandoned. Therapy itself is not in isolation from the realities of life. Therapy for blacks and with blacks has not been successful because of some very basic misassumptions and misapplications of the process we so loosely refer to as therapy; some basic misunderstandings, and ignorance about blacks and their lifestyles; prejudice against blacks; and a social environment that nourishes fear and suspicion of people of different races. We have done a terrible disservice to poor blacks when the black client, based upon standards of behavior which may be irrelevant to him, is told that something is wrong with him and is *required* to participate in a tenuous process called therapy, which is typically administered by a culturally different person who may or may not be sensitive to blacks.

Given this background of therapy and blacks, we really do not have an accurate picture of whether or not therapy actually works. In cases where therapy was not successful, we do not know if the process was inadequate, the therapist failed, or the client was unwilling. What must be done if we are to implement a meaningful form of therapy in a with blacks in prisons is to re-evaluate the whole concept of therapy. The old stereotypes and false assumptions about black mental health and therapy must be removed. Mental-health practitioners must not simply take unproven and erroneous therapeutic concepts used with black nonoffenders and transplant them onto a black prison population.

Though limited, there have been some successful applications of therapeutic techniques with blacks (Redfering, 1972; George, 1975). However, as presently provided, psychological treatment techniques still fail to meet the needs of those incarcerated in prisons and other institutions, particularly black offenders. There are many difficulties which contribute to misguided program design and faulty application.

A discussion of therapy with offenders is not a task specifically related to corrections or the criminal-justice system, but in a much broader sense it demands an understanding of the basic dynamics of black culture and black survival in our society. It is important to be aware of the perspectives that blacks outside the criminal-justice system have toward psychotherapeutic intervention because in spite of the unique environment which exists inside prisons, the attitudes, practices, and beliefs held as free individuals help to shape the attitudes, acceptances, and prohibitions of the inmate culture. For example, very demanding allegiance is required among delinquent groups. They must swear to silence and heed the wishes and commands of the leader or leaders without dissent. In correctional settings, inmates who communicate with guards are viewed as rats, squealers, or "stoolies" because they break one of many rules in the inmates' code of behavior.

With incarcerated blacks, effective therapeutic intervention is a difficult and unpredictable undertaking. The outcome is shaped by a number of factors, including the inmate's experience, resistance to therapy in general, and racial differences.

The Inmate Experience

The difficulties inmates have in just living in prison are complex. The many anxieties, fears, disappointments, and discouragements that inmates experience promote an unhealthy and a tense environment. The "us versus them" relationship existing within prison walls and the distorted psychological dynamics which many blacks possess does not facilitate ideal therapeutic conditions. The impact of these factors is compounded by racial differences.

In addition, the prison's administrative operations preclude latitude for day-to-day fluctuation in the inmate's coping behavior. Any staff member can come to work depressed, hungover, tired, or angry. In these cases, the staff member expects and usually gets interactional concessions. The inmate's behavior, however, is categorically expected to be consistently stable.

As the inmate population experiences excessively punitive controls and restrictions, they react by making the atmosphere tense and dangerous for staff and other inmates. Often the anger exhibited by them has not as much to do with character pathology as with personal retaliation for injustices. These responses are a matter of pride. The emasculating environment of prisons demands that one maintain self-respect by any means possible. Rarely able to receive favorable recognition and support from staff, inmates seek it among their own ranks.

Indeed, homosexuality is the most predictable and pervasive phenomenon of prison life. Homosexual acts or other anti-social behaviors, such as stealing and lying, if engaged in by anyone other than an inmate population, would be diagnosed as psychopathic. Yet in prison, these may simply be coping behaviors. Many blacks serving time are able to adapt to prison life, having only the severity of the coping difficulties increased. Some, however, actually undergo personality changes.

Resistance to Therapy

Unquestionably, the alienation inmates feel from the "havers of freedom" constitutes the greatest obstacle to establishing meaningful communication. Resistance to counseling or psychotherapy revolves around inmate resentment of having liberties stripped, being ordered about, and being reduced to the status of a caged animal. Correctional staff are cognizant of the problems encountered in attempts to obtain accurate information from inmates. Many reports critical of promoting and releasing inmates from the system state: "Much of the information obtained in this report was obtained from the resident and therefore may be subject to discrepancy." Black inmates do tend to withhold the truth, but it is important that any person working extensively with black clients be aware that deceit may not be the intention of the evasive reply.

Being black in America has taught them well not to be too trusting of others. In one instance after another, openness has led to abuse of individual liberty, loss of property, and embarrassment before family and friends. The black response to these humiliating situations has been to avoid them by design— by studying the nature of the situation and trying to say or do whatever will reduce the invasion of privacy. Those engaged in therapeutic contact with black clients can attest to many sessions where they received information which appeared inconsistent with the client's abilities or resources. Later in their relationship, the subject revealed the truth. This "coming clean" may have little to do with the therapist's techniques alone; rather, it is a reflection of the inmate's own feelings that the worker can be trusted. The process of trust is a personal one based predominantly on nonverbal cues—the "feeling" level of the client. In some instances the therapist may be quite empathic and yet still not be accepted by the black client.

If the helper forces the issue of honesty too quickly (that is, before the inmate feels comfortable in therapy), the black client may manipulate the therapeutic encounter by simply assuming the expected role. The key lies in allowing sufficient opportunity for the black client to adjust before beginning the work of psychotherapy or counseling. Inmates find it difficult to retract statements later because this requires them to admit to having been dishonest. Blacks particularly hate to show fault of any kind in interactions with whites. The pervasive belief is that all whites think negatively of all blacks. Thus blacks believe each opportunity to prove worth must be capitalized upon. This accounts for the observation made by some whites that blacks tend to overdo— spend too much, hoard too much, live too big. In the black view, the road to success demands twice as much of everything: first for being black and second for what it takes for anyone else.

A common characteristic of people sent to prison is that they project blame on others. "My lawyer's fault . . . the judge . . . a bum rap," are lines heard all too often by correctional employees. Such staff realize that in many instances injustices may indeed have been meted out. These truths are not the issue, however; the denying of individual responsibility, and all too often attributing personal irresponsibility onto others are the main concerns here. Therapists who work in corrections must demand that the rapport established between themselves and their clients include the inmates' acknowledgment of personal responsibility for their present lot, and recognition of the need for future growth. Once this groundwork has been laid, other modes of mental-health intervention can be implemented.

Another significant problem is the continued perception by blacks that once you begin therapy you have admitted to a most embarrasing situation, that is, "your mind is in need of help." That is not an acceptable form of suffering to blacks. It somewhat follows an archaic belief that once a woman has been raped, she will never be clean again.

Racism as a Topic in Therapy

In an environment where survival is paramount, black offenders will attempt to latch onto anything in their surroundings that will put them at an advantage. This can include using the issue of race and racism in therapeutic settings to either make the therapist feel guilty and evoke feelings of sympathy or as a means of diversion from subject matter too painful to confront. Both Wicks (1974) and Yochelson and Samenow (1976) have alluded to this misuse of race in therapeutic interaction with blacks. Wicks addressed this issue when he discussed his counseling relationship with a seventeen-year-old black offender:

> When John first entered therapy, he spent a great deal of time detailing his disadvantaged background and berating the society around him for the way it had perpetrated his poverty and continued to reject him. He also verbally attacked the therapist for being part of the system. He condemned the therapist as rich, condescending, unfeeling, and prejudiced to try to force him to become angry and reject him as others had done in the past.

Yochelson and Samenow (1977, pp. 500–501) expressed their views on the discussion of racial concerns by black offenders:

> Invoking the racial issue is another way of diverting. Clearly, there has been racial bigotry and discrimination by both blacks and whites, but racism is irrelevant to the issue at hand. The criminal knows that race is a sensitive issue, and that is why he raises it; he takes the offensive with charges of racism after he has failed to gain agreement on some point. . . . Of course, an examiner seriously complicates the transaction if he fails to perceive it to be a smokescreen.

It is irrefutable that some blacks do indeed use the issue of racial discrimi-nation for devious purposes and perhaps at inappropriate times. But it must be clear to therapists that there are blacks who are sincerely and honestly con-cerned and affected by racism in America.

To carelessly dismiss all racial responses in therapeutic interactions as only evasive gestures is to deny not only a very real part of being black in America but to summarily erase the assertions of countless numbers of black psycholo-gists, and even white psychologists who feel that racism continues to be a serious problem for blacks.

Undoubtedly, by reducing racial remarks in therapy to the common de-nominator of a defensive mechanism, it can be labeled as maladaptive and the therapist does not have to come to grips with the issue. For many therapists unprepared to deal with racism this may be a convenient solution.

The White Problem: White Staff and Black Inmates

The two principle obstacles that white staff encounter in working with black inmates are alienation and distrust. Alienation is a carry-over from the issues of racism and hostility on the outside. Prior to incarceration, blacks or other minorities confronted with racism had little way in which to retaliate and as prisoners they could not act on it. The lack of trust is a by-product of not having empathic support. Of course, there are nonminority staff who are quite profes-sional and concerned about the plight of incarcerated minorities. However, inmates view them as sympathetic, not empathic; they want someone who understands and cares, not just someone who cares.

Being black, of course, does not give one a patent on empathy. It is true, however, that the inmate perception is that black staff are much more likely than white staff to have grown up in a manner similar to their own. This also explains why inmates prefer to racially segregate themselves in prison. There are no guarantees that sleeping next to another black inmate ensures the likelihood one will wake up the next morning, or wake up not having been raped or bur-glarized; as a matter of fact, statistics on black on black crime suggest the pro-pensity is greater! The comfort afforded comes from sleeping beside one whose lifestyle you understand, whose behavior you can predict, and whose culture you understand and can identify with. Thus alienation and distrust are not unique to blacks in jails and prisons, but constitute a magnification of racial conflicts brought in from the outside.

The race of the mental-health worker need not necessarily be a barrier to a good working and therapeutic relationship with black offenders. Race only becomes a problem if either the client or clinician makes it an issue. If a client refuses to trust the therapist because he is white, or if the clinician can not empathize with the offenders, if either the client or therapist brings racial hang-ups into the therapeutic settings, or if either is reluctant or afraid to confront racial feelings, then the chances of a meaningful interaction is thwarted.

Given the small degree of trust black inmates feel toward white staff members, establishing rapport is a constant priority. One effective means of building good and credible communications is to spend as much time as possible with the inmate away from the office. The office design carries with it the stigma of "knowing all, placing blame, having all the answers." In this environment the black offender does not feel his best interest is at heart; feeling instead that such therapeutic contact serves only to demean and remind him of his sinful ways. In facilities which incarcerate maximum- and medium-custody inmates, flexibility is often limited because of security. "Limited" is a key term, however; one can be quite innovative within such limitations. Talking together in an empty dining hall is helpful, as is walking to the gym with the inmate, or meeting in the library. The goal is to remove a distant, hostile, or alienated client from the atmosphere of offices, and allow latitude for the offender to express himself in a less threatening environment.

Language can be a barrier to effective therapeutic intervention. In America it is true that the lower the black client falls on the socioeconomic scale the more divergent is his dialect from that of standard American English. Given the fact that the incarcerated black is more often the poorer black, it becomes paramount that any helping agent understand the inmate's mode of communication among his peer group, as well as his cries of distress and grief. If questions are asked of a black client in a way that person understands, a wealth of suffering and pain comes forth. The subsequent challenge is for the therapist to understand the heavy symbolism and emotional aspects of black expression.

In many therapeutic interactions there is a communication gap, and not actually a nonverbal client! Thus if the nonminority therapist accepts this perspective (of a communication gap) the problems of communication among blacks and whites assume the focus of cultural differences, as opposed to an orientation of a "deficit" model. Such an orientation allows the nonminority therapist to accept the black client for what and where he is, rather than looking upon him for what he is not.

For many white clinicians it is important to obtain a broader perspective of the minority offenders' culture. Attempting to extract such information from printed literature is the slowest means. A better way is for white therapists responsible for treatment with blacks to attend more black conferences. It is not insinuated that revolutionary concepts in helping people will be forthcoming; the purpose is to hear about ethnic idiosyncracies and rehabilitation from a black perspective. Although many such conferences are labeled "black only," such meetings seem not only to have nonminority participants, but also white panelists and presenters! The purpose of such conferences is to stress to black professionals the need to meet collectively and address issues which relate to minorities from a minority perspective. However, these meetings should no more be "all black" than should meetings of the American Psychological Association, the American Medical Association, or the American Bar Association be "all white." The need for black-sponsored workshops arose from minuscule input that minority members were afforded at other professional meetings. White mental-health staff can gain additional access to minority culture by subscribing to black journals, periodicals, and newsletters, in order to become familiar with modes of expression and feeling which differ from Anglo orientations.

The level of interaction among therapists and the families of offenders is critical for both black and white therapists. This is doubly important for white staff because of inherent lack of familiarity with cultural, familial, and social differences among nonwhites. Many a clinician is faced with the client statement: "But you just don't know where I'm coming from." Without family contact, all that correctional staff have to go on is their contact with the inmate and whatever correctional data are available. Many families do not visit for one reason or another and in these cases a phone call may be helpful.

The Black Problem: Black Staff and Black Inmates

The barrier to communication and honesty most likely to handicap a relationship between the black therapist and the black inmate is value disparity. The therapist may initially provoke the same alienation and mistrust normally directed toward white staff. In fact, black clinicians may observe total rejection by an inmate, which indicates that the inmate (1) rejects the personality-value system of the therapist; (2) believes the therapist has not been genuine— "for real"—in the initial contacts; (3) believes the minority staff member is an Uncle Tom (that is, one who has sold out to white culture); or (4) is punishing the therapist for being a success in life. This reemphasizes that black inmates expect the therapist to care and understand; failure to do so reinforces feelings of alienation and distrust which make the likelihood of anyone reaching the inmate quickly remote.

The advantage afforded a minority therapist is that the minority inmate may be willing to be honest, to communicate much sooner, and to respond on a more consistent basis than with nonminority staff. The benefit should not be overestimated, however, because correctional staff still represent "havers of freedom," the ultimate desire and envy of the inmate population. Therefore, as outsiders, minority staff, too, can anticipate that inmates will try to manipulate them if the end result is either personal or general inmate benefit.

Black therapists will have greater rapport with inmates if they set conflicting personal values aside. Black therapists have every right to personal value systems, of course. However, middle-class values simply cannot accommodate the personal demands of prison life. Understanding the realities of prison existence—

the attitudes and personal orientations which negatively affect the therapists' relationship with clientele—reemphasizes the fact that alien values should be left at home.

Therapeutic-Intervention Techniques

There are a number of therapeutic-intervention approaches that can be utilized in a correctional setting with black inmates. They range from insight therapies to the more action-oriented therapies. In some therapeutic approaches the therapist does not become actively involved in solving the client's problems and in others the clinician not only makes suggestions to the client but actively challenges and confronts the individual. Both group and individual approaches are used.

Some of the major therapies and their possible applicability to black offenders are discussed below.

Psychoanalytic Psychotherapy

Traditional psychoanalysis was the first, and remains the most comprehensive explanation of human behavior, interaction, and thought, addressing itself to the present and past of the individual, his conscious and unconscious functioning, and most significantly the development and maturation of the physical and mental functions (Freud, 1935; McCary, 1955).

Psychoanalysis is considered an insight-oriented therapy which implies that once an individual understands his problem or gains insight into his behavior he is much more capable of changing his behavior. The psychoanalytic psychotherapist attempts to help the client understand the root of his conflict using therapeutic techniques such as dream interpretation, free association, and projective testing. The individual's early childhood relationships are extremely important.

This approach to treatment is based on the medical model. The medical model assumes that there is something wrong with the individual, that the malfunction is diagnosable and treatable. The treatment is long in nature, often lasting for several years. Thus psychoanalysis is neither brief nor cheap. In general, analysts prefer that their clients be well-motivated, able to pay for services promptly, and able to express themselves verbally in a language the analysts can understand.

There are a number of criticisms of the use of traditional psychoanalysis with blacks. The first has to do with the fact that it relies heavily on the sickness or medical model, and consequently the black client is often the one who has to make the adjustment or readjustment. The medical model does not encourage the therapist to intervene into the negative aspects of his client's environment. The problems are not conceptualized as problem of living in a complex, mechanized, uncaring, racially conscious environment, as Thomas Szasz (1976) has stressed continuously. Unfortunately, many of the problems blacks face are very much related to their race and socioeconomic level.

The criteria for the successful client are that he be verbal, able to do the psychological work, and be highly motivated. This has caused a great deal of concern because incarcerated blacks are often required to attend therapy rather than voluntarily participate in the process. In some cases therapy is recommended as part of the classification ritual and sometimes probation or parole may be contingent on therapy attendance. Therefore, the black offender's motivation for therapy may not meet the criteria required by psychoanalysts. In addition, because of the language differences between the therapist and client, and the prison environment of fear and suspicion, the black offender may be resistant to sharing information with the therapist.

The therapist, in order to understand and interact with black offenders, must have an understanding of black culture. This requirement is one that many therapists have not been trained to meet and/or have not deemed a necessary endeavor. Consequently, the degree of competency in implementing psychoanalytic concepts and principles is reduced.

Although the more contemporary psychoanalytic approaches differ in some respects from classical psychoanalysis, such approaches are still subject to many of the criticisms that have been levied against classical psychoanalysis. They pay more attention to the influence of environmental factors, but they continue to adhere to the medical model.

Client-Centered Psychotherapy

"Client-centered" as a psychotherapeutic technique was originally developed by Carl Rogers (1961). The hypothesis postulated by Rogers states that a client's potential for growth and positive personality change optimally occurs in an environment where the therapist is empathic, warm, and demonstrates genuine concern and unconditional positive regard. The assumption is that each individual, barring major organic-physical abnormalities, has the potential to be competent, that is, to be in charge of one's own life and immediate environment. Further, such self-actualizing abilities have either been inhibited in development by lack of exposure, insensitivity, or personal or psychological weakness. According to Rogerian theory, a therapeutic environment characterized by warmth and unconditional regard allows the potential of the client to be actualized, and in other ways helps the client to return to a state of rational decision making.

A client-centered approach to therapy is antithetical to directive psychotherapy. The directive approach portrays the therapist in the role of expert, which means there are things he must know, and things he must do, to become involved in the life of the client. The therapist using the client-centered approach does as little as possible to interfere with the client's own perceptions of what he feels or is experiencing, as such individual perceptions determine what will be done about the problem. The therapist's suggestions are based on the self-actualizing potential of the individual!

Client-centered therapy, also an insight therapy, has received criticism similar to that of psychoanalysis regarding its applicability to blacks. It also has been shown to be more effective with college-level students. One of the major concerns with this approach is that it requires the therapist to be empathic with low-income black offenders who may have committed violent crimes, which may be a difficult task for many middle-class punishment-oriented therapists.

Client-centered therapy does not encourage therapists to actively intervene in the black offender's environment, even though there may be a clear link between the client's behavior and some external event. Many have said that blacks tend to seek aid in emergency situations. When they look for help they are seeking answers and solutions at that moment.

Client-centered therapy is a long process and is basically oriented toward individual therapy. Since there is a shortage of mental-health professionals, group therapy is generally considered more efficient and economical.

Rational-Emotive Psychotherapy (RET)

The rational-emotive form of psychotherapy, formally developed by Albert Ellis (1973), began around the 1950s. This form of therapeutic intervention seeks to denote and eliminate irrational thoughts and beliefs held by individual clients which may interfere with their being in control of personal thoughts and emotions. Five very general statements can be made regarding the process of therapy: the interview is very structured; treatment focuses on overt symptoms to a great degree; little attention is paid to childhood experiences; minuscule focus is placed on more traditional constructs (such as the unconscious or infantile sexuality); and insight is not considered necessary to alleviate problems.

RET is considered to be more active than passive, and includes in treatment a number of tasks (such as homework assignments and roleplaying) which the client must be involved in, obtaining practice toward more desirable thinking and behavior. RET assumes that human beings are born with the potential to be rational decision-makers. But it also postulates that culture and social conditions increase the likelihood that irrational thought and behavior will ensue as a result of the belief system the individual builds about the world he lives in, and what "ought" to be his reaction to various stimuli.

RET seeks to rid the offender of the "musts" and "shoulds" in his life in order to help him toward a more happy life. This form of treatment has found wide acceptance because people generally agree that what a person tells himself about a situation, or about life has a major bearing on the way he feels. The techniques the therapist employs toward therapeutic intervention are quite plausible, however difficult they may be to accept. The very style and theory of Ellis's RET is clear and explicit.

RET purportedly works well with delinquents and criminals. The type of patient not viewed as a good candidate for RET is the psychotic person, with organic impairments of a seriously debilitative nature, the person of borderline and lower mentality, and possibly the person in highly manic states.

The most serious criticism of RET is that it is generally considered to be most effective with populations that have achieved a high academic level. Most black offenders have a low academic achievement level. A real danger is that because RET is so academically oriented, it might create a condition where the offender may feel that he is inadequate because he does not understand what his therapist is attempting to communicate.

Reality Therapy

Reality Therapy was developed by William Glasser (1975). It was his firm belief that in order for reality therapy to be effective the therapist must become involved in the life of the client. The two points most essential to the principles of reality therapy are (1) the requirement that the patient accept full responsibility for his behavior and (2) that there be a warm, involved, and caring relationship between client and therapist. It is most helpful if there are others in the patient's life with whom he has, or can potentially develop, similar relations.

The therapist teaches the patient new behaviors and how to plan for new behaviors. Because of intense involvement in the life of the patient, the therapist directs all suggestions toward present life activities. Such goals should be success programmed, in order not to perpetuate a failure identity. There must also be a commitment by the patient to succeed; this commitment should involve at least one other caring person. Finally, no excuses are accepted (because they are easy ways off the hook), and there are no punishments that could interfere with the involvement necessary for the patient to succeed.

Deberry used the basic concept of reality therapy successfully with inner-city black offenders in a maximum security correctional setting. His approach allowed for the prisoners to confront the reality of being black and poor in America. He noted that once they came to accept this reality they were then able to display more adaptable and constructive behaviors and to act more responsibly.

Behavior Therapy

Behavior therapy focuses on the here and now, does not tend to rely on information from the past, and treats the problems of the client in a scientific and quantifiable manner. The principles of behavior therapy assume that all behavior is learned and that the maladaptive behavior demonstrated by clients can be systematically unlearned. The therapist, using psychological acumen and learning theory, plans a treatment regime with specific, clearly defined treatment goals. In the process of using this technique the form of treatment designed is based upon the therapeutic needs of the client (that is, the presenting problem) and thus requires his active involvement in establishing the plan and goals (Franks, 1969; Lazarus, 1971).

Behaviorists acknowledge environmental factors as the principal determinants of individual behavior. Behavior therapy seeks to provide relief to the individual by consideration of variables in the person's life, such as employment, marriage, or finances. The goal in therapy is to either remove or change the discomfort.

There are a number of techniques that are employed by behaviorists in therapy. These include, but are not limited to, systematic desensitization, modeling, assertiveness training, contingency management, and aversive conditioning.

Behavior modification has received the most negative criticism thus far as compared to all the other therapy techniques. While the typical insight therapies have only been passively ineffective and considered inappropriate, behavior-modification techniques have been considered actively abusive. There are two basic complaints about behavior modification:

1. There have been a number of instances where certain components of behavior modification have been used abusively, flagrantly, and irresponsibly on inmates. Electric shock treatment as a consequence of undesirable behavior is one instance. The most notorious use of behavior modification has been the START program (Special Treatment and Rehabilitative Training), conducted at the federal medical facility in Springfield, Missouri. This program was designed to alter the behavior of inmates considered incorrigible, uncooperative, and assaultive. It was based on behavior-modification principles, especially contingency management. But in implementing this program the inmates were deprived of their basic freedoms and rights, such as regular recreation, showers, and contact with others. These rights were given only after the offenders displayed desired behaviors. The program was eventually canceled because of its harsh nature.

2. The term behavior modification has become synonymous with any kind of mind control and behavior alteration techniques. Thornton (1977) voices this view:

The penal institutions, then, have served as a testing ground for the perfection of new behavior control techniques. While testing and perfection take place in the penal institutions, the ultimate objective is to develop more advanced techniques for controlling all black people.

These advanced and most commonly used techniques are: chemotherapy psychotherapy, electrical therapy, neurosurgery, and sensory deprivation.

There is no doubt that behavior modification can be effective in changing and maintaining behavior. The principles of behavior modification are used in our everyday lives. For example, we perform for pay, praise, or grades. These same principles have been successfully applied with mentally retarded and psychotic individuals, and even autistic children. In prison, "good time," "leaves," and "passes," and other rewards are clear examples of behavior modification in action.

The biggest problem with the use of behavior modification as it applies to black offenders is that they usually have very little input into making the decision about what behaviors are to be changed and how.

Therapeutic Community

The therapeutic community concept was first employed by Maxwell Jones (1968). The focus was to involve the total institution, including staff, in the therapy of individuals confined in the institution. The process allows for decisions to be made by the total group, including the patients.

The first implementation of the therapeutic community concept in a correctional setting occurred in 1969 at the U.S. Federal Prison in Marion, Illinois. The concepts of the Synanon therapeutic community were combined with the treatment methodology of transactional analysis (T.A.) and the actual treatment was conducted by trained inmate therapists. Policy was determined by the residents themselves in consultation with the staff and each person had input into the operation of the community. This was in direct contrast to the general population where inmates had little or no voice in the policymaking process of the institution.

Therapeutic communities appear to be a treatment of choice for the federal prisons. Norman A. Carlson, Director of the Federal Bureau of Prisons, speaking before the U.S. Senate Committee on the Judiciary (1978), endorsed the self-help voluntary therapeutic community programs, and reported that there were therapeutic community programs in eighteen federal correctional institutions that involved about 2,700 inmates, which is about 10 percent of the federal prison population.

The therapeutic community, when implemented properly and endorsed by the administration, is an excellent treatment modality for black offenders because it incorporates so many of the ingredients blacks have struggled for since slavery. It allows for equal partnership, which means that the black offender has input into making decisions that govern his life. It provides an environment of sensitivity and maturity with individuals who have an opportunity to come to grips with their own racial prejudices. Therefore, blacks are accepted as individuals, and color may not be an issue. It also allows for blacks to confront their blackness and their place in the world and how being black might have influenced their interactions with others. Finally, there are other black role models who are able to provide direction.

There is a striking similarity between the therapeutic community and the Black Muslim prison community (chapter 2). Both provide a confrontative format, allow for peer-group support, provide learning exercises to keep the person mentally alert, and give the black offenders a chance to come to grips with being black in a supportive structure. These environments appear to be healthy settings for black offenders to develop emotionally.

Undoubtedly, each of the therapeutic approaches have been used in a correctional environment and each therapist will claim some success with black offenders using their particular style. This is understandable since black offenders differ in their responsiveness to different therapeutic approaches. In the final analysis it may be that if the client believes in the therapist whatever approach the therapist uses will work, as long as the offender has trust in him. For mental-health professionals, the most difficult task may not be the selection of an appropriate therapeutic approach but rather gaining the trust and confidence of black offenders.

Conclusion

Perhaps one of the most used and abused terms with regard to mental-health professions is therapy and/or treatment. It is abused because therapy is not clearly understood and has not been shown to be highly effective with poor and minority groups. Undoubtedly the treatment modalities preferred and practiced by most mental-health professionals will be the direct or confronting type of therapies where responsibility for attitude or behavior change is placed directly on the offender. These techniques are much more comfortable because they relieve clinicians of the responsibility of having to understand blacks and their culture.

What is perhaps needed in most mental-health therapeutic intervention programs in correctional institutions is a movement away from the narrow and restrictive use of the term therapy, toward programs and services that are more reflective of the problems faced by black offenders. It appears that for a great majority of the people in prison, what is wrong with them is that they get caught, they are poor, they do not have access to the same things as noncriminals or noncaught criminals, and they have not received educational opportunities, positive rewards, and other self-enhancing opportunities.

It seems reasonable that any type of treatment should be geared toward eliminating these inequitable conditions. While black offenders may have psychological problems, it may be that their social and economic conditions were responsible for their criminal activities rather than any deep-rooted psychological problems. Therapy for these individuals will not correct social inequities.

6 Preventing Black Crime

The Reverend Jesse Jackson outlined very succinctly why we need to increase our crime prevention efforts when he said: "If a young man or woman goes to any state university in this country for four years, it will cost less than $20,000. If he or she goes to a state penitentiary for four years, it will cost anywhere from $50,000 to $120,000. Education and employment cost less than ignorance and incarceration" (Chambers, 1979 p. 1607).

It is becoming increasingly apparent that if we are to curb the flow of black crime and to prevent more younger blacks from getting involved in the criminal-justice system we must place a high priority on crime prevention. Mental-health professionals can become involved in crime prevention efforts by understanding the factors in the family, schools, and community that encourage criminal activities and creating and conducting programs that either strengthen these units as crime prevention influences or reducing the factors that foster criminal behavior.

The Black Family

Typically, low-income black parents are seen either as significant causal factors in their child's delinquent and criminal activity or at best ineffectual and impotent in preventing the antisocial activities of the child. This negative perception of the black family is anchored in earlier research that has tended to characterize the lower-class black family as disorganized, dysfunctional, and unhealthy (Billingsly, 1977). In addition, the black family has been described as a violent unit. One-fourth of all black homicides in 1972 took place among family members—either spouse killing spouse or killings which involved parent and child. In 1967–1968, the child abuse rate reported for black children was more than three times the ratio for nonblack children (Staples, 1975). The black family is generally stereotyped as a single parent family, which is viewed by some as being a significant causal factor in criminal behavior (Moynihan, 1965).

The acceptance of crime as a way of life may be inevitable for a great percentage of black parents who are poor and feel estranged from the larger society; who feel powerless in controlling their own lives; whose employment may be temporary and who may live in an environment where criminal behaviors are pervasive. And heads of many single-parent families cannot and do not provide the parental supervision which will allow them to continuously monitor the activities of their children. Consequently, when their children become involved in criminal activities, they may simply accept it.

Indeed, in some instances children are encouraged to participate in illegal behavior by significant others, including parents who sanction the acts, either by encouraging them or by routinely ignoring their behavior. And some parents are incapable of preventing their children from committing delinquent acts.

Unfortunately, the above description may accurately depict some black families. The majority of poor black families, however, are sincerely interested in keeping their children out of the clutches of the juvenile system. They want the same things for their children that other parents want including equal access to educational and employment opportunities. The parent is rare who has a goal to make his or her child a criminal.

Because there are many poor black parents who care about what happens to their children and their neighborhoods, they form a valuable, untapped resource for preventing crime. Unfortunately, because of the negative stereotypes that prevail about them, they have not been seriously viewed as an asset in crime prevention efforts. The area where black parents can be the most effective is in keeping their own children from becoming delinquent.

In most major urban areas there appears to be no concerted effort to utilize the services of parents or to increase their effectiveness as a crime prevention resource. Parents are left to use their own prescriptions for diverting their children from committing delinquent acts. Not unlike other parents, black parents do not receive lessons, instructions, or guidelines about how to keep their children from a life of crime. Somehow we assume that parents should know these things. However, black parents may be affected more by this oversight because their children are more likely to enter the criminal-justice system.

Unfortunately, most of the help or attention black parents receive comes after the child has been apprehended. Even though the facts support that a life of crime is most preventable before the child receives reinforcement for successful delinquent acts, it appears that most social agencies prefer to become involved after the child becomes a legal problem.

The controversial film "Scared Straight" is indicative of society's preoccupation with focusing attention and resources on individuals who become delinquent and ignore the potential valuable role of the family. "Scared Straight" describes the program at Rahway State Prison in New Jersey which is designed to frighten adjudicated juvenile delinquents away from further delinquent activities by interacting with hard-core convicts. One of the precautions given to the viewing public was that abusive language would be used in the program, with the implication that young children and adolescents (who had not been exposed to such vulgar language) should be discouraged from viewing the program. A much more beneficial and useful approach would have been to communicate with parents how to view the program constructively with their children who were not delinquent and to discuss with them the possible consequences of becoming criminal. The program could have been an excellent graphic weapon for parents to use to discourage their nondelinquent children from future delinquent acts.

Realizing that many black juveniles have committed a number of delinquent acts by the time they are apprehended by the police, it might be feasible to strengthen the capacity of black parents to deter their children from a life of crime. At the point of detection, the youngster may have experienced many criminal successes that have reinforced the positive consequences of a law-breaking lifestyle. However, some delinquent behavior is generally known to someone in the child's environment such as their parents, relatives, or neighbors before the juvenile comes into contact with the police. There are both direct and subtle clues that alert relatives and others that he or she may be participating in delinquent acts or at least engaging in questionable activities, such as the sudden acquisition of new wealth or behaviors such as secretiveness and a high degree of anxiety.

When parents become aware of their child's illegal activity, they attempt to resolve the problem to the best of their knowledge. Too often, the alternatives are limited. One option, to call the police and report their child's delinquent behavior, seems the least likely course that a black parent would pursue. For those parents who have not been involved with the police, the involvement of their child with the police may be considered a family disgrace. Thus they are not likely to make a referral to the police in this case. Also, a parent may be un-likely to submit a child for arrest or incarceration after he or she successfully escaped capture. The lack of trust in the law-enforcement agencies, the loss of time from work for hearings, and the possible court and legal fees further serve to dissuade parents from pursuing this course of action. Finally, many parents hope that their children will change and will not become more deeply entrenched in delinquency.

Another alternative would be to notify institutional representatives such as social workers and teachers. The adoption of this course of action is contingent on many conditions. First, the information that black parents tell individuals outside of their immediate family will probably depend on the degree of trust that exists between the parent and the social worker or teacher. However, it is doubtful that black parents will seek aid and advice from these people partly because of the assumed linkage with the police, and partly because of the lack of knowledge of how this negative information about their children will affect various services and programs that they might vitally need. In the final analysis, contacting institutional representatives would not seem to be a popular course of action for black parents to pursue in seeking help for their delinquent child.

One other possible choice for many black parents is to talk to those family members and friends who are very close to them. This interaction can result in receiving advice or, in some cases, having the relative or friend intervene directly by talking to the child. For other black parents, however, even this may not be a viable option, as they may not share the type of relationship with friends and relatives that would stimulate them to share their concerns about their child's potential delinquent behavior with others.

For these and other reasons, most parents probably attempt to solve the problem alone. There are several ways in which parents may try to solve the problem: (1) threats, where the child is told of all the negative consequences that might accrue to him, such as prison; (2) punishment, such as a beating or being restricted from leaving the house; (3) appeals and reason, where the parent attempts to reach the child emotionally or intellectually; (4) restitution, in which the person replaces the object stolen or in some way makes amends for the criminal act; or (5) any combination of the above.

The knowledge of how black parents relate to their offspring, prior to the time the child is apprehended by police, is extremely limited. We know neither what has worked for black parents nor what has not worked. Thus there are no known effective solutions. Perhaps one specific method which was effective for one family, and may have been all that was required to deter a potential offender, may have had no effect for another parent using the very same method. For all we know, what black parents say or do to their children could unintentionally motivate them to criminal behavior.

By the time a child is apprehended it is possible that many black parents have grown to accept the fact that their child has committed many delinquent acts. Many police officers, juvenile workers, and mental health workers who come into contact with parents are surprised that black parents are not shocked or disappointed when they tell them that their child has been involved in delinquent behavior.

The reports of those involved in processing the black delinquent will usually reflect that black parents are apathetic and unconcerned about the child's rehabilitation program. However, what they might be seeing in some black parents is very similar to what Seligman (1969) described as "learned helplessness." This label describes a condition where people, after many unsuccessful attempts to accomplish a goal, realize that they cannot succeed and eventually quit trying. In essence, they learn to be helpless and hopeless. Black parents, after countless unsuccessful efforts to direct their child from delinquent acts, may eventually realize that they are powerless to affect the child's behavior and simply accept the reality of the situation.

A number of valuable services are needed if the black family is to become a viable crime prevention resource. Many of these services can be performed by mental-health professionals. Child rearing and communication skills that can strengthen closer relationships through effective communication among family members can be taught to parents. Programs that reduce the negative influences in the environment by helping family members to obtain needed medical educational and employment services are very much needed.

The Black Community

Black communities have historically and typically been characterized as environments conducive to fostering mental illness rather than mental health. Within
this environment high unemployment, apathy, powerlessness, alienation, lack of
community services, inadequate housing, a high transient population, ineffective
schools, and antisocial behaviors abound. These conditions contribute not only
to the poor mental health of its inhabitants, but also to a high crime rate in the
communities. The chances of becoming a victim of a criminal act increases for
those living in these areas and many black residents, including the elderly, live
in constant fear.

However, in spite of the fear, anxiety, and tension generated by delinquents
and criminals, black communities have traditionally protected its deviant members by not reporting many law breakers and law breaking activities. This protective nature of black communities was understandable in light of the injustices
experienced by blacks within the criminal-justice system, the blatant abuse
directed at black offenders, and the resulting lack of identity with a justice
system that was not designed to protect the interests of blacks. Consequently,
many community members could justify the illegal behavior with the belief
that "he's just trying to make it," or more directly, "That's the only way the
black man can make it in a white society."

In the past, not turning a black man in to the police may have been a realistic and sound decision, especially when statistics revealed that there were critical
shortages of blacks throughout the system who were in decision-making positions.

As many obstacles and barriers to equal treatment and justice throughout the
system are removed, and as more blacks are absorbed in the ranks of the police,
judges, correctional officers, probation and parole officers, and attorneys, the system becomes less oppressive and abrasive. The decision to protect black criminals
in the community thus is less valid. Protecting someone or groups that may be
harmful to oneself and others in the community is in many respects evidence of
poor community mental health. While there continues to be injustices in the system, this does not now reflect the callous nature that was so characteristic earlier.

There is no doubt that the first priority in preventing and reducing crime
by members of the black communities against other black residents is to provide
employment opportunities, access to institutional services such as adequate
health care, recreational opportunities, law enforcement protection, and other
positive elements that other communities with low crime rates enjoy. These
services can at least reduce some of the motivations and frustrations that play
a prominent role in delinquent and criminal behaviors.

Ultimately, however, crime can only be reduced or prevented in any community when the residents themselves decide to reduce crime. One of the

valuable resources in most communities, including black communities, is that there are more residents who want to be law abiding than there are who want to be criminals. Individually and collectively, members of the black community have to realize that they are responsible for their lives, and can have a share in controlling the crime in their community. Black residents should not have to live under a state of tension and the fear of being assaulted, robbed, and killed by other blacks. Swan (1977), in his review of black communities, noted that, when black community residents feel powerless to control their community, they become uninvolved. The more black offenders feel that their chances of being detected, reported, and captured in the black community are minimal, the more they feel free to continue their criminal behaviors.

While racism is responsible for many of the present ills of black people, and there is ample evidence to document this phenomenon, focusing on racial injustice as the main factor responsible for the financial and social condition of blacks and the reason for black-on-black crimes excuses all sorts of deviant behavior in the black community. Consequently, all the responsibility for failure, for lack of motivation and delinquent and criminal acts, is shifted to external factors and individual responsibility is thwarted.

Community residents must assume some responsibility for changing their social environment. In areas where black community members have taken responsibility for what goes on in their neighborhoods, there have been noticeable reductions in delinquent and criminal behaviors (U.S. Department of Justice, 1979).

All community members have some responsibility in preventing and controlling crime in the community. This responsibility must be accepted, shared, and transmitted to the children. The young must be helped to understand what is expected of them, particularly as new elements are introduced into the community.

An example of how this responsibility must be accepted is demonstrated by the following anecdotes: A tennis court had been placed in the heart of a black community in a large southern city. After a number of weeks, slight signs of deterioration caused by vandalistic acts were noticed, such as holes in the windscreens, tire tracks on the tennis court surface, and torn nets. These were eventually repaired after many weeks of delay. Ardent tennis players were angry because it meant that they were inconvenienced. One day later, a group of people were playing tennis and some kids came over and blatantly started running their bikes into the net at a vacant court. Most of the participants and onlookers either were unaware of the incident or chose not to intervene. However, one young man who was playing tennis on the opposite side of the tennis court stopped his game and went over and told the kids to stop damaging the property. He said it in such a way that made the kids realize that they had a responsibility to keep equipment in good condition in the black community. After that, others began to confront the destructive behavior on the courts, and the courts remained in relatively good playing condition.

Still another example: young children were beginning to play tennis on tennis courts and used some of the same loud language that one is accustomed to hearing on outdoor basketball courts. Many people chose to ignore the loud, distracting language, even though it interfered with their own game. Finally, one day someone told the kids who were using the loud language that in tennis people have to concentrate and it would be appreciated if they would not scream at each other. They looked angered, but they eventually stopped.

The point is that these young people really did not know that loud talking was not acceptable in tennis. They had participated in a game for which they did not know all the rules. They were not trying to be antisocial purposely; it was just that, up to that point, no one had taken the responsibility to make sure that they knew what was expected of them.

One can only wonder about how much of black children's behavior we label as antisocial could be attributed to gaps in their experiences. Since their inappropriate behavior is not corrected, they continue it. Then when they display this behavior outside their community they get into trouble because others label it as disruptive.

The community mental-health center is one mechanism for the involvement of the mental-health professionals in improving community mental health and reducing crime. However, it should be stressed that a mental-health center is not the total antidote for black crime. Community members may not utilize the services of the center for a number of reasons. It is imperative that the staff be able to relate to the community and be accessible and responsive to the needs of the residents.

Regardless of the particular structure through which mental-health professionals work, there are a number of services that they can provide to community members and those who come into contact with community members such as the police. Palmer (1976) recommended the establishment of Neighborhood Centers that would implement programs geared to help citizens cope with crime in their communities. He proposed a series of coordinated program activities, including family meetings.

One of the most critical services needed in black communities is crisis intervention. Most mental-health programs are set up to serve populations from 8:00 A.M. through 5:00 P.M. However crisis situations occur regularly within the black community after 5:00 P.M. Most of the assaults, rapes, and murders occur late at night and on weekends (Amir, 1971). Community members are generally helpless because they have limited resources to go to with their emotional problems other than the police and the hospital. This lack of access to a listening ear can breed frustration. Of course, some situations can be handled by the individuals themselves, with a little help from friends and relatives. Other situations may rquire a higher level of intervention.

In order to handle the emergency problems that occur in black communities, crisis centers with twenty-four-hour phone service should be available. Members staffing the crisis center should be qualified to handle a variety of personal problems that might be common in the black community including potential suicide victims, substance abusers, violent family members, potential child abusers, and battered children. The staff should be trained so that they will know what to tell parents who find out their children have committed criminal acts; what to tell the elderly who are alone and fearful; and what to tell the woman who has been raped but is afraid to report the crime. Needless to say, the crisis center should be able to reach out and pull in other services both in the immediate community and the larger society. This crisis center service can help ease the trapped feeling that many community members might feel in crisis situations.

Mental-health professionals can also use their clinical skills in teaching police how to effectively interact with black community members as a whole and intervene in family conflict situations. A number of models for training police in crisis family interventions (Bard, 1976) and black relationships (Hughes, 1976) have been reported. This training is vital because the policeman is the first line of defense for the criminal-justice system. The abuse black communities have endured from police has reinforced their powerless position. Their relationship with the community may significantly affect the community's attitude toward the criminal-justice system. It is important that the criminal-justice system be perceived as being concerned about the positive mental health and survival of the black community. Community members should feel that they can be protected from criminal elements in their midst and that, if they intervene in criminal activities, abusive treatment will not result from becoming involved. They must concurrently feel that black offenders will not be unfairly treated in the system. Courteous, efficient police who understand the culture of the black community, who have been trained to use effective listening and helping skills, can reduce some of the negative feelings that blacks have had toward the police and the criminal-justice system.

Finally, mental-health professionals can expand their services to the victims of criminal acts. In all too many cases, the victims suffer more than the offender, both in terms of financial loss and psychological damage. The need for post-assault counseling has been pointed out for both rape victims and victims of kidnappings and hostage holdings. Victims of muggings and robberies have the same need. This has been shown most clearly by the Karen Horney Clinic in New York which specializes in providing free counseling services to the victims of violent assaults (Innovations, 1975). A clinic report revealed that after an attack, victims sometimes go through periods of depression, self-blame, indecision, anxiety, and other crippling emotional states.

We know that blacks in urban areas stand a much greater chance of being a victim than those in nonurban areas. Mental-health professionals in clinics in the urban areas equipped to help black victims come to grips with their emotional reactions to the crime, and to make many of the countless decisions one might have to make after a crime pertaining to family maintenance, employment, financial support, and others, would be a valuable asset in black communities.

The School

One obvious fact about criminals is that almost all of them at some period in their life are enrolled in a school system. Even though they may quit school earlier than other students, the schools have a chance to influence the direction of their lives. Attitudes about criminals and criminal activities, law enforcement, getting caught, reporting criminal activities, and values about right and wrong are sometimes planted and often nourished in the school environment. At many junctures, youngsters both in school and after school face the fears and anxieties related to criminal acts—fear of capture, fear of detection by parents, moments of regret and doubt, indecision about repeating a crime, and, of course, moments of pleasure and excitement. What happens in the school does influence how these fears and anxieties are resolved.

In spite of the awareness that the schools have daily contact with the future law violators of America, and can influence their behaviors, very few schools have structured programs that are specifically designed to keep them from becoming offenders. Visibly missing from most school curriculums are systematic and coordinated crime prevention and crime education programs from kindergarten to high school that equip black students to make intelligent decisions about criminal acts; that discuss realistic alternatives for poor black children; that encourage law-abiding students to become involved in crime prevention; that allow the potential lawbreaker to realize the consequences for his actions; and that simply motivate students to remain within the confines of legal behavior.

Not only does it appear that schools have failed to assume an active role in deterring black students from criminal acts, but periodically they may be centers for teaching students about crime. Members of the Senate Juvenile Delinquency Subcommittee (1975) found from their survey of 757 elementary and secondary schools that each year about 70,000 teachers and hundreds of thousands of students are physically assaulted. More than 100 students were murdered in 1973. Between 1970 and 1973, there was an increase in all categories of aggressive behavior. Assaults on teachers increased 77 percent; assaults on students increased 85 percent; rapes and attempted rapes were up by 40 percent; robberies of teachers and students increased 37 percent; homicides in schools increased 19 percent; and the number of weapons confiscated form students in schools increased 54 percent. In addition, the number of security personnel now employed in school settings is over 15,000.

Little research has been conducted on teaching criminal-justice courses in public schools; consequently, little is known about what teachers are doing or teaching with respect to crime and lawbreaking or what cues are being emitted by teachers that either deter or encourage crime. Teachers are generally not trained to teach criminal-justice classes to youngsters. The most qualified usually have had only one criminal justice class as a college elective. With no structured system for teaching about crime, what is presented on the subject is left up to the discretion of the teachers and is probably reflective of the instructor's value system. Teachers might, for example, feel that all lawbreakers are psychologically disturbed, and convey this to the class, or that all lawbreakers are victims of society, and present this view to the class. Either position, of course, will inevitably affect the perception of the students.

Urban schools have not accepted the responsibility for providing leadership in crime-prevention programs. It seems very probable that black students who are considered high risk candidates for criminal careers by and large acquire their values about crime from their natural environment, without structured school intervention.

The school a student attends will influence the types of delinquent and criminal behavior to which he or she is exposed and the type of criminal behavor he or she is most likely to exhibit. In other words, since the school is at best neutral, the peer group becomes an important influence on subsequent criminal careers. Sutherland's theory of differential association (1973) supports this perspective by noting that, where there is an abundance of criminal activities in one's environments, a person is more likely swayed in that direction.

It has also been suggested that schools are very much like prisons both physically and psychologically. Haney and Zimbardo (1975) noted striking similarities between the two: the long, bleak corridors; the alignment of rooms; movement by the clock; and security guards. In many respects, the daily routine of a student in the school system is as structured as the day of a prisoner. The control that the school system exercises over the lives of the students is almost as complete as the control prison systems exercise over the inmates.

Schools parallel prisons in other important aspects. Prisons range from maximum security prisons, where the most dangerous prisoners are supposedly kept and where there is a much tighter security, to the minimum security prisons, where the least dangerous are assigned and security is more relaxed.

The inner-city schools are more similar to the maximum security prisons, where tensions are higher, much less trust exists, and more severe criminal behavior is evident. In this setting, there is a higher probability of personal injury and property damage. Even teachers live in fear and many are assaulted in these schools. The expectations for learning, for achievement, and for success are low and defeatist attitudes prevail. Most of the emphasis in these schools, as in maximum security, is on control and order rather than on freedom and creativity.

In contrast, the schools outside the inner city display much more freedom for the students, much less fear, and much less security. The suburban schools exemplify the minimum security status. There is very little emphasis on control and more concern with creativity and learning. The expectations for achievement and success are high. These students, much like the minimum security prisoners, have more freedom of movement and more control over their environment. Students from schools that approximate medium and minimum systems will be exposed most often to nonviolent crimes—the so-called white-collar crimes. Students are more likely 'to be exposed to violent and destructive crimes in the schools that are similar to the maximum security prisons. These are the schools in which most black students will be.

However, even if school systems decide to get involved, they must address the real concerns and lifestyles of black children. We cannot simply teach that the criminal-justice system is colorblind or that all policemen are helpful and courteous. While policemen may be helpful and courteous in some areas, they may not be perceived in such a positive light in urban areas. The criminal-justice system should be presented realistically and in a manner that is relevant to the lifestyles of blacks. Black children need guidance that will help them to over-come the type of criminal activities they may be exposed to on a regular basis. The type of situations black children may face and which should be discussed in schools, are being poor and having to steal to eat; or what to do when a relative is breaking the law; or how to resist your friends when they challenge you to do something illegal.

Schools which fail to intervene neglect an important opportunity to reduce a student's chances of being influenced by the criminal elements in his or her environment. Unfortunately, students are left to fend for themselves. Those who need intervention programs the most are black students in the inner-city max-imum security schools, because they have the greatest exposure to an environ-ment of crime.

There may be many students who will not benefit from intervention by the schools. It may be that the behaviors of black children fit into the psycholog-ical triage concept of therapy, where one-third will not get better no matter what treatment is administered, one-third will get better without any treatment, and only one-third will be influenced by any treatment program.

Or, it may be that the early behaviors of black schoolchildren form a bell-shaped curve. On one end are a very small number of students who will exhibit deviant behavior. Because of the interaction with their environment, their genetic makeup, and other factors, most of these children will populate our mental hospitals, mental retardation facilities, and correctional institutions. By the time they reach the school, if they get that far, they will probably be firmly anchored in their behavior patterns. Negative school experiences will probably accelerate their academic and social demise.

On the other extreme of the bell curve are a small group who will probably not exhibit deviant behavior except under the most extreme circumstances. These black children, because of a positive family background, a highly developed conscience, a successful educational experience, or other reasons, will not become part of the criminal-justice system. This group by and large is not sensitive to the failing and inadequacies of the educational experience. They will make it in spite of the school environment.

The larger percentage of black children, however, are sandwiched between these two extremes. These are the students who have not committed themselves one way or the other to crime and delinquent acts. Their future may hinge on what happens to them during their school years. They are most sensitive and vulnerable to the academic experience and to peer pressure. Many of them can be influenced to become criminal or noncriminal, depending on what happens with them and to them in their environment. If, for example, their educational experiences are rewarding and positive and they develop positive self-concepts and coping skills, they will respond to nondeviant elements. The most vulnerable students in this group are the ones who have suffered either physical or emotional abuse from significant others, have difficulty navigating the academic and social environment, or receive reinforcement from peers for participating in criminal acts.

Unfortunately, for most of these marginal black students, as the educational process continues, the education experience becomes skewed in a negative direction. The Coleman Report (1966) documented that the educational gap between black students and white students increases throughout the educational experience. By the time black students reached the twelfth grade, standardized test results showed that they were much farther behind white students than when they started out in the first grade. As a result of academic failures and frustrations, many black students either drop out or are pushed out by teachers. Many leave school with good intentions of joining the employment market. Finally, because black youth possess few academic skills and a higher than average unemployment rate for teenagers, these black youths subsequently become prime candidates for coming into contact with the criminal-justice system.

Early intervention (especially for the marginal student) through crime-prevention programs, counseling, and other services and activities becomes especially critical. There will generally exist an excess of criminal behaviors in their environment and they can just as easily become criminal as noncriminal. Many will, in fact, become entangled in the juvenile-justice system. If caught, it is highly probable that this group will be the most rehabilitative because their criminality evolved mainly as a result of restricted options or lack of positive intervention in their lives rather than as a result of a real commitment to crime.

We must assume and/or believe that the majority of black youth do not want to commit crime. Programs, therefore, must be geared toward tipping the scales so that the temptation to commit delinquent and criminal acts is not a viable option for black youth.

What is needed for these marginal students is a program in a nonthreatening school environment that can assist students in coming to grips with their unresolved concerns, myths, fears, and values about crime; to ventilate some of the feelings they might have about the criminal-justice system; to understand peer-group pressure; to analyze all the other negative elements that might be influencing the youngsters to a life of crime; and to make rational decisions about criminal activities. This program should be a sequential, purposeful course of study from grade one through twelve that provides for gradual growth in scope and content in keeping with the stages of development of the child. The program should provide the child with the knowledge, understanding, appreciation, and values needed in order to become a worthwhile citizen in society. It should be structured to give the child a sense of stability, as well as desirable attitudes and standards of behavior in keeping with an acceptable way of life.

This criminal-justice-education program should be structured around the main reasons why people commit crimes: (1) economic reasons, (2) emotional reasons, (3) pathological reasons, (4) peer influence, (5) drug related, (6) a habitual lifestyle, or (7) any combination of the above. With this typology as a base, the criminal-justice program should be designed to equip young people to resist (peer pressure and drugs); to understand or control (emotional or pathological states); and explore alternatives (economic deficiencies and lifestyles). In order to accomplish these goals, the objectives of the criminal-justice curriculum should be to (1) increase awareness of crime and the operation of the criminal justice process; (2) decrease negative peer influence; (3) develop a sense of social responsibility with an awareness of values and the consequences of one's actions; (4) expand awareness of the alternatives to criminal acts; and (5) increase coping skills for emotional and social pressures and conflicts.

It is important for the criminal-justice-education program to be systematically presented for a specified period of time in each grade level. The focus may shift, but the goals should remain the same. The program should be realistically presented by trained teachers. Students should know that crime does pay, for some; that not all offenders get caught; that some offenders, if they do get caught, don't get punished; and that the criminal-justice system has not been completely blind. However, students should also know what the punishment is for various types of offenses; the rights of offenders; what jails and prisons look and feel like; the reasons people commit crimes; what happens to families while inmates are incarcerated; and, finally, what alternatives there are to crime. There should be a major focus for each developmental stage (elementary, middle school, and high school), as the need of each age group is different. For example, peer influence may be more of a problem with elementary school children, while drug abuse may be more pertinent to older groups.

Elementary school children aged six to twelve are in their most formative years and, therefore, this period of development is crucial for setting the foundation for future attitudes and perceptions toward criminal activities. Modeling appropriate behavior by significant adults is extremely critical. Noncriminal role models should be presented and discussed regularly. In addition, discussions of various antisocial behaviors, consequences, and alternatives can be a regular activity. Specific childhood behaviors that may occur in the classroom such as restlessness, stealing, lying, and destructiveness could serve as focal points for discussion. The school environment should be structured so that inappropriate behavior will be less likely. If inappropriate behavior is displayed, the teacher must be prepared to discourage the behavior immediately and to present appropriate behavior.

Audio visual aids, field trips to criminal-justice agencies, show and tell, and other techniques used in the school for other academic activities could be utilized. Activities such as crime prevention week or a contest for the best crime prevention poster are certainly worthwhile and appropriate.

In the middle school years (thirteen to fifteen), early adolescents are in the process of making new friends, pulling away from parental influences, and questioning old values, They will be exposed to new challenges during this period and will be highly vulnerable to peer influences. This is the stage when many youngsters begin their delinquent behavior, either individually or in gangs. The criminal-justice curriculum should focus primarily on how our behavior is shaped by those in our environment and the needs that are satisfied by participating in delinquent behaviors. Stressing the importance of the consequences of behavior is encouraged. Young adolescents should be allowed to vent their feelings and attitudes in groups so that feedback can be obtained from their peers in a nonthreatening environment. Role models, both the ex-offenders and employees in the criminal-justice system can provide a global view of the operation of the system, the ramifications of lawbreaking behaviors, and possible future employment opportunities. Visits to correctional institutions should be a part of the early adolescent experience.

In high school during late adolescence (sixteen to eighteen), students are striving to assert themselves as individuals, to carve out an identity, to become independent, and to be concerned about their future. The criminal-justice emphasis could be shifted to more sophisticated and specialized subject matter such as the theories of crime or special categories of criminals such as the rapist, the mentally ill offender, the mentally retarded offender, the mugger, and the elderly inmate. The duties of specific criminal-justice professionals or biographies of famous criminal-justice figures could be researched and presented as projects. These activities can help the students to understand the dynamics of criminal-justice organizations and also broaden their scope about employment opportunities in the criminal-justice fields.

Since a significant number of young people will be unable to find summer employment and some will be considering dropping out of school, there should be a strong emphasis on alternatives to criminal behavior, individual responsibility, and consequences of behavior. The opportunity to discuss feelings and attitudes and to visit institutions where interaction with both offender and nonoffender role models is possible should be a necessary part of the curriculum.

What must be threaded throughout the criminal-justice education program, however, is the theme of responsibility, both for one's own life and for crime prevention in the environment. In all too many situations, black students feel that they have no control over their environment and do not accept responsibility for what happens to them or what happens to their environment.

A school superintendent in Michigan described a successful program that was initiated by an industrial organization to train poor and black youngsters for employment at its plant. These youngsters had no employment skills, were unemployed, lacked initiative and direction, and were considered apathetic. In order to inspire these youngsters to become involved in taking responsibility for their lives, one of the early aspects of the training session was to make them aware that between birth and death all of us make decisions that help to determine whether we will be successful in life.

After this idea was presented to students, they were instructed to list all the situations, conditions, and events that contributed to making people failures in life. The students listed all possible reasons including race, sex, age, physical handicaps, emotional handicaps, racism, unemployment, poverty, lack of initiative, lack of confidence, lack of information, peer influence, and lack of education.

From these completed lists the students were directed to eliminate all those factors that the individual could not control. Those factors eliminated tended most often to be biological, such as race, age, sex, and physical handicaps. Students eventually came to realize that, while they lacked control over some aspects, there were many more elements they could control which could make a difference between success or failure. Many of them came to realize that the reason they were in their present situation was because they had failed to take responsibility for improving their lives. After this realization, students began to concentrate on maximizing their ability to influence the course of their lives. Teaching responsibility should be an integral part of a criminal-justice-education curriculum.

In conjunction with a structured program to discuss crime and criminal-justice issues, there should be a good relationship established between school members and law-enforcement agencies. It is desirable that students not believe that all police are "out to get them" or that they will be treated unfairly if they are arrested. Building this relationship may take a great deal of time and effort, but the dividends are worth the investment. A school relations bureau was established within the police department of Montgomery, Alabama, in 1972. After three years, a questionnaire revealed that students from all-black schools expressed more positive feelings toward the school relations bureau officers than did students from an integrated school. In addition, 70 percent of the parents of the black students expressed support for the officers (Clements, 1975).

Conclusion

Crime prevention in black communities must be seen as an important and necessary area for the involvement of the larger society. It is critical not only because of the economical savings to our country, but also because of the savings in terms of needless suffering and agony that accrue to the offender and significant others in his environment.

Parents, school officials, and community are all influential elements in the lives of black youth. It is only when these important socializing segments accept individual and collaborative responsibility for deterring blacks from criminal activities that we will see any significant reduction of crime in black communities and among black youth in general.

The potential skills that mental-health professionals possess are critical in crime-prevention efforts. However, all the training they have received will be meaningless until they begin to believe in the potential of black parents to be effective crime prevention agents, the ability of the school to offer meaningful academic and vocational programs, and the desire of black neighborhoods to control and prevent criminal activities.

7 Mental-Health Professionals as Agents of Change

There is no doubt that a number of positive changes have occurred in criminal justice settings. Almost every agency of the criminal-justice system can attest to new procedures or requirements. The police are now required to attend academic courses; the standards for correctional officers have been upgraded; prisons are becoming less overcrowded; there has been an increase in postrelease services; and more mental-health professionals are becoming involved in criminal-justice affairs and offering more services and programs.

These innovations will inevitably affect the quality of the treatment the black offender receives from the input through the output stage of the criminal-justice process. There are other changes, however, that more directly influence blacks. Although personnel shortages still remain, there has been an increase in the number of black criminal-justice personnel in most agencies: judges, police, correctional officers, administrators, and even mental health professionals. A consortium of predominantly black schools now offers criminal-justice programs which should enlarge the pool of black professionals eligible to work in criminal-justice settings. In some correctional institutions black culture programs are conducted.

There have been several reasons contributing to these changes. Many have occurred as a direct result of court intervention. Some have been caused by pressures from special interest groups and concerned citizens. Still others have occurred because of strong administrative leadership and some have resulted from staff dedication and commitment.

For every change that has taken root and been implemented there are probably as many innovations that have been squelched and prevented from becoming a lasting reality for many of the same reasons: lack of court intervention and pressure from the citizenry; poor administrative leadership and weak staff support.

While there have been a number of improvements in the area of mental health in some criminal-justice settings, much still remains to be done if mental-health professionals are to function effectively and efficiently. In order to provide new and creative services they may have to transcend the narrow operational boundaries usually prescribed for them. The result may be that recommendations for both behavioral and attitudinal changes of staff and administrators have to be made which might be unpopular and generate negative feelings toward mental-health programs. These feelings may be manifested by resistance to the implementation of new or existing programs. Resistance may be expressed in a number of ways, ranging from direct program sabotage to more subtle forms of passive-aggressive behaviors. The experience of a group of psychologists wanting to start group sessions with inmates in a local jail vividly demonstrates one of the many faces of resistance (McCarter, Colwick, and Goodwin, 1978). Although a number of seemingly practical reasons were given by correctional staff for resisting group sessions, such as security problems and the use of jailor time, the mental-health professionals felt that the real reason was that the staff traditionally had negative feelings about psychological and psychiatric treatment for incarcerated individuals.

It is clear that the mental-health worker must become an agent of change if mental-health programs are to be implemented in environments resistive to change. The role of the change agent might not appear to be inconsistent with one's academic and experiential background since mental-health professionals are generally trained to change behavior and attitudes. Unfortunately, for so many professionals their experiences have been designed to be used on and with powerless people (clients) and those with problems, not with powerful people (administrators, supervisors, peers, and other staff) and those without personal problems. As a result they are not prepared to be effective system change agents. The perception of their role is to change the people in the system and not the system, which implies strict adherence to the medical model.

Their role perception is reinforced by the fact that mental-health services are typically labeled as supportive services, which suggests their purpose is to support the system and maintain the status quo. As a result, some mental-health professionals prefer to be called facilitators and helpers rather than change agents. There are reasons for this preference. A change agent is a person or group who attempts to influence decisions and change in a direction desired by the change agent. This person or group of persons plans, systematically, for the change and maps out strategy to get the desired results. The term change agent implies behavior manipulation which is still viewed negatively by some clinicians who cling to the belief that counseling and therapy is most effective when the client makes decisions without interference from the therapist.

A change agent accepts responsibility and accountability for changes in the system, including both improvements and failures. The role of a facilitator removes the individual from responsibility and accountability. A change agent also intervenes in the operation of the system to influence its direction. Facilitators and helpers do not.

This is a dilemma many of those providing psychological services will face. Their understanding of human behavior qualifies them as the most likely system change agents and yet their commitment to the individual blame model directs their energies and skills away from system changes. This dilemma merges into a larger issue of whom the mental-health practitioner is to serve—the offender population or the administrative structure.

Brodsky (1973) explains the conflict in terms of dichotomized roles for psychologists. These polarized roles he labeled as "system professional" and "system challenger." The system professional accepts the basic policies of the system and focuses his efforts on changing the client's behavior through services and programs such as therapy and counseling. The system challenger is much more critical of systems, and believes that the injustices of systems and institutions share responsibility for the problems that individuals experience. The system challenger, therefore, directs his energies toward system change rather than individual change. For black offenders, the resolution of this dilemma is critical, for in the final analysis the quality and focus of the services offered to them will be based on who the mental-health worker perceives his real client population to be.

The professional who decides that he is to be an agent of change increases his worth in his role if he has an understanding of the deficiencies in the system and is aware of changes that are needed throughout the system to correct the shortcomings. A multitude of fragmented complaints and concerns have been voiced about the operation of various criminal-justice agencies. Countless federal, state, and city committees, task forces, and boards have formed and investigated the functioning of almost every criminal justice component. As a result, a number of impressive reports have been written containing elaborate recommendations for improvements in the system. The sum total of all these recommendations is that at all levels and at each stage in this criminal-justice process each individual, regardless of race or socioeconomic status, is assured of the protection of individual rights, humane treatment, competent and professional practitioners, nondiscrimination, ethnic representation, placement in the least restrictive environment, maximum community involvement and sustained emphasis on reintegration into society with employable skills.

Specifically with respect to mental-health services, the following are minimum requirements for an acceptable system:

1. The use of assessment instruments that are appropriate and that minimize racial or cultural influences. There should be periodic reevaluation of these assessment instruments.
2. The implementation of a classification process that can identify those persons with specific problems (emotional, physical, and educational) and can generate individual treatment plans for each inmate.
3. Mental-health services that are not linked to decisions for parole or used solely for or inappropriately by prison administrators, parole boards, or correctional officers.
4. Mental-health professionals who are accountable for their programs and services. There should be regular in-service training sessions for staff.
5. Mental-health services that are voluntarily administered and will allow offenders access to services and a right to refuse services.
6. Mental-health services that will assure that offenders will have the same rights and benefits in treatment as those clients who are not incarcerated.
7. Mental-health services that function not only to improve offenders' internal psychological functioning, but also to facilitate the maintenance of an environment conducive to positive mental health.
8. Minority representation on mental-health staff.

Resistance to Change

One of the main reasons that the system has not evolved to the ideal state is because there has been a great deal of resistance to change throughout the system. Until recently, the criminal-justice system has been a closed system that excluded outsiders and innovations. A climate of fear, distrust, and suspicion prevailed throughout. In fact, the very nature of criminal-justice processing makes it highly resistant to change. Carlson (1965) identified three conditions which hindered the adoption of innovations in public school systems that seem equally relevant to criminal-justice systems. These three conditions are (1) domestication, (2) lack of a designated change agent, and (3) lack of research.

A "domesticated" system is resistant to change because it is assured of survival by society, regardless of the quality of services of success with its clients. It does not have to compete for its clients, nor does it have to improve the quality of its services to attract new participants. The criminal-justice system is a "domesticated" system and will continue to exist whether its operation is good, bad, or indifferent. Second, there is no designated change agent or change component built into the criminal-justice system. Criminal-justice systems focus primarily on regulation and control. There has been limited planning for change or improving its operation. Changes in the system have mostly been in response to agitation from riots and concerned citizen groups and direct court orders. As a result, changes have been of a defensive rather than offensive nature. Third, there has been a lack of quality research in the area of criminal justice. This lack of research prevents the implementation of programs based on sound empirical data. It also reduces the chance of convincing decision-makers that new techniques or programs will bring more positive results or reduce their problems.

Institutions and individuals resist change when it exceeds the financial and philosophical boundaries set by society. This is especially true in situations where criminals are involved. Individuals tend not to be supportive of programs that will allow offenders to get more than those who are law abiding. This attitude was demonstrated in New York, where proposed legislation to provide educational opportunities and facilities to inmates was strongly opposed by the wives of Attica guards, and eventually was defeated because they thought that the inmates would have been getting more than the guards and their families (*The New York Times,* 1975). Resistance to programs and services for offenders diminish when they do not make it better for criminals than for those in society who are law abiding.

In addition, criminal-justice staff and inmates resist change for the same reasons other people do. People resist change if they do not have input into the decisions that affect their lives; if there is no incentive to change; if the change is not going to make their lives better or easier; if there is a strong support group against the change; and if the innovation ignores the informal groups within the institutions.

In order for a change agent to overcome resistance and to assure adoption of the program, it would certainly be advantageous to include those individuals in criminal justice to be affected by the change in the decision-making process; to provide a highly attractive reason for the necessity of program; and to provide convincing data for its chances of success. Additionally, there are basic suggestions that the mental-health professional must follow in setting up change strategy.

Plan for Change

In order to be an effective agent of change, change must be planned for in the same manner that important changes in one's personal life are planned. There should be a master plan. This requires that targets be isolated and identified to be changed and the desired end result be clearly specified. Unattainable goals create a sense of powerlessness and frustration. There should be concrete realistic short-range goals and attainable long-range goals. Time tables must be scheduled so that progress and/or failure and/or lack of progress can be measured. By setting time tables and realistically looking at obstacles, the change agent can focus on the accomplishments of the set goals.

Understand the Population

The characteristics of the target population to be influenced should be clearly understood. This applies to the prison population, law-enforcement personnel, correctional officers, criminal-justice administrators, probation and parole officers and others. The change agent should be aware of their motivations, value systems, fear and priorities. This understanding will be helpful in devising strategies that may influence the population in a planned direction. One young, attractive mental-health professional was able to start a group counseling session with inmates in a jail where other male clinicians had failed. When asked what she said or did to get the program started, she simply said, "It's amazing what a little flirting will do."

*The Same Principles of Behavior Change Can Be
Applied to Everyone*

Mental-health professionals have been trained to change behaviors and attitudes of those who are powerless, who seek help, and who have some problems. However, those individuals who do not seek help are just as amenable to behavior change techniques as those considered the "client population." More patience, time, and planning may be required, but professionals can apply their skills to those individuals who hold decision-making positions. Chambers and Owens, using the concept of rewards and punishments, designed an experimental commitment workshop format to influence the participation of concerned citizens in improving and changing the criminal-justice system (Appendix 1).

The commitment workshop evolved from observations that most meetings and workshops on criminal justice were largely unsuccessful in evoking change in the system. These programs followed a similar format. Presentations would be made on the state of affairs of criminal justice and enthusiasm would be generated in the audience. Those in attendance would usually ask what could they do to change or improve the functioning of the criminal-justice system. The speakers and workshop leaders would respond by suggesting that they call or write public officials, organize committees, get the media involved, or support some specific project such as the Wilmington Ten or Jo Ann Little's Defense Fund. While all of these recommendations were worthwhile and could potentially contribute to change efforts, neither the audience nor the speakers typically accepted responsibility for implementing the suggestions. Pessimism that their individual efforts would not affect change in the criminal-justice system or not understanding the total criminal-justice system prompted many individuals to do nothing. Consequently, once the speaker left, the audience dispersed and nothing really happened to change the system.

The purpose of the commitment workshop was to stimulate participation of concerned citizens in the criminal-justice processes and to allow for measurement of this participation. Participants are encouraged to commit themselves to perform acts related to criminal-justice needs. These acts were to be realistic and only ones that they felt that they could complete within six months. They could be simple ones, ranging from calling a sheriff to inquiring about jail facilities, or writing a letter to a congressman to congratulate him for his endorsement of a particular criminal-justice bill, to more complex ones, such as initiating a church program to adopt a prisoner for a year or arranging for a comprehensive court monitoring plan. After a commitment was made, a contract would be negotiated detailing the service to be completed along with contingencies (Penalty Clause) for failure to complete the behavioral task. The contingency could be stated in terms of money (check to an inmate or to The American Civil Liberties Union) or materials (curtains to be contributed to a work release center) or individual time (volunteer to be a big brother). After six months the contracts would expire and an evaluation of whether the person had fulfilled the terms of the contract would be made.

Informal Situations Can Be Used to Effect Change

It is naive to think that all or even most of the important decisions are always made in formal settings. Many decisions are made in informal situations, such as at social gatherings, or even in casual conversations.

Changing Negative Racial Relationships

One critical area where an agent of change is needed is in race relations. There is an obvious need for mental-health professionals to become aggressively involved in eliminating racism and reducing racial conflicts throughout the system. The task panel report to the President's Commission on Mental Health (1978) noted that racism is still a major problem confronting blacks. The problem is no less severe in the criminal-justice system.

Racial tension and racial discrimination have always existed and continue to exist throughout the criminal-justice process and at all levels of the system. Racial friction has surfaced among policemen, as exemplified by open confrontations between black and white policemen (Darnton, 196; Delaney, 1970). A number of prison riots were stimulated by the racial friction existing between black inmates and white guards. In July 1978 U.S. District Judge Alaimo ordered the dormitories at Georgia State Prison at Reidsville to be racially segregated based on evidence that the chronic fights among inmates were racially motivated (Clearinghouse, 1979), and the disparate sentences received by black offenders have been a clear indication that the color of a person's skin is a factor in the criminal-justice system.

Mental-health professionals are not exempt from racial influences and strained relationships between blacks and whites can exist in helping relationships. This is of particular interest to mental-health professionals since it extends the issue of race relations to implications for personality development, stereotyped thinking in the therapeutic process, and interaction with inmates and mental-health constituents of different racial and cultural background. A psychologist newly employed at a southeastern prison describes how racial friction can interfere with therapeutic processes:

> And we do have a racial problem. We have one black psychologist and two black social workers and they won't have anything to do with us. I had lunch with them one day—and not because they had invited me, either, and it was really painful. I mean—they wouldn't talk to me. It gets very hairy—our right hand doesn't know what our left hand is doing. And black inmates want black group leaders—and white inmates will tell me they won't be in groups with blacks. I really don't know what to do about this. Even though I've grown up in the South, this is the first time somebody's racial prejudice was hampering my performance. Do you have any ideas? You see, nobody is saying I want to work on my racial prejudice—they say I want to look at why I keep coming to prison, but not with blacks in the group. And the three black professionals are not saying anything. They are just wooing black inmates away from white group leaders and pushing white inmates out of groups. . . .

The American Personnel and Guidance Association (1969) recognized the susceptibility of mental-health professionals to racism and suggested the following guidelines for those who administer mental-health services to racially and culturally different populations: (1) become informed about racism and prejudice and how these are manifested in behavior; (2) learn about racial, cultural, and individual differences and similarities so that they can relate to persons of different racial and cultural groups more realistically and with greater understanding; (3) examine personal attitudes and behavior toward individual members of different racial and cultural groups to determine whether they represent rational reactions to the person or expressions of a prejudgment based on his race or cultural background; (4) attempt to broaden personal contacts and experiences with members of all racial and cultural groups. These contacts, when made under conditions that present all persons as individuals of equal status, can do much to counteract stereotypes, fears, and misinformation on which racism and prejudice are based.

It is becoming increasingly evident that a cooperative effort must be instituted if constructive programs are to succeed and if diverse and culturally distinct populations are to live and work together. In order to insure a harmonious relationship, mental-health professionals must be sensitive to overt or covert racism and racial tensions in the offender population as well as the professional and nonprofessional staff.

The Kerner Commission report was perhaps first to recognize that the great magnitude, seriousness, and extreme permeability of racial attitudes and resulting conflicts are certain to give rise to persistent and increasing communication problems. While there have been improvements in black-white relationships, stereotypes about blacks seem to continue. Brigham and Weissbach (1972) reviewed the research on social attitudes and concluded that while most whites are ready to accept eventual desegregation and complete legal equality of blacks, they are not yet willing to concede black equality in motivation, personality characteristics, or intelligence. Williams, Tucker, and Dunham (1971) studied the attitudes of whites over a six-year period and found no significant change in white views of blacks as bad, strong, and passive, while whites were seen as good, weak, and active. Negative stereotypes of blacks remain. The color of one's skin is still considered to be an important part of American society.

Black-White Race Relations Group

During the late 1960s, primarily in response to the civil rights movement, discussion groups were formed in many states to enhance racial sensitivity and understanding. These were generally biracial groups that dealt specifically with racial issues and attempted to bridge the racial gap. They were called by various names: cross-cultural, race relations, and racial growth groups.

Biracial groups are not new. There has been some research on biracial groups, but most of these were concerned with the interaction of blacks and whites in cooperative problem solving situations and how the participants communicated with each other. These studies have shown that whites have generally been more active in discussions, talk primarily to other whites in the group, and are more influential in the group's final decision. Blacks, however, make fewer proposals and are less influential (Cohen, 1962; Cohen and Roper, 1972; Katz and Benjamin, 1960; Katz, Goldston, and Benjamin, 1958).

Biracial groups focusing on racial issues are important for a special reason. They were the nation's attempt to resolve racial problems utilizing mental-health professionals and the therapeutic group process. These groups tended to follow similar patterns. Blacks would tell white group members their experiences as blacks in a white society and how it felt to be discriminated against. The group sessions were generally cathartic for black participants because it offered them an opportunity to express their true feelings toward whites in a safe, therapeutic environment. Whites, on the other hand, typically responded with a wide variety of reactions, including utter disbelief, sympathy, and even guilt. The group sessions were painful for many whites who were the recipients of the anger that blacks unleashed, but, for those who endured the sessions, it supposedly made them more sensitive to the problems of blacks and other minorities.

Many problems that affected the overall success of the groups emerged. Since they were novel and there was very little research on black-white groups focused on racial conflicts, there were virtually no guidelines for the group leaders to follow in terms of either content or process. No requirements or standards were necessary, nor was additional training recommended, so that almost anyone could become a group leader or use whatever group techniques they desired.

Group goals and purposes were not consistent. Some groups met to discuss the "black" problems and to better understand racial issues. Others chose to be action-oriented and to perform community services to alleviate racial problems. Some groups assembled merely to cleanse themselves of racial prejudice and guilt feelings.

These groups eventually lost their popularity and ceased to be utilized on a large scale for improving race relations. Whether the biracial group format was effective in increasing racial sensitivity and decreasing racially motivated behavior remains a mystery because, unfortunately, little empirical data were collected on the results of participation in the groups. Many questions were left unanswered. For example, as a result of being in the group did racial attitudes change? If there was change, what types of individuals were most likely to change? What content was most effective in producing attitude change? Perhaps the most critical unanswered question is, did the experiences in the groups generalize to the outside world in a manner that affected behavior?

One of the criticisms of insight-oriented groups such as the race-relations groups has been that the insight gained within the group setting did not necessarily generalize to real-life behavior. This was noted with police who attended group sessions to increase their understanding of juvenile delinquents. An examination of the police treatment of juveniles in the San Diego and Philadelphia police departments revealed that sensitivity gained through insight into the causes of delinquency was not translated into actual techniques of dealing with delinquents, as discrimination against juveniles and especially black juveniles still existed (Winslow, 1968).

Offenders and Racial Attitudes

Just as racism exists in the free world, racial problems exist in prison. In correctional settings, racial conflicts may simply be a reflection of external societal attitudes and policies toward black and white interactions. While the larger society is able to diffuse and dilute racial problems because of larger geographical areas, the prison becomes a microcosm of these racial problems in a condensed area. Because the physical space is reduced, all the fears, ignorance, and misunderstandings brought into this environment from the outside world are intensified. In addition, staff in some prisons (for various reasons) try to keep inmates racially divided by accentuating and nourishing racial conflicts. In many of these racially torn environments violent confrontations have resulted.

While in prison, inmates tend to maintain the cultural and social environment that is most comfortable to them. Because of this, it is a very natural process for inmates to conform to group racial norms as a powerful mandate, especially in a condensed area. Some racially divided prisons have been useful primarily for survival.

Additionally, the inmate population is composed primarily of individuals from low-income, racially segregated areas, and they will probably return to the same neighborhood after prison. In view of this, it is perhaps unrealistic to expect individual offenders who come into prison to undergo a racial reawakening or to change their attitudes or behavior with respect to their primary reference group. Some inmates do become close friends with inmates of different races; however, most inmates will maintain their preprison racial attitudes and behaviors, for they, like the rest of the society, have been programmed to respond to racial situations with certain prescribed actions. While it would be expedient, from an administrative perspective, if there were no racial cliques or racial tension, offenders are not incarcerated to become racially integrated, and perhaps the most that can be expected is that the races coexist and tolerate each other.

However, in those correctional facilities where there is concern about racial friction from the administration and the inmate population, mental-health professionals can take an active role in easing racial tensions among inmates. Racial concerns and racism can be discussed as one part of regular group meetings. In some cases, special groups can be set up specifically to discuss racial feelings. Cotharin and Mikulas (1975), for example, successfully used systematic desensitization to reduce racial prejudice in white high-school students.

Mental-health professionals can use their influence with black and white group leaders to assist them in resolving their differences. They can also assist in identifying and reducing the influence of those environmental factors, including staff, that might be aggravating and nourishing a racially tense environment.

However, mental-health professionals must not believe that all racially segregated environments are destructive. In fact, it may be psychologically healthy for some inmates to remain in a racially segregated environment in prison. There is a secure feeling about being in the same interactional milieu as one's home environment. There are familiar and common grounds for communication. The language, mannerisms, and similar tastes in music all help to facilitate interaction. As long as the inmate remains in his reference group, the likelihood of making racial slips and the resulting racial hassles are minimized. Irvin (1970) noted from his evaluation of inmate groups that black inmates do tend to be more nationalistic than other races.

Because of the natural racial grouping in prison, it could be beneficial for black inmates to have all-black discussions or therapy groups. The main focus of the group could be on black inmates' racial concerns and relationships. This idea might not sound appealing and may appear to be anti-American, but homogeneous groups are not a new idea.

In fact, there is some evidence to suggest that homogeneous groups can be an efficient method to deal with problems. Clients with similar problems and concerns can assist each other, even though they bring different experiences to the same problem. Lazarus (1961), for example, conducted groups utilizing systematic desensitization with clients displaying common problems such as phobias and obsessive compulsiveness. Assertive training groups are designed for those who have problems asserting themselves in our society and have been conducted specifically for women. The concept, then, of groups being restricted to a specific population who have similar problems is acceptable. And blacks do share common problems.

On the positive side, all-black groups can be educational and provide a forum for blacks to talk specifically about black culture, black pride, black relationships, and black responsibility to self and others. These concerns are generally not discussed in interracial circles.

On the other hand, all-black groups can stagnate. If all group members come from similar environments, their experiences and range of topics may be limited. Opportunities to experience opposing viewpoints and to understand different opinions will be restricted. Without proper leadership, the group discussions may dissolve into gripe sessions that simply complain of the black man's relationship to the white society and blaming the system for their incarceration. These groups can become counterproductive to individual or group progress and prevent an understanding of racially different populations in the institution.

Conducting racially segregated groups is an extremely sensitive and potentially volatile endeavor. The implications of these groups must be carefully thought out and the advantages and disadvantages must be weighed. Those considering implementing racially segregated groups should address the following questions: (1) Do we only focus on black-related issues? (2) Is race the common denominator in the population, or are the type of crime, geographical area, education, or age more relevant variables? (3) Will such a group facilitate racial understanding? (4) Do black criminals have different problems in society than white criminals? (5) Will all-black groups increase or decrease racial tension?

Race Relations and Criminal-Justice Personnel

It is naive to expect that criminal-justice employees become less biased or that all prejudiced individuals will be weeded out of the system or that all racial hate will dissipate automatically as a consequence of working in the system. Most typically, individuals bring their biases from the community in which they reside and merely act them out at some level in the criminal justice system.

The emphasis and concern over race relations in criminal justice settings vary. There seems to be no universal pattern for training those who will come into contact with and control the lives of black inmates.

The Correction Officers' Training Guide prepared by the Committee on Personnel Standards and Training of the American Correctional Association contains no provisions for or reference to race relations, interpersonal relations, or sensitivity training for the correctional officer (ACA, 1975).

The Interpersonal Relations Workshop conducted by the Federal Bureau of Prisons for its new employees consists of a total of two hours. While racial awareness is considered, it is only one of the other "minority situations" such as age, long hair, and women that is addressed during the allotted two hours (U.S. Department of Justice, 1975). The objectives of the two-hour workshop are to qualify the participants to (1) list three major causes of interpersonal conflicts in our institutions, (2) write the definitions of minority, and (3) write the definition of ethnic.

Using a consensus statement format, participants state whether they agree or disagree with ten statements such as black correctional officers can handle black problem inmates better; women correctional officers do not belong in a male institution; and the use of terms like "shrink," "hack," and "screw" reduce the professional image of correctional officers.

The race relations training with correctional officers in the Florida correctional system, by contrast, places heavy emphasis on race relations. The race relations program is a four-day intensive training session designed to aid in cross-cultural communication among correctional officers and inmates (Wittmer, Lanier, and Parker, 1975). This program presents a communication model which consists of facilitative responses that increase communication and interaction. Using structured exercises, the guards practice these responses. Integrated and segregated groups are used for appropriate exercises. Mechanisms for positive feedback and self-disclosure are built in throughout the workshop. Communication barriers between blacks and whites are discussed and concrete plans of action for positive racial interactions are constructed. Subjective feedback from the officers who have gone through the program suggests that the program did help in their cross-cultural interactions.

Hughes (1976) conducted a three-hour weekly training program for police recruits to assist them in interacting with residents in urban ghetto settings. The program was a part of a thirteen-week police academy program. Of the total forty-seven police recruits participating, twenty-one were black. A variety of instructional methods were used, including role-playing; racial situations; small group discussions; discussion of a ghetto glossary by recruits; lectures; and visits to criminal justice agencies involved in crime control and prevention.

Smith and Bierdman (1976) reported on a program model designed for both staff and patients to reduce racism in the forensic unit of a state hospital housing the mentally ill male offenders in Missouri. In this maximum security unit, over one-third of the patients were urban black offenders and 99 percent of the male staff members were from rural areas. For the staff, sessions on racism, the black family, and black history were conducted. A variety of techniques were used, including lectures and small and large group discussions. A black studies program, focusing on the positive aspects of black history, was presented to black patients. An informal conversational approach was used initially and then changed to more formal and structural experiences.

Two of the positive and concrete changes occurring from this program, as noted by the authors, were that the content of black history and culture and their meaning for treatment was incorporated into the hospital orientation program for all disciplines and levels of staff, and overt racist remarks aimed at black patients diminished.

While the group format with different variations has been the most standard mechanism for race relations, simulation and gaming is a structured technique that may be useful in facilitating racial understanding. Simulation and gaming is a process that provides real-life situations and allows participants to experience, firsthand, these life situations. For example, to illustrate the point that racism and poverty are conditions that provoke feelings of powerlessness, specific games can be utilized that enable the group members to actually experience these feelings. It moves individuals from a level of verbalization to actual participation. Some of the games available that may be of assistance in reducing racial friction or promoting racial understanding are given in table 7-1.

Conclusion

The concept of changing systems and changing behavior, other than for those who are poor, troubled, afflicted, and powerless, is foreign to most mental-health professionals. This is understandable since there is generally little in most

Table 7–1
Selected List of Simulations/Gaming

Name	Purpose	Number of People	Time (Hours)	Cost (dollars)
Understanding the Criminal-Justice System				
Guilt by negotiation	Understand plea bargaining	4+	2–5	Under 10.00
Innocent until	Jury trial	13–30	4–10	35.50
Social seminar	Drug abuse	32	4–6	13.75
Understanding others				
BAFA	Understand another culture	24–40	3–6	20.00
Center city	Understand problems of inner-city youth	12–27	3–5	15.00
Culture contact	Understand another culture	20–30	2–5	36.50
Dignity	Understand ghetto life	4	2–4	6.95
Equality	Become familiar with black history and pressures of blacks	20–40	20–30	12.00
Ghetto	Experience frustration and pressures of ghetto life	8–10	5–7	24.00
Government preparation for minority groups	Develop awareness of problems and frustration of minority groups	15+	3–5	1.50
Horatio Alger	Experience of powerlessness of the poor	13–32	2–4	1.00
Poverty game	Understanding poverty	15–35	2–4	Under 10.00
Power game	Demonstrates rejection, power, and powerlessness	12+	2–3	1.00
Raid	Demonstrates urban racketeering	5–15	3–5	31.50
Starpower	Understand power and its effect on powerful and powerless	24–45	3–5	25.00
Sunshine	Understand dynamics of racial attitudes and problems	20–36	25–35	12.00
Welfare week	Understand welfare and its effect on the poor	Any number	4+	50.00
Yes, but not here	Understand social rules and community-interest groups	20–40	4–6	12.00/kit

Table 7-1 *Continued*

Personal Understanding				
Cruel, cruel world	Examine personal goals and laws	2–4	1+ hrs.	8.95
Hang-up	Understand racial attitudes	2–6	2–4	15.00
Shrink	Analyze individual traits and characteristics	Any amount	3+	3.50
T-puzzle	Understand how frustration affects performance	6+	1–2	3.00/ 12 puzzles
Together	Awareness of need for cooperation in successful group problem solving	2–36	½–1	5.30

Source: Ron Stadsklev, *Handbook of Simulation Gaming in Social Education.* (Part 2: Directory) (Alabama: Institute of Higher Education Research & Services, The University of Alabama, 1975). Reprinted with permission.

academic curriculums that addresses this critical area. One rarely finds, for example, courses preparing students to move into criminal-justice settings which consider the students as change agents or as armed with the skills to effectively change systems.

This means that, either by omission or commission, professionals leave their academic environments with the intention of maintaining the status quo of the system they enter. They enter criminal-justice systems to change the offender population, since this is what they have been trained to do.

Unfortunately, many of the problems affecting the lives of blacks, even in criminal-justice settings, continue to be race related, and if mental-health professionals are to become truly effective with black offenders they must begin to see eliminating racism and reducing racial tensions within the system as a necessary part of their professional and social responsibility. They must then develop programs to provide the type of environment that can truly nourish the concepts of democracy and equality, thus enhancing black mental health.

8 Black Mental-Health Professionals

The possibility of being the only black psychologist, social worker, or counselor within the criminal-justice system is enhanced by the critical shortage of blacks among all of the mental-health professions. An estimated 2 percent of psychiatrists, 4 percent of psychologists, and slightly over 7 percent of social workers are black (President's Commission on Mental Health, 1978). While sometimes being the only one carries a status of distinction and may be highly sought, the black professional may pay a high price for being the only one in criminal-justice settings. This dubious status may mean being confronted with obstacles and challenges that other mental-health workers may not understand or have to contend with. In addition, there is no one to guide him through the maze of problems that accrue to him because of his position.

One of the major challenges faced by black mental-health professionals is personal and professional survival in a racially unbalanced environment that has historically been abusive to blacks. In most cases, there is no guarantee that the professional will be prepared to meet this challenge because, unfortunately, programs which train behavioral scientists are often void in sensitivity to this aspect of the black experience. Educational institutions by and large have not been pressed to teach large numbers of blacks aspiring to become psychologists, social workers, counselors, and other human-service professionals. Academic preparation, therefore, has not focused on racially oriented problems that blacks may encounter simply because they are black. Consequently, many black mental-health professionals enter criminal justice environments unaware and unprepared for the unique experiences they will face in these settings.

Oblivious to the unique problems that black professionals face within criminal-justice settings, administrators and other colleagues can offer, at best, only limited assistance. In the final analysis, psychological survival and professional effectiveness will depend on the person's own ability to integrate the divergent and contradictory racial forces in his environment.

Some criminal-justice environments create more problems for black professionals than others. Settings such as research agencies, criminal-justice planning agencies, and high-level administrative offices which are not divisive and oppressive are less stressful. Correctional settings, however, are potentially the most taxing and hazardous to their personal and professional survival. For blacks, prisons symbolize their struggle with servitude as slaves. They are intense climates where the incidences of racial discrimination will be told over and over again by black inmates and the black professional will be constantly reminded of the bleak role of blacks and poor in America.

In prisons conflicts occur between weak and strong inmates, old and young inmates, and black and white inmates. The kept and the keepers are separated into distinct categories of the powerless and the powerful, and the haves and the have nots. The administrative staff, predominantly white, are on one side and the inmates, mostly blacks, comprise the other side, the powerless and the have nots. Each side forms a distinct group and everyone knows where his allegiance belongs. Both the inmates' code and the guards' regulations help to maintain the clear-cut division between the opposing sides. Role expectations are clear and well-defined.

While all mental-health professionals may face the initial problem of role expectations from both the kept and the keepers to some degree, this problem is more pronounced for black clinicians. Their roles probably will not be as clearly defined or delineated as their constituents' role, and neither will the perceptions and expectations of others in the system likely be the same for them. The clinician will be in a rather strange predicament. A new ingredient in the prison equation, the mental-health worker, has a certain degree of power, and yet he is black. Where does he fit? Is he the champion of blacks? Is he going to be a system challenger? Will he be assigned to only black inmates? Is he to be the person who gets information from both black guards and black inmates?

The concerns of race and racial allegiance are not unique to black mental-health professionals in the criminal-justice system. One of the chief concerns that white guards had when black guards were to be finally hired in prison settings was that the black guards would become friendly with the black inmates and unite against them. When John Boone was hired as the first black Commissioner of Corrections in Massachusetts in 1972, the governor said (Profile/Massachusetts, 1975, p. 43):

> I said the job is yours, but I want to mention three strikes that you're going to have against you. First of all, you're from out of state and, therefore, will be mistrusted. Two is that you're a reformer and that's even worse in the eyes of this department. But the worst and toughest strike of all is that your skin is black, and they're going to hate your guts.

So the biggest problem any black mental-health professional will have will be that of clearly defining his role with the various segments of the prison community, both professionally and racially. This includes his colleagues also, because even they may have stereotypic perceptions and unrealistic expectations of him. There will be the temptation to assume that because he is black his behavior and attitudes are predictable; he is against capital punishment; he feels the criminal-justice system is biased; he believes that all blacks in prison were unfairly put there; and he can talk to all black inmates, and so on.

The relationship with the white inmate population, while important, poses much less of a threat to the survival of the black mental-health professional than does the relationship with the black inmate population, for it is in the black sector that the credibility of the black mental-health professional will be evaluated most severely and either affirmed or denied.

Even black inmates may have unrealistic initial expectations and perceptions of black professionals. The professional will be seen as someone with some degree of influence and because of the similarity in color and other common cultural experiences with them, they may expect extra favors and services. Undoubtedly, some inmates will attempt to use the common racial backgrounds to their advantage.

The following experience of some black guards at a prison with black inmates might be useful as a reference point. A group of black guards at a southern prison echoed these sentiments:

> Black inmates talk a good game about black pride and unity, but they are just using it to make you feel guilty for your being employed in the system and to get you to do special favors.

Some black inmates evaluate black staff members solely on the basis of how they interact with both the whites in the prison and the black inmates. Chishom (1974) found that in one southern prison system, black inmates had their own classification for black staff members. Specifically, they classified them according to the titles "Colored," "Negro," and "Black," with "Black" being most positive. The "Colored" category referred to a black person who did everything the white man wanted without any black pride. He was a system's person, an Uncle Tom. The "Black" label identified the staff member who stood up to the system as a challenger. This person generally related well to other black inmates and displayed pride in being black. The term "Negro" was reserved for that category in between the two extremes, the person who was not completely subservient, and yet not completely autonomous. He could act black or side with whites depending on which was most advantageous to him.

If black clinicians can clearly establish comfortable role definitions, the opportunity for job satisfaction increases. If roles are not clearly defined, strained and unhappy relationships with inmates and/or others can result in job dissatisfaction. This can inevitably create an atmosphere of stress and frustration which may cause the professional to seek new employment. Being alone in a punishing environment, without a support group and others in the environment sensitive to the dilemma of being black, is a psychologically lethal situation for the black professional.

The problem may be a bigger one for blacks in environments where they have been lured into criminal-justice settings because of pressures from various federal and state equal opportunity agencies to hire blacks. In these situations, administrators and other staff members may not only be insensitive to the mental-health professional's dilemma, but fail to see and appreciate the valuable services that they render. They may question why black mental-health professionals are needed in criminal justice, and most importantly, what can they contribute to mental programs and services that white mental-health professionals cannot? This question is especially crucial when it is noted that the majority of black clinicians will be graduated from predominantly white schools, which implies that their education is identical to that of whites. They too are just as likely to be strong followers of the medical model. The assessment instruments that they will utilize and interpret are identical to the ones that whites will use. The same therapeutic techniques they employ will be the same ones white professionals learned.

All of the above concerns are quite legitimate. However, it is a rare occurrence when any black individual grows up devoid of exposure to those elements of his environment that allow some insight and understanding of the black experience, even those educated in a predominantly white school. The awareness of and sensitivity to these experiences may be very minimal in many individuals, but it exists. These differences in experiences and background will more than likely be manifested in how black practitioners interact with other blacks. Many will relate well to black inmates. Some may not relate well to other black inmates due to different values. Some may be insensitive to black inmates in order to show the institution that he is fair to all inmates. Others may relate poorly due to rejection by the black inmates.

In spite of these problems, there are many possible contributions that black mental-health professionals can make in general that can be beneficial to correctional staff, offenders, and their families. The insights and judgments black assessors may be able to share about black test behavior and responses may help in accurately determining functioning levels of black inmates. This input is especially critical in making decisions about those black offenders suspected of being mentally retarded. In fact, there has been some research to suggest that test performance can be influenced by the race of the examiner (Sattler, 1973).

Black professionals can interpret the black experience and black adaptive behavior to those staff members unfamiliar with black behaviors and communication patterns. For example, in one prison a classification team member remarked that black offenders seldom make eye contact with classification team members, especially females. This was interpreted as a lack of self-confidence. While this may have been generally true, a black professional suggested that this behavior was a survival tactic for many black offenders. He explained that blacks have been exceedingly vulnerable to accusations of rape, and not making eye contact reduces the chance of being unfairly accused of having ideas of rape. When this was pointed out, some still did not accept this explanation because they felt that social conditions had changed so dramatically that blacks did not have to be concerned about being falsely accused of rape. The professional then pointed out that prisons lagged behind in social changes and that many blacks had been in prison for a long period of time. In fact, there were several black inmates in the prison who had previously been on death row for allegedly raping white women. This sensitivity and awareness of the black experience can be beneficial to both staff and inmates.

Black professionals can serve as role models for black offenders. It would seem that adult male offenders would not need role models; however, many black offenders have matured without positive black role models. Contact with an adult professional may be a significant influence in the lives of young black offenders. There are also many older black offenders who are sensitive, knowledgeable, articulate, and mentally alert, and who would enjoy and possibly profit, both intellectually and emotionally, from interactions with black professionals. Professionals can also serve as a liaison among institutions, programs, and the family members in correctional situations and climates that might appear unfriendly.

There have been some limited data to indicate that black therapists and counselors are more effective in counseling situations with black clients. However, the real value of being a black clinician with black clients seems to be that rapport is much easier to establish and may occur earlier. This suggests that blacks may see black clinicians as allies and come to them for emotional assistance. However, merely being black does not guarantee that a black clinician will achieve any more effective outcomes than a white clinician. Although he may have an edge with black inmates, he must be able to be an effective and competent professional if blacks are to be helped. All in all, when criminal-justice administrators consider the total range of services that blacks can provide, the pressure from the courts and/or governmental agencies to hire blacks seems appropriate.

Once employed, however, the black mental-health professional must assume some responsibility to enhance his effectiveness as a professional and must create positive situations and take advantage of all opportunities that can contribute to his own professional and psychological survival. First of all, setting priorities and budgeting time are a must. As a result of the variety of services he can perform, he will usually find an inordinate demand for his time (Jones, 1972). The more one does the more one will be called upon to do more. Not only will this be true at work, but the demands on his free time will increase. In some cases, the professional may be seen as the "true solver" of all black problems. Proper budgeting of time can help to prevent the professional's becoming "burned out."

The professional should consider attendance at professional workshops and conferences as a high priority. In addition to professional growth, annual conferences can satisfy needs that might not be fulfilled on the job. Conferences can also serve as a periodic "where-are-you checkup." Some mental-health professionals attend conferences for this explicit purpose. Every year at a designated conference they meet and set individual goals to be accomplished during the next year. Some goals are personal, such as "I will become more understanding of my children" or "I will spend more time with my wife" or "I will get out and socialize more with others in the community." Other goals articulate more professional aspirations, such as "I will read more books in my discipline," "I will write one article for publication," "I will devote more time to improving my therapy skills," or "I will commit myself to organize a group for the family of inmates."

The group makes a pledge to convene at the next annual conference to evaluate what has happened to its members in the preceding year. They discuss the racial conflicts, the frustration of being black in a predominantly white environment, and share solutions and survival strategies with each other. This meeting enables them to evaluate their utilization of the past year and any personal and professional changes they have made. But most of all, it provides feedback and a support group for the black mental-health professional that may be unavailable on his job.

There is an obvious shortage of research on mental health and the black offender conducted and published by black professionals. Those who do publish may enhance their own professional advancement while making valuable contributions to the field. Black clinicians must continually get involved in activities and situations where they can share their experiences with larger audiences. If too much time is spent trying to cure the world, little time is left to let the world know how one has been saving it. In order to accomplish this, they must remain in the mainstream of professional activities which afford them an opportunity to keep abreast of professional opportunities and events that they might ordinarily be left out of through normal channels. Volunteering to present papers at conferences and to speak to concerned citizens are worthwhile activities.

Within the correctional atmosphere, black therapists can have an impact by becoming involved in all levels of staff training. They must be responsive to conduct in-service training. In addition to the excellent experience obtained by leading workshops, this is a viable way to bring an understanding of their talents and capabilities.

Spending time periodically with the offender population beyond the business day is an excellent technique to devise a better understanding of the real problems of black inmates. The impromptu conversations which take place with inmates during these times afford them further opportunity to talk and express their concerns. Extra availability to the inmate population can also have an impact.

Black Mental-Health Professional Survival Guidelines

Many of the survival guidelines that were suggested for mental-health professionals, in general, are equally pertinent to black practitioners. However, blacks may find that they need additional suggestions to survive in criminal-justice environments. The following are minimal suggestions:

Black Mental-Health Professionals Must Establish Their Own Identity

Regardless of their efforts to prevent it, many will live in two worlds—one black and one white. At times one may predominate over the other. Both blacks and whites will try to influence how they should be, how they should think and dictate their total lifestyle. Black mental-health professionals must be sensitive to two cultures, but for their own positive mental health, they must be individuals and define their own existence. It is vital that they maintain a positive attitude toward themselves. At times confusion as to whom they are and what they are about may have to be dealt with; these periods may be painful but should be viewed as necessary and growth producing experiences.

Black Mental-Health Professionals Cannot Resolve All the Black-White Problems in Their Lifetime

Many of the racial problems that are interwoven in the fabric of society existed before black mental-health professionals came into the world and will probably exist long after they depart. Racism, sexism, classism, and favoritism unfortunately are facts of life. This does not mean that black professionals do not have any responsibility for eliminating or, at best, reducing these negative aspects of the environment. It does mean, however, that they should be aware of the limits of their power and the realities of their environment. They must set priorities for those racial problems that they consider most important and then focus their energies on those.

Black Mental-Health Professionals Cannot Solve All the Black Problems

There are a number of blacks in the world who are vicious and cruel, just as there are many who are very loving and caring. Being black does not guarantee one type of behavior or another. In criminal-justice settings black professionals will come into contact with all types. Being able to make the distinction between those who are sincere and those who can be helped from those who are not sincere and those that cannot be helped is crucial to their success. They will not be able to change the behavior patterns of all black offenders.

Black Professionals Should Have at Least One Person with
Whom They Can Sincerely, Honestly, and Openly Discuss
How They Feel about Being Black

There will be times when blacks may feel very much alone in their work situation. They may feel lonely because of differences with others in values, priorities, or just philosophical differences. There will be times when they may question their own commitment and responsibility to black people. Many black professionals will not discuss their personal problems with white colleagues for the same reasons that offenders are hesitant to seek therapy from white therapists. There is a lack of trust and the feeling that whites are not capable of understanding blacks. During these periods of depression and loneliness, it is critical to their mental health that they be able to relate to someone with whom they can be truly open and honest. There should be a person with whom they can communicate job-related problems as well as racial feelings.

Conclusion

Being a black mental-health professional in criminal-justice settings can be both a curse and a blessing. It can be a curse in that the person will inevitably be endorsed as a part of a system that punishes, which may serve to alienate him from black offenders. Additionally, he is a new kid on the block and as such he is an unknown quantity. The perceptions and expectations held for him will vary according to the perceptions held generally of blacks. Administrators may expect that he simply keep blacks from rioting and being unhappy. Other mental-health professionals may expect that he work with black and white offenders. Black offenders may expect special favors. White offenders may expect him to show favoritism to blacks. Through all of these expectations the black mental-health professional must attempt to respond to his internal value system and expectation level—whatever they may be.

It can be a blessing because the professional has an opportunity to abort many of the negative stereotypes that have existed about black offender intelligence and emotional behavior. In addition, because he is black, the opportunity is available to bridge gaps between black offenders and other segments of the environment, including family, employers, and social agencies.

Unquestionably, the need exists for more blacks to become involved in all areas of criminal justice that affect the emotional functioning of black offenders. Hopefully, their employment will not simply be for cosmetic purposes but will be based on their ability to provide a real service to the total mental-health effort. In order to reduce the attrition rate of these clinicians, administrators must become sensitive to the potential problems to be faced by black mental-health professionals and allow them opportunities to resolve the conflicting racial demands and expectations in criminal-justice settings.

9

Moving Away from Dead Center: The Challenge

The challenge to the mental-health professionals who work with black offenders is great. Services must be provided in criminal-justice environments to a population that has been historically underserved by the mental-health professionals and that has been largely unresponsive to those mental-health services provided. They must also shed the vestiges of racism and ignorance that have influenced their assessment instruments and behavioral analysis of blacks.

There are a number of positive courses of action that must be vigorously pursued if the professions are to fulfill the mandate they espouse in criminal-justice settings.

Training for the Black Offender Experience

When psychologists, social workers, psychiatrists, counselors, and others in the helping professions graduate from programs that have not prepared them for contact with black offenders, they may be unprepared and incapable of offering the types of services and programs that can truly be responsive to blacks in criminal-justice settings. If behavioral scientists are to be effective with this population, it is imperative that they have an understanding of blacks and the black experience in America.

Educational programs must be established that bridge the gap between the classroom and correctional settings. In order to accomplish this objective, traditional programs and methods may have to be revamped to accommodate bold and creative strategies for training future professionals. Fields (1979) reported on an innovative program in California designed to reduce the gap between therapists and low-income minority patients. For potential psychiatrists, a seminar is conducted focusing specifically on low-income black lifestyles and various therapeutic techniques to use. Potential clients are shown a media presentation that prepares them for the therapeutic experience.

Courses can be redesigned or altered so students can get direct or indirect exposure to black experiences. This was the case in an undergraduate seminar psychology course focusing on the role of psychologists in criminal justice. Students in the class had had limited or no interactions with blacks. Since the class met at a distance too far away from the major penal institutions to travel to them on a regular basis, arrangements were made so that the students could write to a number of black inmates in the Alabama prisons.

However, this correspondence was much more systematic and intensive than a routine pen-pal experience. Students were assigned to a specific inmate and they were required to maintain regular communication with that inmate. Each inmate's letter was analyzed and discussed by the class so that the student who was responding, and the class, could get a glimpse of the concerns of each black inmate. After feedback from the entire class, the student would then prepare a response to the inmate, using language that was designed to facilitate responses from the inmate.

The students were also required to read a number of books that reflected black experiences, such as *The Autobiography of Malcolm X, Native Son, Dark Ghetto, Soul on Ice, Blacks and Criminal Justice,* and others. They used these books as a basis for stimulating interaction and maintaining communication. The students asked questions and made statements based on the contents of these books. For example, "How do you compare yourself with Malcolm X?" "How do you feel about *Native Son?*" "After reading *Dark Ghetto* what do you think is the biggest problem in crime prevention?" "Based on *Soul on Ice,* what do you think psychologists should do in prison?" "A number of books have said that poverty and racism is the basis for so much black crime. Do you feel that this was true in your situation and in most of the other inmates in prison?" (appendix 2).

Since most inmates were generally idle, it was hoped that they would find the communication a worthwhile activity and would be stimulated to read new materials to broaden their awareness of themselves and their environment. Another goal of the project was to improve offenders' writing and communication skills through student examples and tactful comments about sentence and paragraph construction, grammar, and so on.

Those who apparently profited most from this interaction were the students. The experience served to dilute the culture shock of moving directly from the classroom into the correctional settings, while providing them with some understanding of the black experience. Students who had had limited contact with blacks or the black experience had an opportunity to interact with black inmates on a relatively safe level. They could gain insight about the concerns of black inmates without having face-to-face interaction in a prison environment. By communicating through the mail, they had a chance to think through the inmate's responses and to evaluate their own value system. Since they used books about the black experience, they became acquainted with black literature. Finally, it allowed the students an opportunity to look at dimensions of being black other than as a person with problems.

There is no doubt that there are a number of other techniques that can be implemented to assist students to become acquainted with black experiences. The most important first step however is to consider it necessary that students be exposed to culturally different populations.

Identifying Special Groups of Black Offenders

One of the unfortunate legacies of racism has been that blacks have generally been seen as a group, not individuals. Even today, there is the temptation to speak in terms of "the black problem" or "the black offender" as though these global descriptions characterized all blacks. While it has been convenient in many respects to refer to blacks as a single homogeneous unit, there is considerable heterogeniety among blacks. Although blacks share many commonalities, they are also very different. However, programs and services have been developed based primarily on the needs of larger groups. This has recently become apparent by the small number of correctional programs designed to deal with various subgroups of offenders with special needs. Consequently smaller groups of blacks in prison have not received services that may have been of benefit to them.

Undoubtedly, it will be difficult to resist the urge to refer to blacks as a singular unit, but mental-health professionals must be cognizant of the diversity existing within the black offender population. When this happens, programs that are responsive to the total black offender population can be implemented. In order to make this concept a reality, mental-health professionals can become involved in identifying and delivering relevant psychological and educational services to those smaller groups of black offenders who have needs similar to the larger group of offenders, but also have a variety of special needs. Two of these groups that have traditionally been ignored in criminal justice are the black mentally retarded offenders and black married offenders.

Mentally Retarded Offenders

Although mentally retarded offenders constitute a minority in most prison settings, surveys have consistently revealed that at least 60 percent of all male offenders labeled as mentally retarded on the basis of IQ scores are minority, with some reporting percentages as high as two-thirds of the mentally retarded inmate population (Santamour and West, 1977).

There are a number of possible explanations that may account for the disproportionate number of blacks represented in the mentally retarded offender population: (1) more mentally retarded blacks commit crime and are caught than do whites who are mentally retarded, (2) mentally retarded whites commit just as many crimes but are diverted from the criminal justice system more readily than black retardates, or (3) the tests used to detect mental retardates are biased against blacks, and therefore at least some of the blacks labeled as mentally retarded are labeled inaccurately.

There may be some truth in each of the statements. Unfortunately, since many criminal acts are not reported and there is little research available, it is not possible to accurately assess the extent to which black or white retarded offenders commit crimes and are funneled into or diverted from the criminal-justice system.

Data which focus on the use of intelligence level tests with minority groups are, however, more available. Generally, it is known that blacks as a group score lower on intelligence tests than do whites. However, as discussed in chapter 4, the practice of using IQ tests to determine the intelligence level of blacks has been criticized as an inaccurate assessment measure for a number of reasons.

Since black offenders typically have experienced difficulty and dissatisfaction with the academic process, with many subsequently not completing high school, the possibility exists that those inappropriately labeled as mentally retarded children have not made significant progress in academic learning. Their poor academic records, coupled with application of similar intelligence tests for classifying mental retardation and similar clinicians for interpreting these test results, may very easily place black adults in the same inappropriate category they were in as youngsters.

While some black offenders may be inaccurately labeled as mentally retarded, there will be some who may be appropriately classified. In this case, the task is to provide social and learning environments where they can maximize their abilities and learn skills that facilitate their survival both in prison and after release from prison.

The preponderance of research suggests that, on the basis of IQ scores, the majority of the inmates labeled as retarded are classified as mildly mentally retarded (Santamour and West, 1977). Only a very small percentage of those offenders labeled as retarded score within the moderately retarded range. Those individuals likely to be classified as severely or profoundly retarded will usually not be found in prison. Individuals in the severe or profound categories would more than likely have displayed the type of intellectual and social behaviors that would lead to detection of their retardation at a much earlier age and subsequent institutionalization in a mentally retarded facility or an environment with strict supervision.

Since most mentally retarded inmates are eventually released from prison, environments that help them to cope with individuals who are nonretarded provide positive preparation for nonprison life. Only those mentally retarded inmates who demonstrate an inability to function responsibly and independently in a general prison population should be removed and placed in an environment that is designated for the mentally retarded. These are the inmates whose retardation makes them highly vulnerable to abuse by other inmates and who require a more structured environment, both in prison and possibly after their release into the community.

However, since most are classified in the higher ranges of retardation, they will be capable of remaining in the general population with some environmental support. This means that in order for them to survive and to profit from the experience, the environment must not be a predatory environment, or one that causes frustration.

According to cited research, retarded inmates, because of their low intellectual functioning level, are usually taken advantage of by other inmates, are extremely vulnerable to abuse, and get into trouble in the institutions (Santamour and West, 1977). These stereotypes of the retarded offender must be interpreted with caution, however, because retarded offenders, like nonretarded offenders, display a wide range of behavior in prison settings.

This emphasizes again the need to assess black offenders as individuals, not as a group. While some of these inmates may be victimizers, still others seem to be able to maintain at least satisfactory relationships with both inmates and correctional officers.

In order to make the correctional environment safe and productive for mentally retarded offenders and to minimize frustrations and failure experiences, mental-health professionals can assist in training staff to be responsive to the needs of these inmates. If instructors and correctional officers are aware of the limits of the learning capacity of these inmates, material and instructions can be presented to them in a manner equivalent to their ability to understand. Many disciplinaries received by mentally retarded inmates may be a function of their retardation rather than a function of antisocial behavior. They may get into trouble because they use poor judgment or are impulsive or are set up by other inmates. If mentally retarded offenders are to remain in the prison environment, the treatment task is to make the environment a safe, learning environment rather than an aversive, predatory one. This reduces the opportunity for retarded offenders to get into trouble while in the institution. In these environments they can be trained for employment after prison.

Since mentally retarded offenders are represented by a large black population, an understanding of black experiences and needs is necessary if relevant treatment programs are to be implemented. Based on the types of environments that many blacks have left and the urban inner-city areas that most will more than likely return to, programs and training that will facilitate their survival in these social environments are crucial. In fact, many of the same relationships and conflicts that black inmates experience in prison are quite similar to the ones they will encounter in their community. Programs and strategies that teach these inmates how to recognize con games, how to resist being the butt of jokes, how to say no, how to be cool under pressure, and how to compensate for deficiencies are useful survival techniques.

Drug and alcohol abuse needs should also be included in the program for retarded offenders who have such problems. Programs that assist the retarded black inmate in recognizing his tolerance limit for alcohol, in abstaining from drinking, and in refusing alcohol may be beneficial in helping him to control his impluses.

Finally, many of the problems that blacks experience are related to being black in a society that has historically been color conscious. Important to the development of any program for blacks is the recognition both that blacks must be able to accept and like themselves as *blacks*, and that they must understand their relationship to the larger white society. It is no less important for the black mentally retarded to be able to come to grips with being black in a predominantly white society. In the development of a treatment program, whether it is labeled social studies, current events, or whatever, some provision for the discussion of minority groups should be included. Discussion on how to be assertive about getting a job, and how to make it as a black person in today's society, are survival techniques that may strengthen a black mentally retarded offender's chances of remaining in the community after release.

Black Married Offenders

In spite of the fact that black married offenders have always been represented in correctional settings, they have not been a popular subject of research. Further, concern for the maintenance of the black family has not held a high priority ranking among correctional programmers. The reason for this lack of concern may relate to the historically negative image of the low-income black family unit and especially the black male. In the earlier literature, the black family was typically seen as a poor socializing unit with weak values. What little strength there was, if any, was attributed to the black female. The black male was generally depicted as weak, ineffectual, unemployed, and absent. Consequently, it seems logical that correctional officials should feel no compelling need to strengthen or maintain black family relationships through programming, because they do not acknowledge that there is anything to maintain.

Most minority inmates are single at the time of arrest. A smaller percentage are married, are living with their families, and are the primary breadwinners when they are arrested. In 1972, of all minority prisoners received into federal correctional institutions, approximately 41 percent were single, 29 percent were married, 10 percent had common-law relationships, and 12 percent were separated (U.S. Department of Justice, 1975).

There are many problems the married offender continues to face as he attempts to build a positive relationship with his wife and children during his incarceration. He now has little control over his life or that of his family members. In most cases, because of the meager amount of money received in prison, he is less able to support his wife or children. Consequently, even his role as a potential contributing family member is diminished. Instead, he becomes the dependent family member.

In addition, once released he must readjust to society and his family. While readjustment to society is a problem for any offender, regardless of his marital status or race, a black married inmate faces additional challenges. Not only must he adjust to a society that continues to discriminate against him because of his inmate status and race, but he also must concurrently readjust to a family that has been surviving without him. He must interrupt the coping and interactional pattern that his family has formed during his absence. He must assert himself as the head of the family at a time when he is, perhaps, most sensitive to other aspects of manhood. He has to reconstruct a sexual relationship with his wife and a fatherly relationship with his children. In short, he has to meet the demands of others at a time when he may be readjusting to himself in a new environment. If the inmate has maintained a healthy and close relationship with his family during his imprisonment, this adjustment to his family becomes easier.

A major obstacle to a smooth and successful reintegration of the black married inmate with his family, is the apparent inability of prisons to rehabilitate or habilitate offenders and to become seriously involved in helping build or strengthen family relationships. Conditions and factors such as the unnatural environment of prisons, the treatment of offenders, the overcrowded conditions, the sexual abuse of inmates, the emphasis on punishment rather than rehabilitation, and lack of training opportunities have all been highlighted as contributing causes for the many inmates who return to society more embittered and antisocial than when they entered. In a study by Erickson et al. (1973) of the perception of parolees about the prison experience, parolees were asked to evaluate their time in prison. Seventy-one percent considered the time spent in prison as a negative experience, and no one saw it as a positive experience.

In addition to the problems associated with surviving in prison, the geographical location of the major correctional institutions contributes to the weakening of ties with families and friends. Prison locations in rural areas are a long distance from the urban centers where black inmates lived before imprisonment, establishing a handicap to visitors in terms of both time and cost. As a result of diminished communication with significant others and negative experiences in prison, a smooth transition to one's family and society may be hampered.

The importance to the ex-offender of building and maintaining harmonious relationships with the family is accentuated by Glaser's (1969) findings from his study of the federal prison and parole system. Glaser found that successful release from prison is related to the interaction of the ex-offender with his family or others with whom he lived. The study showed that the failure rate of parolees was more than three times greater among those reporting conflict in the home than those never experiencing conflict.

Correctional facilities that allow family members to remain in close proximity are a viable alternative for keeping a family intact. In reality, however, large rural prisons will continue to exist. As partners lose contact with each other, they may share different experiences which influence their relationship. A dependent wife who assumes more responsibility for the maintenance of the family and becomes less dependent on a spouse may react a little differently once the husband returns. An offender who left the family as the main bread-winner, but is no longer occupying this status, rejoins a family where he is now dependent and may have a difficult time adjusting. Being a major contri-buting member to the family is crucial to many black males.

Staples (1976) commented on male dominance and power relationships in low-income black families and suggested that the person generally providing the most resources in the marriage has the most power in the relationship. He notes that money has typically been the source of power that maintains male dominance in the black family. Since it is generally acknowledged that inmates go to prison poor and return from prison poor, there may be a shift in the balance of power and possible establishment of conflict areas during the inmate's absence. One study found that 58 percent of the jail population, prior to incarceration, had a reported income of less than $3,000 (U.S. Depart-ment of Justice, 1974). Lenihan (1975) reviewed the savings of all inmates released from prisons in one eastern state during a twelve-month period, and found that almost 56 percent had $50 or less to start a new life; almost 75 percent had $100 or less; and only 8 percent had over $400.

The importance of the family to resettling a former inmate cannot be ignored. Thus various levels of assistance, including counseling programs for inmates and the members of their families, may possibly mediate a smoother transition from the prison community to the family community. Efforts must be made to assure that black married offenders who will eventually return to their families be exposed to opportunities during their confinement that enhance the continuity of a positive marriage and facilitate a smooth reentry. This is certainly important to the offender, but it may be even more critical to the wife and children who may be indirectly penalized by the absence of the husband. In order to meet the needs of this population, programs should be varied to meet individual needs. As with retarded black offenders, married black offenders are individuals, not a homogeneous group. The programs should allow for differences within black married offender populations.

1. Reduce excessive pressure on the wives and maximize contact with the husbands. Since some married inmates are satisfied with their spouses and their relationship, there should be programs that simply assist both parties to endure the period of imprisonment without creating new areas of conflict. An early orientation of both the husband and wife about possible problem areas during the period of incarceration, and survival techniques while they are separated, may better prepare both parties. Provisions for financial support for the wife and children through employment and other services, coordinated through social or community agencies, will reduce some of the financial pressures on the family. Employment opportunities for the husband, while

imprisoned and after release, will help him to continue to support the family and to feel that he has continued to be a contributing member of the family.

Other services and programs that reduce obstacles are providing inexpensive travel service through group bus trips to the institutions at regular intervals; allowing flexible visiting hours for the wives who may have time conflicts because of employment hours; and frequent passes and furloughs for the married man can make the separation a little less painful.

2. Increase marital and parental coping skills. There is a segment of the black married male population who will be adversely affected by the prison experience. For these inmates a different type of program may be needed. A class on marriage and family should be available. This course could focus on possible family conflict areas. In addition, group counseling sessions composed of married inmates could help inmates to develop coping and problem-solving skills. Toward the end of imprisonment, more intensive transition counseling, focusing on reentry concerns, could be offered for those who are experiencing reentry anxiety.

The area where the most concerted effort may be needed is in the black male offender-child relationships. Since the child is not in contact with his father as much as the mother, the possiblility of a loosening of emotional ties is heightened. As a result of his absence, he misses stages of the child's development. It would certainly help the father to reintergrate into the family and reduce the uncertainty of resuming the role of father if he were aware of the present developmental level of the child, including the child's needs, dislikes, and fears.

3. Divorce counseling. A number of inmates will grow emotionally apart from their families during their absence. It must be clear that marriage is not the answer for every black male inmate. Neither the wife nor the husband should have to remain married simply because the latter is incarcerated. In some cases, the separation may have been the final straw that helped to sever an already intolerable family situation. It is possible that maintaining an already emotionally depleted relationship may not be in the best interests of either the husband or the rest of the family.

There is a noticeable shortage of counseling programs that help black families and their incarcerated spouses during the period of separation. If black families are to be a positive influence in the inmates' lives and are to survive the negative effects of the removal of the breadwinner, and if black inmates are to obviate some of the adverse effects of the prison experience in order to make the transition to the family a smooth one, correctional programs must be focused on this population.

There are a number of other subgroups of black offenders that will be found in the criminal-justice system, including the elderly, the illiterate, and the mentally ill. Each subgroup, while sharing many similar problems as the larger group, will have its own set of unique needs and concerns. Mental-health professionals need to be sensitive to the heterogeneity within the black offender population.

Rehabilitation of Black Offenders

The question of whether mental-health professionals have really provided meaningful rehabilitation programs for black offenders remains largely unanswered. It is exceedingly difficult to analyze and measure accurately the effect that so-called rehabilitation efforts have had on black offenders. Indeed, many blacks feel that the results have not been encouraging. Some have questioned whether there has been a sincere and relevant rehabilitation effort. Some have even felt that programs so facilely referred to as rehabilitation programs were not designed to work, were implemented without an adequate understanding of blacks, or were sabotaged by incompetent or unscrupulous staff and administrators. However, the impression generally conveyed to the public is that these programs failed because blacks were generally incorrigible, too hard core, too unresponsive, or too disinterested to benefit.

Barnett (1975) suggests that, in order to differentiate the superficial programs from the rehabilitation programs designed to succeed, the following questions should be addressed:

1. Are the services designed to help poor black and other minorities compete equitably with the white majority?
2. Does the program attempt to deal with the interrelationship and interplay between mobility, cultural conflicts, economics, the labor market, racial, religious, and political differentiation as the basis for much of black criminal behavior?
3. Does the program consider the relationship between self-concept and the historical attempts of America to keep the black American in a position of second-class citizenship or lower self-esteem?

It is only when program planners begin to ask these kinds of questions about current rehabilitation for black offenders that relevant and responsive programs for blacks will become a reality—not before. So far these questions have not been asked or answered. If rehabilitation is to be successful, mental-health professionals must not offer the dead-end type of program that has not been shown to be effective and/or simply maintain the status quo. They must not operate within the criminal-justice system with narrow perspectives or goals—simply to use their skills to change the behavior of the offender. Rather, they must be prepared to evaluate and, if need be, alter the organizational structure that influences the mental health of black offenders and control their destiny.

Current studies indicate that less than 1 percent of the general black population will manifest behavior serious enough to be diagnosed as mentally ill. Blacks do have emotional problems, but the overwhelming majority of those manifesting aberrant or maladaptive behavior appear to be reacting to the stress and pressures associated with their socioeconomic and racial status in a class- and race-oriented society. High rates of substance abuse, hypertension, and even violent crimes are all symptomatic of a serious malady. The types of therapeutic and rehabilitative programs that will be of assistance to black offenders will be those that will first of all provide them with the skills and wisdom to face the unpleasant racial and economic realities of life, and second, help them successfully navigate through the complex social and political structure to actualize their full potentials.

In order to make a significant contribution to rehabilitation, mental-health professionals must make a commitment to get involved in the total life space of black offenders. They must determine their role in the criminal justice system and how they can best have an impact on influencing positive mental health throughout the system. Their services and programs must not be dictated by administrators who simply want to use them to maintain the status quo of the system.

Increased Representation of Black
Mental-Health Professionals

There is a critical shortage of black mental-health professionals at all levels in the criminal-justice systems. With a balance of black sensitivity and understanding and professional competence, they can provide invaluable services in all stages of the criminal-justice process. At the present time, only limited use has been made of their talents. For the trial of black activist Angela Davis black psychologists were called upon by the defense attorney to assist in the selection of jurors who would be sensitive to her. A black psychiatrist was involved in assessing the mental functioning level of Tommy Lee Hines, a black mental retardate accused of raping three white women in Alabama. In Atlanta, a black psychiatrist was called upon to eavesdrop on a telephone conversation between a black gunman, holding a female hostage, and the local police. He was asked to provide a psychological profile of the black gunman. A need still exists throughout the criminal justice process for blacks to become involved in the classification of offenders, staff training, and therapeutic programming.

With the reluctance of many black community members to cooperate with white researchers and the tendency to be suspicious of white mental health professionals, black professionals can provide a valuable linkage between the mental-health profession and black communities. They can work in black communities with more ease and access, and thereby facilitate services to ex-offenders, establish communication with family members, and conduct needed research.

Methods for increasing the numbers of black psychiatrists, psychologists, social workers, and counselors must be implemented. Recruitment efforts must be directed toward enlarging the pool of black candidates to be educated to work as mental-health professionals in criminal-justice settings.

Educational and training programs must assure that blacks receive the same exposure to the black experience as other students. It would be especially beneficial if the program allowed black students to gain a deeper appreciation and understanding of their biological and psychological roots so that they could successfully come to grips with their particular black concerns.

Just as much concern for keeping black mental-health professionals in the system must be expressed as there was in getting them in. There must be an awareness of the unique stresses and strains that blacks may experience, while working in a predominantly white-controlled and oppressive environment. In-service training and open discussions about racial concerns may be beneficial in eliminating the problems that may be potential contributors to a high attrition rate among black professionals.

However, there must not be an assumption that because a mental-health professional is black, he or she is automatically qualified to work with black offenders or that they want to. Black mental-health professionals are individuals with varied backgrounds and experiences. Some blacks may have very negative experiences with the black experience and feel much more comfortable interacting with nonblacks. It is important that black professionals be allowed access to all populations and a wide variety of experiences.

Conclusion

Mental-health professionals in criminal justice have the unique opportunity for a new beginning with black offenders. As of yet, they have not become so embedded in criminal justice settings that their roles have become completely cemented. This allows them the freedom to set up their own philosophical base and operating procedures and to challenge myths and negative stereotypes about black offenders that have historically influenced mental-health professionals and their assessments of, and interactions with, blacks.

There are a number of pressing concerns facing mental-health professionals. Issues such as the right to treatment, confidentiality, therapist responsibility, use of human and animal subjects in experimentation, licensing, and others are still very much in the forefront. While these issues affect both black and white offenders, the larger issue for blacks continues to be whether or not race will continue to be a factor in any decisions or interactions with mental-health professionals. It is only when those in the helping professions come face to face with this concern by blacks, and resolve it affirmatively, that mental-health services for black offenders will be relevant and mentally healthy for all concerned.

Appendix A
Commitment Workshop in Correctional Change: Schedule

Charles Owens and
Bill Chambers

Objectives

1. To assist participants to understand the dynamics of the criminal-justice system.
2. To commit participants to an acceptable and realistic change objective.
3. To follow up for evaluation purposes the attainment or lack of attainment of the stated changed targets.

Materials

1. A two-part questionnaire which will collect demographic data and have questions designed to assess the degree of commitment that an individual has to changing the criminal-justice system. This will be administered pre and post with only the second part related to commitment being taken after the workshop is completed.
2. Questionnaire to be used in discussion groups related to the amount of knowledge the individual has about the criminal-justice system.
3. Contract format—to be used to assist the individuals or group to state succinctly what they intend to do and to be used as part of the follow-up evaluation (approximately six months) to see if the contracts were followed through.

Workshop Schedule

9:00-9:30 A.M.	Overview of the criminal-justice system; national, state, and local.
9:30-10:00 A.M.	Subgroups responding to questionnaires on facts regarding the state and local system which will later be presented.
10:00-10:45 A.M.	Information on recidivism, cost, philosophy about the state and local criminal justice system.
10:45-11:00 A.M.	Coffee break.
11:00-noon	Overview of groups, organizations, individuals, and types of activities which individuals can become involved with

147

or can initiate. Inclusion of state resource book and any slides or films to familiarize the workshop participants with these possibilities.

noon-1:00 P.M.   Lunch.

1:00-2:00 P.M.   Workshop groups based on interest areas which have evolved from the 11:00-12:00 session or for a group that fits in the "I don't know" category. Groups will discuss possible courses of action: What interests me? What could I do in my area? How do I implement what interests me? How much time or money or people will this take? Leader will circulate and facilitate these discussions in any way possible.

3:00-4:00 P.M.   Completion and signing of the contracts after presentation of some alternative models.

Commitment Workshop: Questionnaire

Part I

Demographic Data

1. Mark the following statements in relation to contact you have had with the criminal-justice system (CJS).

    A. Check the parts of the system with which you have had contact:

    Public Police _____ Judges _____ Guards _____ Private Police _____ (Sec. guards, etc.)

    Probation Officers _____ Parole Officers _____ Sheriffs or Deputies _____

    District Attorneys _____ Public Defenders _____ Juries _____ Parole

    Boards _____ Juvenile Delinquents _____ Truant Staff _____ FBI _____

    Corrections Officials _____ None _____

    B. Type of contact with the criminal-justice system:

    As a member of any of the components of the criminal justice system _____, please indicate which part(s) of the CJS _____.

    As a personal friend to anyone who is in the CJS _____, please indicate which part(s) _____.

    As a client of the CJS _____, please indicate which part(s) of the CJS _____.

    As a relative or close friend of anyone who has been a client in the CJS _____, please indicate which part(s) of the CJS _____.

    C. Do you currently hold any strong opinions related to any part of the CJS? Mark below which direction these opinions go and in relation to what part of the CJS.

    Positive _____

    Negative _____

    Indicate which area(s) of the CJS _____

    _____

2. In one or two sentences would you try to summarize your reason for coming to this workshop?

3. We would like to have the following demographic information on you. How-
    ever, we certainly do not intend to pry and please feel free to respond only
    to those questions which you would not mind us analyzing group data for.

    A. Your occupation _____

    B. Your socioeconomic level _____

    C. Married _____ Single _____ Widowed _____ Divorced _____

    D. Age _____

    E. Educational Level _____

    F. Amount of hours per week or per month which you might consider
        yourself to have available to work on some criminal justice project
        in any of many related areas such education, legislation, group develop-
        ment, personal contacts with criminal justice clients, writing letters
        or editorials, participation in the development of filmstrips or film
        series, or other areas which might occur to you that are not listed here.

        Time: _____ Area: _____

        I do not know whether I would be interested in any of these particular
        areas and have not thought of any areas of my own at this time, but I

        believe I would _____, would not _____ want to explore the pos-
        sibility of involvement further.

4. Would you indicate on the scale of 1 to 5 below the degree of activism you
    have demonstrated in the past in relation to public or social issues you have
    been interested in. This could include the organization of a garden club, the
    membership chairman for your church, serving as a member of the board
    in any of your religious affiliations, initiating or participating in writing
    campaigns, actively working for the election of a politician, actively seeking
    to change legislation in some area that concerned you, etc.

1	2	3	4	5
Totally inactive		Moderately active		Totally active

Part II

Check whichever is appropriate Pre Workshop _____ Post Workshop _____

The following questions ask you to make an assessment of yourself at this point
and time. The questions are for the workshop leaders' purposes in analyzing data
regarding the usefulness of these workshops and are to be treated anonymously.
We hope that you will feel free to give us your honest and candid responses in
relation to yourself to assist us in assessing the value of the workshop as it currently is, and ways in which we might change it to be more beneficial.

1. At this point in time, which of the following statements would be most descriptive of how you see yourself in relation to this workshop?

    _____ A. I am here because I am curious about what a workshop of this nature might be all about.

    _____ B. I am here for the purpose of becoming more informed about the CJS.

    _____ C. I am here for the purpose of finding some active way to become involved in the CJS.

    _____ D. I think there are a lot of things wrong with different parts of the CJS and I came because I want to find ways to change these.

    _____ E. I am already involved in actively working towards change in some areas of the CJS and I want to find ways to become involved in other areas of it.

    _____ F. I am already involved in working towards change in some aspect of the CJS and I hope to find other people at this workshop to work with me in these areas.

    _____ G. None of the above is particularly true of me. It would be more

    accurate to say _____

    _____

2. At this point in time, the following would be the most true for me:

    _____ A. I desire more information on the following part(s) of the CJS

    _____

    _____

    _____ B. I am curious about the effects of some types of programs related to the CJS, but would like to hear about them primarily as a concerned citizen rather than getting involved with them.

    _____ C. I am curious about what my involvement in some aspect of the CJS would lead to, but am not prepared at this point to make a commitment to becoming involved in that.

    _____ D. I am prepared to become involved with some aspect of the CJS from a supportive standpoint, but not in terms of trying to change

    it. Which part(s) of the CJS _____

    _____

3. Please mark the degree of commitment you have to becoming involved in the CJS on the line before

1	2	3	4	5
I wish to stay uninvolved		I wish to become more involved than I have been		I am committed to becoming very involved

Commitment Workshop: Contract Format

I. Contracts are hard to make and we are not trying to get you to commit yourself to something which you have not thought out well for yourself at this point; however, we would like to present a couple of models for you and, if you desire at this time, we would like to write contracts with you. If you are not prepared to do that but think that you might want to after you have had some time to think it over during the days to come, we would like you to discuss the contracts with us in our subgroups so that you may later be better able to write your contract and send it to us then.

Example A: Contract with BRACELETS

I commit myself to joining BRACELETS and wearing my prisoner's bracelet so that I can have the opportunity to explain to my friends and contacts what BRACELETS is all about and what I am learning from it. I realize that this contract means I am committing myself to writing to some inmate who is inside the prison and it will allow me an opportunity to become more personally acquainted through correspondence with a client who is at the extreme end of the punishment spectrum in the CJS. I realize that it may also allow me to become better acquainted with that aspect of the system and more knowledgeable when I am talking to friends or to legislators or when it comes to voting on legislation which may pertain to CJS.

Example B

I have become interested in court monitoring and commit myself to seeking the involvement of other members of my community in setting up a court monitoring process for our judges who deal with juvenile delinquency cases. I realize that this will take a lot of organizational effort on my part as well as a fair amount of time to insure that those people who join with me do their monitoring and learn what they need to know to be monitors and that I will also want to participate in some monitoring and a little further training on what monitoring is all about myself.

II. **Open-ended Contracts**

As the above two examples help point out, a closed and specific contract sometimes is very precise and very demanding. Neither of these necessarily has to be true to feel like you have made a contract to be doing something. The following are designed to serve as examples only for what an open contract might be like.

Example A

I have become interested in what a detention home for juveniles is like and enjoyed the preliminary information which I received during the workshop related to these. I think I would be interested in joining with other members of our workshop and gaining more information about what it would entail to set up one of these in our community and how to go about doing so. During the next six months, I propose to have gotten myself or the group I join to become well enough informed for myself and others to either initiate the action necessary to start such a home or to encourage the people we would deem appropriate to do such.

Example B

The only thing I am sure of right now is that I am interested in becoming more involved in becoming knowledgeable about (or in doing something about) the CJS. At this point I am more than willing to commit myself to have taken some active steps toward becoming more knowledgeable (or becoming more involved) in the CJS, and I am confident that I will have done so in the next six months.

III. We are not interested in trying to pin anyone down to a specific type of format which they might be uncomfortable with or which they might not see a very valid reason for. If you were not stimulated by the types of contract forms or statements in I and II, we have provided the following space for you to make any kind of statement which would seem to you more reasonable than making the contract statements which we have indicated above or discussed in our groups.

IV. If you have adopted a contract somewhat similar to those which are in I or II and have committed yourself to achieving that contract within the next six months, we would like to offer you a suggestion which you could use as continued stimulation or motivation in accomplishing your contract. This idea falls into a category which we have called Penalty Clauses, similar to the types of clauses that one might read in a business contract or to the types of clauses that a student goes into with a teacher that he'll perform a certain kind of homework and get a certain kind of grade, etc. At this point in time, we are still exploring how it might be best to use Penalty Clauses, so the examples which we give should be considered rather naive, and we would certainly want you to choose clauses of your own and state them in the kinds of terms which would make sense to you.

Example A

I had anticipated that I would have time to become more involved than I realized that I had after the workshop. In my particular case, often I do

not have the time to do something but I do have the money to help somebody else do something. Since I have not achieved my contract, I am

making an award of $_____ (or _____ materials/goods)

to _____ organization so that they may further the
efforts which I had intended to further myself but found myself unable to.

Example B

I had intended to come to the meetings which our subgroup formed for
the initiation of a detention home in our community, but found that I

could not schedule the time to do so. I therefore pledge $_____

(or _____ materials/goods or _____ individual time)
to the detention center to facilitate the objectives which have been accomplished by others even though I was unable to participate with them.

Example C

At the close of the workshop six months ago, I had anticipated that I
would get quite involved because at that time there seemed to be a lot of
excitement in the air and a commitment at that time was easier for me to
make than I later learned it was to carry out. This has been a new realization for me and I have agreed with myself to help other people I know
to be more realistic in their commitments of themselves in terms of time
and activities and am now prepared to assist others in being a personal
spokesman at the next workshop you hold in my area.

Example D

Here is a Penalty Clause that I thought of which is not really related to me
but which you might be able to use as an example in your next workshop.

We have enjoyed being with you and working with you today. Regardless of the
kinds of contracts we have, we feel like we have learned from this experience
and we hope that you have. Thank you.

Appendix B
Letters

February 1974

Inmate #1

Dear Mr. X,

We were really pleased to hear from you and to know that you have decided to correspond further with us. This last week has been extremely busy, with the conference, so we didn't have a chance to write you until today. Anyway, we hope to write more promptly from now on, and we're sorry for the delay.

The conference was a huge success and there were such prominent people here as Grover Bell, Dorothy Williams, and Sister Patricia. As a result of the conference, a national committee was organized to keep communications open about blacks in the criminal justice system. A future conference was also talked about, and it seems that the university is fast becoming a center for disseminating information about prisoners of all minority groups. So all in all, things went very well. Dr. Owens has much reason to be pleased with all his efforts.

We appreciate your answering all of our questions—we have more, if you wouldn't mind answering them, too! First of all, what did you mean by "Jeff." in your last letter? Do you have a cell by yourself? What kind of "group action" meetings do you participate in, and are you fairly free to say whatever you want during them? In your letter, you talked about guards being "racist" and "sadistic." Can you give us some examples, and finally, could you explain more about your situation in segregation, and why exactly the board won't recommend your release to the general population? Does your case come up at each review meeting? Thank you for being so patient in answering all of our questions. It really does give us a better understanding of how you're having to live right now. Two women from the Link's Society spoke to our class last week and painted a similar picture about prison life.

We were sorry to hear that you weren't able to be more successful in communicating with your brother. You are right, unfortunately, it does seem that people who become addicted to drugs become submerged in their own world and no longer respond to others who do not share in this world.

We're enclosing clippings from the *Montgomery Advertiser* about the prison riots. We hope you'll read them, if you haven't already, and be able to share them with others.

We'll try to answer any questions you have for us, too—even tough ones like the query about our being "class bound." In reply, we have no strict rules of procedure to follow. We won't lie and say we are going to quit school and become a member of a militant organization. It is our hope that contact with you and others in your position can keep us in touch with the real world. But more importantly, our correspondence will hopefully make us get up and do something for others.

Again, we want to thank you for continuing to write to us. We'd just like you to know that if it is agreeable with you, we'd like to continue writing even after school is over for the semester. So for now, take care. We look forward to hearing from you again.

Yours in Unity,

Carol
Noel
Rosemary

March 1974

Dear Students,

This letter is drastically overdue, so I won't waste anymore time with excuses for tardiness, since none would vindicate my procrastination or speed up this matter. I'll try to answer your questions.

First of all my definition of "Jeff" is a flattery subservient mode of behavior. Something very similar to the dim-witted foot-shuffling, eye-rolling and head-scratching character Stepin Fetchit, Amos n' Andy and Aunt Bessie & Sue. A lot of white people expect for black people to be carbon copies of those characters nowadays. Yes Sir, no Ma'am, as long as they are white regardless of age. I am sure yall can envision what I mean when I said Jeff now. This cringing manner of behavior grew out of the repressive and brutal punishment of slavery, the slaves concocted a way to con and cajole the master from punishing them and get something he desired from his Master.

The "group action" that I participate in is Center around basic and political education, since we were all either deprived of an education or taught wrong our fundamental aims and objectives are to rectify this by relating to an education relative to our particular conditions and circumstances and formulate a viable way to change this order.

I'm never free, not even fairly free to say what I want to, however, I take the liberty to express Myself at all time at my own risk. If, I worry about rules and regulations or being beaten from what I say, I'd never open my mouth. I asserted that the guards were racist particularly because of the racial discrimination they practice against black inmates, sadistic because of the pathological euphoria they get from their action which often entails violence and virulent verbal abuse.

For example, black inmates are always assigned to the most sordid and hardest of jobs, they are given disciplinaries for little or no reason.

A more vivid example Tommy Dotson, After he had been subdued by the guards to allegedly attacked the warden a mob came in and lynched him, not because he killed a correctional officer but rather because he killed a white man. Tommy Dotson's and George Dobbins' death can best be defined as ethnocentric revenge. How sadistic and macabre does it seem if I say Tommy Dotson had handcuffs on his wrist at the time they killed him. And the guard strutted around with pick handles and baseball bats with blood on them as though they were Medal of honors!!!

I was really glad to receive the articles from the *Montgomery Advertiser*, Nonetheless, I had read the paper, the *Mobile Press'* report of the incident but it was divorced from the truth—a caricature!

There is much to be ascertained from this correspondence, I agree to continue.

Toward a more human way of life

                                                        Inmate X

Inmate #2

                                              2-74

Greetings,

I'll start by formally introducing myself as Mister Y. Because of procrastination on my Behalf, I'm going right to the HEART of actual issues!

From relating back to adolescent by way of reminisce & analytical research using "BIGGER THOMAS" of "NATIVE SON" to assist in this venture. We're both, characterized to some extent by the same type environment, altho, BIGGER goes through conscious repression where as I'm more familiar with unconscious states of it—I say this because the degrees in mentality that we differ in until its inevitable he was not to the low grades of illiteracy that played more of a primary role in causing my early age fate to turn out the way it did (Speaking of Reality & Prison). And now that I'm more in compatibility with reading, writing, & understanding, I see the necessity when it comes to this tactic for gaining the actual wisdom to really eradicate theses moral Pretexts that refuse to give the Poor Peoples as a class the chance to prove WE'RE of Humanity!!!

As for growing-up in Alabama—I don't really Plan to elaborate on this part of my characteristic—or Past History for long because of my constantly

leaving Ala. for short eras, and this started at a very young age & really, I feel
that time, condition, & knowledge that I was seeking never allow me to get
a good look at these's authentic states of ghetto—I hope it doesn't appear as
evasive along this sector of our correspondence—it's merely an opinion of
whether "You", PREFER fascination or actuality! — The more I heard older
Brother's rap about their miraculous life at my age the more I tried to emulate,
them, so if'n this is what "You" want, then You've got my acquiesce.

Ive, been here (PRISON) 20 mth's Parole month is/or should I say was
this month. (I haven't heard anymore on it) I can't choose where I want to
DIE! BEING this is where they Kill Peoples who favor changes! — I was dead
Before I was born! AND EVERYTHING I RECEIVE HERE INCLUDING
LETTER'S IS CENSORED!

I would like to know more about your classification, and I can always
use certain facts about different Alabama RECORD'S OR REPORTS,

Your's CORDIALLY,

P.S. Disregard all mistakes and all marks for I'm ENDEAVOR STUDYING
TRING TO BETTER MY EDUCATIONAL LEVEL'S

March 28, 1974

Dear Mr. Y:

The prisons, especially Atmore, have been in the news quite a bit recently.
There have been reports of stabbings of guards and of inmates. There probably
is a lot more that hasn't been reported. Could you tell us what the situation
is like? It must be tense, because a few state politicians are clamoring for a
new law regarding the death penalty. Even today I read in the newspaper that
Pennsylvania passed a new death penalty law. This type of thinking seems so
backward and illogical as to be ridiculous. The basic premise of these politicians
seem to be that these prisons are smoldering because the prisoners are treated
too kindly and humanely. No one has ever rebelled against too much kindness
and understanding. It is obvious therefore that prisoners are rebelling against
the racist nature of the prison system and the repression carried out behind
the walls. Still some people on the outside are calling for new and greater repres-
sions. That is the major problem hindering attempts at prison reform. People
on the outside have to be made aware that the many acts of cruelty inherent
in the prison system and those carried out by ignorant officials are done in
their name. If judges would spend even one week behind bars they would
probably be inclined to give more probation and suspended sentences.

Some of the other groups corresponding with prisoners in Dr. Owens class were criticizing the fact that the prison officials refuse to allocate any money for the black religions such as the Muslim faith. In fact the officials refuse to give any encouragement to this black movement. There has not been much information about black religions in Alabama prisons so could you send us a little information. These movements are really strong in the California prisons and in other Northern systems. If you have read the *Autobiography of Malcolm X* it shows how the Muslim religion completely changed his life. He changed from a jive hustler to become one of the most eloquent spokesmen for black unity. By hindering attempts for blacks to have their own religion officials are tacitly admitting that they are afraid of enlightened and eloquent black men.

Hope that you have been able to read Angela Davis' book. This book was the best and most appealing one we've read. Its great appeal came from the fact that it was written entirely by prisoners and former prisoners. These are the people that really know what is happening in America's prisons. Also her concept of the "political prisoner" is straightforward and logical. She is right that there are no wealthy people in prison, and therefore the prison systems are products of an unequal distribution of wealth. Have you given any thought to this idea and how valid do you think it is? It seems that she is right and can understand the blatant hatred and racism between white inmates and black inmates as purposely done in order to divide the inmate population. Do you think that there is any way to get the prisoners united to press for prison reform?

What do you think about the SLA and the kidnapping of Patricia Hearst? Their motives seem entirely political as opposed to ordinary kidnappings. The trouble is that any use of violence in an attempt at social reform makes too many enemies to be effective. The repressive institutions such as the prisons, courts, and police line up solidly against the proposals instead of analyzing them logically as solutions. No one should have to be kidnapped in order for poor families to have food. That is the real tragedy, that it takes so much just to get people to correct wrongs done to poor people.

Any opinions you have on this issue and on the broader issue of initiating social reform would be appreciated.

Sincerely,

Michael
David
Morris

References

Introduction

Baxstrom v. *Herold*, 383, U.S. 107, 1966.

Edward L. McNeil v. *Director of Patuxent Institution*, U.S. Supreme Court, No. 71-5144, Oct. 1971.

President's Commission on Mental Health. Task Panel Report of Black Americans, vol. 3. Washington: Government Printing Office, 1978, pp. 820-873.

Rouse v. *Cameron*. 373, F. 2d 451 (D.C. Cir., 1966).

Chapter 1
Victims of Justice

Abrahamsen, D. *The Murdering Mind*. New York: Harper & Row, 1973.

Attica: The Official Report of the New York State Special Commission on Attica. New York: Praeger Publishers, 1972.

Bainfield, E.C. *The Unheavenly City*. Boston: Little, Brown, 1968.

Barlett, Donald, and Steele, James B. "Crime and Injustice," *Philadelphia Inquirer*, Feb. 18, 1973.

Barnes, Harry E., and Teeters, Negley K. *New Horizons in Criminology*, 2nd ed. Englewood Cliffs, N.J.: Prentice-Hall, 1952.

Bayley, David H., and Mendelsohn, Harold. *Minorities and the Police*. New York: Free Press, 1969.

Baxstrom v. *Herold*, 383, U.S. 107, 1966.

Berman, L. *New Creations in Human Beings*. New York: Doubleday, 1938, pp. 248-249.

Bonger, William. *Criminality and Economic Conditions*. Bloomington: Indiana Univ. Press, 1963.

Brodsky, S. *Psychologists in the Criminal Justice System*. Chicago: Univ. of Illinois Press, 1973.

Bullock, Henry A. "Significance of the Racial Factor in the Length of Prison Sentences," in *Crime and Justice in Society*, ed. R. Quinney. Boston: Little, Brown, 1969.

Chrisman, Robert. "Black Prisoners, White Law," *Black Scholar*, April-May 1971, pp. 44-46.

Clark, Ramsey. *Crime in America*. New York: Simon & Schuster, 1970.

Cloward, Richard, and Ohlin, Lloyd. *Delinquency and Opportunity*. New York: The Free Press, 1960.

Coffey, A.; Eldefonso, E.; and Hartinger, W. *An Introduction to the Criminal Justice System and Process*. Englewood Cliffs, N.J.: Prentice-Hall, 1974.

Dahrendorf, Ralf. "Out of Utopia: Toward a Reconstruction of Sociological Analysis," *American Journal of Sociology*, Sept. 1958, pp. 115-137.

Davis, Angela. *If They Come in the Morning*. New York: Signet Books, 1971.

Davis, J.A. "Justification for No Obligation: Views of Black Males Toward Crime and the Criminal Law," *Issues in Criminology* 9 (1974):69-86.

Dollard, J.; Doob, L.; Miller, N.; Mowrer, O.H.; and Sear, R.R. *Frustration and Aggression*. New Haven, Conn.: Yale Univ. Press, 1965.

Dubois, W.E.B., ed. *Some Notes on Negro Crime, Particularly in Georgia*. Atlanta Univ. Publication #9. Atlanta: Atlanta Univ. Press, 1904.

Fanon, Frantz. *The Wretched of the Earth*. New York: Grove Press, 1965.

Franklin, J.C. "Discriminative Value and Patterns of the Wechsler-Bellevue Scales in the Examination of Delinquent Negro Boys." *Educational Psychological Measurement* 5 (1945):71-85.

Geis, G. "Statistics Concerning Race and Crime," in *Crime, Criminology and Contemporary Society*, ed. Richard Knudten. Homewood, Ill.: Dorsey Press, 1970, pp. 27-33.

Goddard, H.H. *Feeblemindedness: Its Causes and Consequences*. New York: Macmillan, 1914.

Goring, C. *The English Convict: A Statistical Study*. London: His Majesty's Stationery Office, 1913.

Grier, W.H., and Cobbs, P.M. *Black Rage*. New York: Basic Books, 1968.

Haley, Alex. *The Autobiography of Malcolm X*. New York: Grove Press, 1965.

Halsted, D.K. *The Relationship of Selected Characteristics of Juveniles to Definitions of Delinquency*. Ed.D. diss., Univ. of Michigan, 1967.

Hooten, E.A. *Crime and the Man*. Cambridge, Mass.: Harvard Univ. Press, 1931.

Johnson, G.B. "The Negro and Crime," in *The Sociology of Crime and Deliquency*, ed. M. Wolfgang. New York: Wiley & Sons, 1970, pp. 419-429.

Kretschmer, E. *Physique and Character*. New York: Harcourt, Brace, 1925.

Lange, J. *Crime and Destiny*. New York: Charles Boni, 1939.

Lenihan, K.J. "The Financial Condition of Released Prisoners," *Crime and Delinquency*, July 1975, pp. 266-281.

Letkemann, P. *Crime as Work*. Englewood Cliffs, N.J.: Prentice-Hall, 1973.

Lombroso, C. *Crime: Its Causes and Remedies*, trans. H.P. Horton. Boston: Little, Brown, 1912.

Marx, K., and Engels, F. *Selected Works*. London: Lawrence and Wishart, 1965.

McKay, Robert. *Attica: The McKay Report*. New York: Bantam Books, 1972.

McNeil v. *Director of Patuxent Institution*. U.S. Supreme Court, No. 71-5144, Oct. 1971.

Merton, R.K. *Social Theory and Social Structure*, rev. ed. New York: Free Press, 1957.

Miller, W.B. "Lower-class Culture as a Generating Milieu of Gang Delinquency," *Journal of Social Issues* 15 (1958):5-19.

Nagel, S. "The Tipped Scales of Justice." *Trans Action*, May-June 1966, pp. 3-9.

Overby, A. "Discrimination in the Administration of Justice," in *Race, Crime and Justice*, ed. E. Reasons and J. Kuykendall. Pacific Palisades, Calif.: Goodyear Publishing, 1972, pp. 264-276.

Owen, E.R. "The 47 XYY Male: A Review," *Psychological Bulletin* 78 (1972): 209-233.

Piliavin, I., and Briar, S. "Police Encounters with Juveniles," *American Journal of Sociology* 70(1964): 206-214.

President's Commission on Law Enforcement and Administration of Justice. *The Challenge of Crime in a Free Society*. Washington: Government Printing Office, 1967.

Reckless, W.C. *The Crime Problem*. New York: Appleton-Century-Crofts, 1967.

Rouse v. *Cameron*, 373, F. 2d 451, (D.C. Cir., 1966).

Sheldon, W.H. *The Varieties of Temperament*. New York: Harbor, 1942.

Sutherland, E. "Differential Association," in *Edwin Sutherland: On Analyzing Crime*, ed. Karl Schuessler. Chicago: Univ. of Chicago Press, 1973.

Taft, Donald. *Criminology*. New York: Macmillan, 1956.

Terry, Robert M. "The Screening of Juvenile Offenders," *Journal of Criminal Law, Criminology and Police Science*, June 1967, pp. 173-181.

Turk, A.T. "Conflict and Criminality," *American Sociological Review* 31 (1966):338-352.

Watts, F.P. "A Comparative Clinical Study of Delinquent and Non-delinquent Negro Boys." *Journal of Negro Education* 10 (1941): 190-207.

Wicker, T. "The Men in D Yard." *Esquire Magazine*, March 1975, p. 59.

Williams, Daniel. *The Lynching Records at Tuskagee Institute*. Tuskagee, Alabama: Tuskagee Institute Archives, 1969.

Wolfgang, M. *Patterns in Criminal Homicide*. Philadelphia: Univ. of Pennsylvania Press, 1958.

Wolfgang, M. and Cohen, B. *Crime and Race: Conceptions and Misconceptions.* New York: Institute of Human Relations Press, 1970.

Yaker, H.M. "The Black Muslim in the Correctional Institution," *Welfare Reporter* (Trenton) 13 (1962): 158-165.

Yochelson, S., and Samenow, S.E. *The Criminal Personality: A Profile for Change*. New York: Jason Avonson, 1976.

Recommended Readings

"Black on Black Crime," *Ebony Magazine*, special issue, Aug. 1979.

Fanon, Frantz. *A Dying Colonialism*. New York: Grove Press, 1965.

Newman, D.J. *Introduction to Criminal Justice*. Philadelphia: J.B. Lippincott, 1975.

Owens, C.E., and Bell, J. *Blacks and Criminal Justice*. Lexington, Mass.: Lexington Books, D.C. Heath and Company, 1977.

Poussaint, A. *Why Blacks Kill Blacks.* New York: Emerson Hall, 1972.

Chapter 2
Black Offenders: Psychopathology and Mental Health

Beto, D.R., and Claghorn, J.L. "Factors Associated with Self-Mutilation Within the Texas Department of Corrections," *American Journal of Corrections* 30 (1968): 25-27.

Brodsky, S. *Psychologists in the Criminal Justice System*. Chicago: Univ. of Illinois Press, 1973.

Bromberg, W., and Thompson, C.B. "The Relation of Psychosis, Mental Defect, and Personality to Crime," *Journal of Criminal Law* 28 (1937):70-89.

Butler, Keith. "The Muslims Are No Longer an Unknown Quantity," *Corrections Magazine*, June 1978, pp. 55-63.

Caplan, N., and Nelson, S.D. "On Being Useful: The Nature and Consequences of Psychological Research on Social Problems," *American Psychologist* 8 (1973):195-211.

Carpozi, G., Jr. *Son of Sam: The 44-Caliber Killer*. New York: Manor Books, 1977.

Cleaver, E. *Soul on Ice*. New York: McGraw-Hill, 1968.

"Competency to Stand Trial and Mental Illness," *Crime and Delinquency Issues: A Monograph Series*. Rockville, Md.: National Institute of Mental Health, 1973.

Cooke, G.; Pogancy, E.; and Johnston, N.G. "A Comparison of Blacks and Whites Committed for Evaluation of Competency to Stand Trial of Criminal Charges," *Journal of Psychiatry and Law* 2 (1974):319-337.

Cooper, S. "A Look at the Effect of Racism on Clinical Work," *Social Casework* 54:2 (1973):76-84.

Costello, R.M. "Item Level Racial Differences of the MMPI," *Journal of Social Psychology* 91 (1973):161-162.

Cross, H., and Tracy, J. "Personality Factors in Delinquent Boys: Differences between Blacks and Whites," *Journal of Research in Crime and Delinquency* 8 (1971):10-22.

Danto, B.L. *Jail House Blues*. Orchard Lake, Mich.: Epic Publications, 1973.

Erlich, A., and Abraham-Magdamo, F. "Caution: Mental Health May Be Hazardous," *Psychology Today*, Sept. 1974, pp. 64-70.

Fisher, J. "Negroes and Whites and Rate of Mental Illness: Reconsideration of a Myth," *Psychiatry* 32 (1969):428-446.

Fried, M. "Social Differences in Mental Health," in *Poverty and Health: A Sociological Analysis*, ed. John Kosa, Aaron Antonovsky, and Irving Kenneth Zola. Cambridge, Mass.: Harvard Univ. Press, 1969, pp. 113-167.

Grier, W., and Cobbs, P. *Black Rage*. New York: Basic Books, 1968.

Gross, H.S.; Herbert, M.R.; Knaterud, G.L.; and Donner, L. "The Effects of Race and Sex on the Variation of Diagnosis and Disposition in a Psychiatric Emergency Room," *Journal of Nervous and Mental Disease* 148 (1969): 638-642.

Gunnings, T.S., and Simpkins, G.A. "A Systemic Approach to Counseling Disadvantaged Youth," *Journal of Non-White Concerns in Personnel and Guidance* 1 (1972):4-8.

Gunnings, T.S., and Tucker, R.N. "Counseling and Urban Americans: A Search for New Forms," *Journal of Non-White Concerns in Personnel and Guidance* 5 (1977):153-163.

Guze, S.B. *Criminality and Psychiatric Disorders*. New York: Oxford Univ. Press, 1976.

Hall, W.S.; Cross, W.E., Jr.; and Freedle, R. "Stages in the Development of Black Awareness: An Exploratory Investigation," in *Black Psychology*, ed. R.L. Jones. New York: Harper & Row, 1972, pp. 156-165.

Halleck, S. *Psychiatry and the Dilemmas of Crime.* New York: Harper & Row, 1967.

Harper, F. "The Impact of Alcohol on Crime in the Black Community," in *Crime in the Black Community*, ed. Lawrence E. Gary and Lee Brown. Washington, D.C.: Institute for Urban Affairs and Research, Howard Univ., 1976, pp. 77-84.

Hinsie, L., and Campbell, R.J. *Psychiatric Dictionary*, 4th ed. New York: Oxford Univ. Press, 1970.

Hollingshead, A.B., and Redlich, F.C. *Social Class and Mental Illness: A Community Study*. New York: Wiley, 1958.

Johnson, R. *Culture and Crisis in Confinement*. Lexington, Mass.: Lexington Books, D.C. Heath and Company, 1976.

Jones, D. *The Health Risks of Imprisonment*. Lexington, Mass.: Lexington Books, D.C. Heath and Company, 1976.

Jones, R.E., ed. *Black Psychology*. New York: Harper & Row, 1972.

Leavy, M.R. "The Mentally Ill Criminal Defendant," *Criminal Law Bulletin* 9 (1973):197-252.

Lefcourt, H.M., and Ladwig, G.L. "Alienation in Negro and White Reformatory Inmates," *Journal of Social Psychology* 68 (1966):153-157.

Lewis, O. *The Children of Sanchez*. New York: Random House, 1961.

———. "A Puerto Rico Boy," in *Culture Change, Mental Health and Poverty*, ed. J.C. Finney. New York: Simon and Schuster, 1969.

London, N., and Myers, J.K. "Young Offenders: Psychopathology and Social Factors," *Archives of General Psychiatry* 4 (1961):274-282.

Malzberg, B. "Mental Disease among Negroes," in *Mental Health and Segregation*, ed. Martin Grossack. New York: Springer Publishing, 1963, pp. 158-160.

McGlynn, R.; Megas, J.C.; and Benson, D.H. "Sex and Race as Factors Affecting the Attribution of Insanity in a Murder Trial," *Journal of Psychology* 93 (1976):93-99.

McLean, H.V. "The Emotional Health of Negroes," in *Mental Health and Segregation*, ed. Martin Grossack. New York: Springer Publishing, 1963, pp. 131-138.

Nash, J.R. *Bloodletters and Badmen*, book 2 abridged. New York: Warner Paperback Library, 1975.

National Institute of Mental Health, Division of Biometry and Epidemiology. "Diagnostic Distribution of Admissions to Inpatient Services of State and County Mental Hospitals, U.S., 1975," *Mental Health Statistical Note, No. 138*. Washington: Government Printing Office, 1972.

Pasamanick, B. "A Survey of Mental Disease in an Urban Population," in *Mental Health and Segregation*, ed. Martin Grossack. New York: Springer Publishing, 1963, pp. 150-157.

Perls, Frederick. "Four Lectures," in *Gestalt Therapy Now*, ed. J. Fagan and I.L. Shepherd. New York: Harper & Row, 1970, pp. 14-38.

Pettigrew, T.A. *Profile of the Negro American*, Princeton, N.J.: D. Van Nostrand, 1964.

Prange, A.J., and Vitols, M.M. "Cultural Aspects of the Relatively Low Incidence of Depression in Southern Negroes," *International Journal of Social Psychiatry* 8 (1962):104-112.

President's Commission on Mental Health. Task Panel Report of Black Americans, vol. 3. Washington: Government Printing Office, 1978, pp. 820-873.

Schleifer, C.B., and Derbyshire, R.L. "Clinical Changes in Jail-Referred Mental Patients," *Archives of General Psychiatry* 18 (1966):153-157.

See, J. "Insanity Proceedings and Black-White State Hospital Admission Rate Difference," *International Journal of Social Psychiatry* (London) 21 (1975):220-228.

Silverman, D. "Psychotic Criminals: Study of 500 Cases," *Journal of Clinical Psychopathology* 8 (1946):301-327.

Simon, R.J. *The Jury and the Defense of Insanity*. Boston: Little, Brown, 1967.

Singer, B.D. "Some Implications of Differential Psychiatric Treatment of Negro and White Patients," *Social Science and Medicine* 1 (1967):77-83

Srole, L.; Langner, T.S.; Michael, S.T.; Opler, M.K.; and Rennie, T.A.C. *Mental Health in the Metropolis: The Midtown Manhattan Study*. New York: McGraw-Hill, 1962.

Staples, R. *Introduction to Black Sociology*. New York: McGraw-Hill, 1976.

Steadman, H.J., and Cocozza, J.J. *Careers of the Criminally Insane*. Lexington, Mass.: Lexington Books, D.C. Heath and Company, 1979.

Stone, A.S. *Mental Health and Law: A System of Transition*. Rockville, Md.: National Institute of Mental Health, 1975.

Szasz, T. *Law, Liberty and Psychiatry*. New York: Macmillan, 1963.

_____. *The Myth of Mental Illness*. New York: Hoeber, 1961.

Terry, R.M. "Discrimination in the Handling of Juvenile Offenders by Social Agencies," *Journal of Research in Crime and Delinquency* 4 (1967):218-230.

Thomas, A., and Sillen, S. *Racism and Psychiatry*. New York: Brunner/Mazel Publishers, 1972.

Thomas, C. *Boys No More*. Beverly Hills: Glencoe Press, 1971.

Thomas, C. "Different Strokes for Different Folks," *Psychology Today* 4 (1970):48-53, 78-80.

Thornton, J.C. *Behavior Modification: The Road to Genocide.* Chicago: Independent Publishers, 1977.

U.S. Bureau of the Census. *Current Population Reports,* series p-23, no. 69. Washington: Government Printing Office, June 1978.

U.S. Dept. of Justice. *Crime in the United States, 1974.* Washington: Government Printing Office, 1975.

Wholey, C.C. "Psychiatric Report of Study of Psychopathic Inmates of a Penitentiary," *Journal of Criminal Law and Criminology* 28 (1937):52-69.

Wilson, D.C., and Lantz, E.M. "Culture Change and Negro State Admissions," in *Mental Health and Segregation*, ed. Martin Grossack. New York: Springer Publishing, 1963, pp. 139-149.

Woodburg, R. "Delinquent's Attitudes toward the Juvenile Justice System," *Psychological Reports*, June 1973, pp. 11-1124.

Wooden, K. *Weeping in the Playtime of Others.* New York: McGraw-Hill, 1976.

Recommended Readings

Grossack, M.M., ed. *Issues in Mental Health: Selected Conference Papers.* Atlanta: Southern Regional Educational Board, Apr. 1978.

_____. *Mental Health and Segregation.* New York: Springer Publishing, 1963.

Kosa, J.A. Antonovsky, and Zola, I.K. *Poverty and Health: A Sociological Analysis.* Cambridge, Mass.: Harvard Univ. Press, 1969.

Chapter 3
The Black Experience Behind Bars

Barnes, H.E., and Teeters, N.K. *New Horizons in Criminology*, 2nd ed. Englewood Cliffs, N.J.: Prentice-Hall, 1952.

Braginsky, B.; Braginsky, D.; and Ring, K. *Methods of Madness: The Mental Hospital as a Last Resort.* New York: Holt, Rinehart and Winston, 1969.

Carroll, L. "Race and Sexual Assault in a Maximum Security Prison." Paper presented at the Society for the Social Problems Meeting, Montreal, Canada, 1974. Copies available from author: Univ. of Rhode Island, Kingston, R.I. 02881.

Carter, J.H., and Jordan, B.M. "Inpatient Therapy for Black Paranoid Men," *Hospital and Community Psychiatry*, June 1972, p. 182.

Davis, A.J. "Sexual Assault in the Philadelphia Prison System and Sheriff's Vans," *Transaction* 6:2 (1968):8-16.

_____. "Sexual Assaults in the Philadelphia Prison System," in *The Sexual Scene*, ed. J.H. Cagnon and W. Simon. New Brunswick, N.J.: Transaction Books, 1973, pp. 219-236.

Frankl, V.E. *Man's Search for Meaning*. Boston: Beacon Press, 1962.

Gettinger, S. "Cruel and Unusual Prisons," *Corrections Magazine*, Dec. 1977, pp. 3-16.

Jonsen, A.R.; Parker, M.L.; Carlson, R.J.; and Emmott, C.B. "Biomedical Experimentation on Prisoners: Review of Practices and Problems and Proposal of a New Regulatory Approach." Discussion paper presented at the Health Policy Program, School of Medicine, Univ. of California, San Francisco, Sept. 1975.

Maslow, A.H. *Toward a Psychology of Being*. Princeton, N.J.: Van Nostrand, 1968.

Nacci, Peter L. "Sexual Assault in Prisons," *American Journal of Corrections,* Jan.-Feb. 1978, p. 30.

Pugh v. *Locke*, 406 F. Supp. 318-335 (M.D. Ala., 1976).

Sykes, G.M., and Messinger, S.L. "Inmate Social System," in *The Criminal in Confinement*, vol.3, ed. L. Radzinowicz and M. Wolfgang. New York: Basic Books, 1971.

U.S. Dept. of Justice. *Crime in the United States: Uniform Crime Reports, 1972*. Washington: Government Printing Office, 1972.

Wicks, R.J. *Correctional Psychology*. San Francisco: Canfield Press, 1974.

Zimbardo, Philip; Haney, Craig; Banks, W. Curtis; and Jaffe, David. "The Stanford Prison Experiment: A Simulation Study of Imprisonment." Slide presentation at Stanford University, Calif. 1971.

Recommended Readings

Atkins, B.M., and Glick, H.R. *Prisons, Protest and Politics*. Englewood Cliffs, N.J.: Prentice-Hall, 1972.

Fogel, David. *. . . We Are the Living Proof. . . The Justice Model for Corrections*. Cincinnati: W.H. Anderson, 1975.

Frankl, Victor E. *Psychotherapy and Existentialism*. New York: Washington Square Press, 1967.

Haney, C., Banks, C., and Zimbardo, P. "Interpersonal Dynamics in a Simulated Prison." *International Journal of Criminology and Penology*, (1973):69-97.

Scacco, Anthony. *Rape in Prison*. Springfield, Fla.: Charles C. Thomas, 1975.

Sykes, Gresham. *The Society of Captives: A Study of Maximum Security Prisons*. Princeton, N.J.: Princeton Univ. Press, 1959.

Chapter 4
Classification and Assessment

Alabama v. *Thomas L. Hines*, cc 78-0-340H, 1978.

"An Armed Man and a Woman Seek Baby of 20 Years Ago," *Washington Post*, Feb. 12, 1977, p. B6.

Barnes, H.E., and Teeters, N.K. *New Horizons in Criminology*, 2nd ed. Englewood Cliffs, N.J.: Prentice-Hall, 1952.

"Black, 'Mad at All Whites,' Holds Officer, Clerk Hostage," *Cincinnati Enquirer*, Mar. 8, 1977, p. A7.

Carter, D.T. *Scottsboro*. New York: Oxford Univ. Press. 1973.

Castro v. *Beecher*, 365 F Supp. 655 (Massachusetts) U.S. District Court, D. Massachusetts, May 7, 1973.

Center for Correctional Psychology. *Minimum Health Standards for the Alabama Correctional System*. Tuscaloosa: Dept. of Psychology, Univ. of Alabama, 1972.

Coleman, J.S., et al. *Equality of Educational Opportunity*. Washington: U.S. Dept. of Health, Education and Welfare, 1966.

Davison, G.C., and Neale, J.M. *Abnormal Psychology: An Experimental Clinical Approach*. New York: John Wiley & Sons, 1974.

Elion, V.H., and Megargee, E.I. "Validity of the MMPI PD Scale among Black Males," *Journal of Consulting and Clinical Psychology* 43 (1975):166-172.

Goddard, H.H. *Feeblemindedness: Its Causes and Consequences*. New York: Macmillan, 1914.

Griggs v. *Duke Power Co.*, 401, U.S. 424 (1971).

Gynther, M.D. "White Norms and Black MMPIs: A Prescription for Discrimination," *Psychological Bulletin* 78 (1972):386-402.

Gynther, M.D., Fowler, R.D., and Erdberg, P. "False Positives Galore: The Application of Standard MMPI Criteria to a Rural, Isolated, Negro Sample, *Journal of Clinical Psychology* 27 (1971):234-237.

Hathaway, S.R., and McKinley, J.C. "A Multiphasic Personality Schedule (Minnesota): I. Construction of the Schedule," *Journal of Psychology* 10 (1940): 249-254.

Jensen, A.R. "How Much Can We Boost IQ and Scholastic Achievement?" *Harvard Educational Review* 39 (1969): 1-123.

Kozol, H., Boucher, R., and Garofalo, R. "Dangerousness," *Crime and Delinquency* 19 (1973):554-555.

_____. "The Diagnosis and Treatment of Dangerousness," *Crime and Delinquency* 18 (1972):371-392.

Larry P. v. *Wilson Riles*, 502 F. 2d 963 (9th Cir. 1974); F. Supp. (N.D. California, 1979).

Levinson, R.M., and York, M.A. "The Attribution of 'Dangerousness' in Mental Health Evaluations," *Journal of Health and Social Behavior* 15 (1974): 328-335.

McKay, Robert. *Attica: The McKay Report*. New York: Bantam Books, 1972.

Megargee, E. "The Prediction of Dangerous Behavior," *Criminal Justice and Behavior* no. 3 (1976):1-23.

Megargee, E.; Bonn, M.; Meyer, J.; and Sink, F. *Classifying Criminal Offenders: A New System Based on the MMPI*. Beverly Hills, Calif.: Sage Publications, Inc., 1979.

Mercer, Jane. "IQ: The Lethal Label," *Psychology Today*, Apr. 1972, pp. 44-47.

Monahan, J. "The Prevention of Violence," in *Community Mental Health and the Criminal Justice System*, ed. J. Monahan. New York: Pergamon, 1976.

Morrow v. *Chrysler*, 3 EDP. 7563 (S.D. Miss. 1971).

Nash, J.R. *Bloodletters and Badmen*, book 1, abridged. New York: Warner Paperback Library, 1975.

_____. *Bloodletters and Badmen*, book 2, abridged. New York: Warner Paperback Library, 1975.

_____. *Bloodletters and Badmen*, book 3, abridged. New York: Warner Paperback Library, 1975.

People v. *Craig*, No. 41750, Superior Court, Alameda County, Calif., 1968.

Peoples, E. "The Dynamics of I-Level Interviewing," in *Readings in Correctional Casework and Counseling*, ed. E. Peoples. Santa Monica, California: Goodyear Publishing Co., Inc., 1975.

Quay, H. and Parsons, L. *The Differential Behavioral Classification of the Juvenile Offender*. U.S. Bureau of Prisons, 1970.

Ridgeway, J.R. "Who's Fit to Be Free?" *New Republic* 156 (1967):24-26.

Rosenthal, R., and Jacobson, L. *Pygmalion in the Classroom: Teacher Expectation and Pupil's Intellectual Development*. New York: Holt, Rinehart & Winston, 1968.

Rouse v. *Cameron*, 373 F 2d 451 (D.C. Cir. 1966).

Samuda, R.J. *Psychological Testing of American Minorities: Issues and Consequences*. New York: Dodd, Mead, 1975.

Santamour, M., and West, B. *The Mentally Retarded Offenders and Corrections*. Washington: National Institute of Law Enforcement & Criminal Justice, 1977.

Singer, B.D. "Some Implications of Differential Psychiatric Treatment of Negro and White Patients," *Social Science and Medicine* 1 (1967):77-83.

Smith, R., and Giles, J.V. *An American Rape: A True Account of the Giles-Johnson Case*. Washington, D.C.: New Republic Books, 1975.

Steadman, H.J., and Cocozza, J.J. *Careers of the Criminally Insane*. Lexington, Mass.: Lexington Books, D.C. Heath and Company, 1979.

Stoffels, K., and Fauber, J. "Psychiatrist Slain in Her Office; Patient Held," *Milwaukee Sentinel*, June 22, 1979, p. 1.

Stone, A.A. *Mental Health and Law: A System of Transition*. Rockville, Md.: National Institute of Mental Health, 1975.

Thomas, A., and Sillen, S. *Racism and Psychiatry*. New York: Brumer/Mazel Publishers, 1972.

Trigg v. *Ray Blanton et al.* (No. A-6047; Chancery Court for Davidson Co., Tenn.), Aug. 23, 1978.

U.S. Dept. of Justice. *Sourcebook of Criminal Justice Statistics-1978*. Washington: Superintendent of Documents, 1978, pp. 464 and 485.

Vold, G.B. *Theoretical Criminology*. New York: Oxford Univ. Press, 1958.

Wallace, C. "Roxanne's Story Bruised Feminist Cause," *Philadelphia Daily News*, Mar. 10, 1978, p. 12.

References 171

References 171

Warren, M. "Classification as an Aid to Efficient Management and Effective Treatment," *Journal of Criminal Law, Criminology and Police Science* 62 (1971):239-258.

Wenk, E.; Robinson, J.; and Smith, G. "Can Violence Be Predicted?" *Crime and Delinquency* 18 (1972):393-402.

Whitehurst, K. "Assessment Strategies and Techniques for Black Clients," *Issues in Mental Health*. Atlanta: Southern Regional Education Board, April, 1978.

Wicks, R.J. *Correctional Psychology*. San Francisco: Canfield Press, 1974.

Williams, Daniel. *The Lynching Records at Tuskagee Institute*. Tuskagee, Alabama & Tuskagee Institute Archives, 1969.

Williams, Robert L. "Abuses and Misuses in Testing Black Children," in *Black Psychology*. ed. Reginald L. Jones. New York: Harper & Row, 1972, pp. 77-91.

Wooden, K. *Weeping in the Playtime of Others*. New York: McGraw-Hill, 1976.

Recommended Readings

Gerard, R. "Classification by Behavioral Categories and Its Implications for Differential Treatment," in *Correctional Classification and Treatment*, ed. Leonard Hippchen.

Handbook on Community Corrections in Des Moines, Iowa: A Coordinated Approach to the Handling of Adult Offenders, An Exemplary Project. Washington: U.S. Dept. of Justice, LEAA, 1968.

Hippchen, Leonard, ed. *Correctional Classification and Treatment*. Cincinnati: W.H. Anderson, 1975.

Owens, C.E. "A Psycho-social Analysis of Black Hostage Holders," in *Final Report of the Fourth Annual Conference of the National Association of Blacks in Criminal Justice*. Atlanta, Ga., 1977, pp. 143-154.

Schwitzgebel, Ralph K. "Development and Legal Regulation of Coercing Behavior Modification Technique with Offenders," *Crime and Deliquency Issues*. Rockville, Md.: National Institute of Mental Health, 1972.

Warren, M. "Correctional Treatment and Coercion: The Differential Effectiveness Perspective," *Criminal Justice and Behavior* 4 (1977):355-376.

Wexler, David B. *Criminal Commitments and Dangerous Mental Patients: Legal Issues of Confinement, Treatment and Release*. Rockville, Md.: National Institute of Mental Health, 1976.

Chapter 5
Therapeutic Intervention

Bailey, W.C. "Correctional Outcomes: An Evaluation of 100 Reports," *Journal of Criminal Law, Criminology and Police Science* 57 no. 2 (1966):153-160.

Banks, G.B. Berenson B., and Carkhuff, R. "The Effects of Counselor Race and Training upon Counseling with Negro Clients in Initial Interviews," *Journal of Clinical Psychology* 23 (1967):70-72.

Brill, N.Q., and Sorrow, H.A. "Social Class and Psychiatric Treatment," *Archives of General Psychiatry* 3 (1960):344.

Carkhuff, R., and Pierce, R. "Differential Effects of Therapist Race and Social Class upon Patient Depth of Self-Exploration in the Initial Clinical Interview," *Journal of Consulting Psychology* 31 (1967):632-634.

Carlson, N. "Statement of Norman A. Carlson, Director, Federal Bureau of Prisons Before the U.S. Senate Committee on the Judiciary." Washington: U.S. Dept. of Justice, Aug. 2, 1978.

Deberry, C. "Psychological Treatment of Black Inner-City Inmates in a Maximum Security Facility." Paper presented to National Institute of Law Enforcement and Criminal Justice, Symposium on Blacks in Criminal Justice, date unknown.

Ellis, A. *Humanistic Psychotherapy: The Rational-Emotive Approach.* New York: Julian Press, 1973.

Eysenck, H.J. "The Effects of Psychotherapy: An Evaluation," *Journal of Consulting Psychology* 16 (1952):319-324.

Franks, C.M. *Behavior Therapy: Appraisal and Status.* New York: McGraw-Hill, 1969.

Freud, S. *A General Introduction to Psycho-Analysis.* New York: Simon and Schuster, 1935.

George, G.O. "An Empirical Case Study of the Systematic Desensitization of Stuttering Behavior," in *The Crumbling Walls: Treatment & Counseling of Prisoners*, ed. Ray E. Hosford and C. Scott Moss. Urbana: Univ. of Illinois Press, 1975, pp. 105-120.

Glaser, W. *Reality Therapy: A New Approach to Psychiatry.* New York: Harper & Row, 1975.

Jones, E. "Psychotherapists Shortchange the Poor" *Psychology Today*, April, 1975, pp. 24-26.

Jones, M. *Beyond the Therapeutic Community: Social Learning and Social Psychiatry.* New Haven: Yale University Press, 1968.

Jones, R., ed. *Black Psychology.* New York: Harper & Row, 1972.

Lazarus, A. *Behavior Therapy and Beyond.* New York: McGraw-Hill, 1971.

Leavy, M.R. "The Mentally Ill Criminal Defendant," *Criminal Law Bulletin* 9 (1973):197-252.

McCary, J. *Six Approaches to Psychotherapy.* New York: Dryden Press, 1955.

Menninger, K. *Theory of Psychoanalytic Techniques.* New York: Harper & Row, 1958.

Miller, B., and Tresserman, T. "Blue Collar Patients at a Psychoanalytic Clinic," *Journal of Psychiatry* 131 (1974): 261-265.

Miller, K.S., and Dreger, R.M., eds. *Comparative Studies of Blacks and Whites in the United States.* New York: Seminar Press, 1973.

Monahan, J. *Community Mental Health and the Criminal Justice System.* New York: Pergamon Press, 1976.

Phillips, E.L. *Psychotherapy: A Modern Theory and Practice.* Englewood Cliffs, N.J.: Prentice-Hall, 1956.

Redfering, D.L. "Differential Effects of Group Counseling with Black and White Female Delinquents: One Year Later," *Journal of Negro Education* 10 (1976):530-542.

Rogers, C. *On Becoming a Person.* Boston: Houghton Mifflin, 1961.

Rosenthal, D., and Frank, J. "Fate of Psychiatric Clinic Outpatients Assigned to Psychotherapy," *Journal of Nervous and Mental Diseases* 127 (1958):36-42.

Rothman, D. "Decarcerating Prisoners & Patients," *Civil Liberties Review,* Fall 1973, pp. 24-28.

Schwitzgebel, R.K. "The Right to Effective Mental Treatment," *California Law Review* 62 (1974):936-956.

Thornton, J.C. *Behavior Modification: The Road to Genocide.* Chicago: Independent Publishers, 1977.

"WA Prison Psychologist Relieved Because of Controversial Program," *Corrections Digest,* July 14, 1976, p. 5.

Wicks, R.J. *Correctional Psychology.* San Francisco: Canfield Press, 1974.

Yochelson, S., and Samenow, S.E. *The Criminal Personality: A Profile for Change.* New York: Jason Aronson, 1976.

Chapter 6
Preventing Black Crime

Amir, M. *Patterns in Forcible Rape.* Chicago: Univ. of Chicago Press, 1971.

Bard, M. "The Role of Law Enforcement in the Helping System," in *Community Mental Health and the Criminal Justice System,* ed. John Monahan. New York: Pergamon Press, 1976.

Billingsley, A. *Black Families in White America.* Englewood Cliffs, N.J.: Prentice-Hall, 1968.

Chambers, M.M. "Grapevine," Illinois State Univ. Dept. of Educational Administration and Foundations Newsletter 254, August 1979.

Clements, C. *Montgomery, Alabama, Police Department Final Report.* Montgomery, Ala.: Expanded School Relations Bureau, 1974.

Coleman, J.S., et al. *Equality of Educational Opportunity.* Washington: U.S. Dept. of Health, Education, and Welfare, 1966.

"Counseling for Victims of Crime," *Innovation: Highlights of Evolving Mental Health Services* 2 (1975): p. 2.

Haney, C., and Zimbardo, P.G. "Stimulus/Responses. The Blackboard Penitentiary—It's Tough to Tell a High School from a Prison," *Psychology Today,* June 1975, pp. 26-30.

Hughes, J.J. "Training Police Recruits for Service in the Urban Ghetto: A Social Worker's Approach," in *Community Mental Health and the Criminal Justice System,* ed. John Monahan. New York: Pergamon Press.

Moynihan, D.P. *The Negro Family: The Case for National Action.* Washington, D.C.: U.S. Dept. of Labor, Office of Planning and Research, 1965.

Palmer, S. *The Prevention of Crime.* New York: Behavioral Publications, 1973.

School Violence and Vandalism, hearings before the subcommittee of the committee on the judiciary, U.S. Senate, 94th Congress. Washington: Government Printing Office, Apr. 16 and June 17, 1975.

Seligman, M.E. "For Helplessness: Can We Immunize the Weak?" *Psychology Today,* June 1969, pp. 42-44.

Staples, R. "Race and Family Violence: The Internal Colonialism Perspective," in *Crime and Its Impact on the Black Community,* ed. L.E. Gary and L.P. Brown. Washington, D.C.: Howard Univ. Institute for Urban Affairs & Research, 1976.

Sutherland, E. "Differential Associations," in *Edwin Sutherland: On Analyzing Crime,* ed. Karl Schuessler. Chicago: Univ. of Chicago Press, 1973.

Swan, L.A. "Improving Police Relations in the Black Community," in *Blacks and Criminal Justice,* ed. Charles E. Owens and Jimmy Bell. Lexington, Mass.: Lexington Books, D.C. Heath and Company, 1977.

U.S. Department of Justice. *We Can Prevent Crime.* Office of Community Anti-Crime Programs. Washington, D.C. Government Printing Office, 1979.

Chapter 7
Mental-Health Professionals as Agents of Change

American Correctional Association, Committee on Personnel Standards and Training. *Correctional Officers Training Guide.* College Park, Md.: American Correctional Association, 1975.

Barnett, S. "Researching Black Justice: Descriptions and Implications," in *Blacks and Criminal Justice,* ed. Charles E. Owens and Jimmy Bell. Lexington, Mass.: Lexington Books, D.C. Heath and Company, 1977.

Brigham, J., and Weissbach, T., eds. *Racial Attitudes in America: Analysis and Findings of Social Psychology.* New York: Harper & Row, 1972.

Brodsky, S. *Psychologists in the Criminal Justice System.* Urbana: Univ. of Illinois Press, 1973.

Carlson, R.O. "Barriers to Change in Public Schools," in *Change Processes in the Public Schools.* Eugene, Ore.: The Center for the Advanced Study of Educational Administration, 1965, pp. 3-8.

"Coddling Myth, The," *New York Times,* Apr. 19, 1975, p. 6.

Cohen, E. "Interracial Interaction Disability," *Human Relations* 25 (1962):9-24.

Cohen, E., and Roper, S. "Modification of Interracial Interaction Disability," *American Sociological Review* 37 (1972):643-647.

Cotharin, R.L., and Mikulas, W.L. "Systematic Desensitization of Racial Emotional Responses," *Journal of Behavior Therapy and Experimental Psychiatry* 6 (1975):347-348.

Darnton, J. "Color Line a Key Police Problem," *New York Times*, Sept. 28, 1969, p. 1.

Delaney, P. "Race Friction Rising among Policemen," *New York Times*, Sept. 13, 1970, p. 86.

Hughes, J.J. "Training Police Recruits for Service in the Urban Ghetto: A Social Worker's Approach," in *Community Mental Health and the Criminal Justice System*, ed. John Monahan. New York: Pergamon Press, 1976.

Interpersonal Relations Workshop, Instructor's manual. Dallas, Tex.: U.S. Dept. of Justice, Federal Bureau of Prisons, 1975.

Irwin, J. *The Felon*. Englewood Cliffs, N.J.: Prentice-Hall, 1970.

"Judge Orders Reintegration, Single Cells." *Clearinghouse on Georgia Prisons and Jails*. Atlanta, Ga.: ACLU Foundation, January, 1979, p. 1.

Katz, I., and Benjamin, L. "Effects of White Authoritarianism in Biracial Work Groups," *Journal of Abnormal and Social Psychology* 61 (1960):448-556.

Katz, I.; Goldston, J.; and Benjamin, L. "Behavior and Productivity in Biracial Work Groups," *Human Relations* 11 (1958):123-141.

Lazarus, A. "Group Therapy of Phobic Disorders by Systematic Desensitization," *Journal of Abnormal and Social Psychology* 63 (1961): 504-510.

McCarter, N.; Colwick, J.; and Goodwin, A. "Mental Health Intervention in a County Jail," Tuscaloosa, Al.: Indian Rivers Mental Health Center. Mimeographed paper, 1978.

Owens, C.E. "New Directions in Corrections," in *Crime and Its Impact on the Black Community*, ed. Lawrence E. Gary and Lee P. Brown. Washington, D.C.: Howard Univ. Institute for Urban Affairs and Research, 1976, pp. 177-194.

President's Commission on Mental Health. Task Panel Report of Black Americans, vol. 3. Washington: Government Printing Office, 1978, pp. 820-873.

Questions and Answers on Human Rights and the Counselor. Washington, D.C.: American Personnel and Guidance Associations, 1969.

Smith, A., and Bierdeman, J. "Combating Institutional Racism," *Innovations*, Fall 1976, p. 37.

Stadsklev, Ron. *Handbook of Simulation Gaming in Social Education*. Tuscaloosa: Institute of Higher Education Research and Services, Univ. of Alabama, 1974.

Williams, J.; Tucker, R.; and Dunham, F. "Changes in the Connotations of Color Names Among Negroes and Caucasians," *Journal of Personality and Social Psychology* 19 (1971): 222-228.

Winslow, R. "Police Treatment of Juveniles," in *Juvenile Delinquency in a Free Society*, ed. Robert Winslow. Belmont, California: Dickenson Publisher, 1968, pp. 84-112.

Wittmer, J.; Lanier, J.E.; and Parker, M. "Race Relations Training with Correctional Officers," *Personnel and Guidance Journal*, Feb. 1976, pp. 302-306.

Chapter 8
Black Mental-Health Professionals

Chishom, A. "Conflicts of Black Correctional Workers," in *Blacks and the Criminal Justice System*, ed. Charles E. Owens, report 26, the Sixth Alabama Symposium on Justice and the Behavioral Sciences, pp. 55-65. Tuscaloosa: Univ. of Alabama Center for Correctional Psychology, 1974.
Jones, F. "The Black Psychologist as Consultant and Therapist," in *Black Psychologist,* ed. Reginald Jones. New York: Harper & Row, 1972, pp. 363-374.
President's Commission on Mental Health. Task Panel Report of Black Americans, vol. 3. Washington, D.C.: Government Printing Office, 1978, pp. 820-873.
"Profile/Massachusetts," *Corrections Magazine.* November, 1975, pp. 41-48.
Hollingshead, A.B. and Redlich, F.C. *Social Class and Mental Illness: A Community Study.* New York: Wiley, 1958.
Sattler, J.M. "Racial Experimenter Effects," in *Comparative Studies of Blacks and Whites in the United States.* New York: Seminar Press, 1973, pp. 8-28.

Recommended Readings

Smith, P.N., Jr. "Black Psychologist as a Change Agent in the Black Community," *Journal of Black Studies* 5 (1973):41-51.
Vontress, C.E. "Cultural Barriers in the Counseling Relationship," *Personnel and Guidance Journal* 48 (1968):11-17.

Chapter 9
Moving Away From Dead Center: The Challenge

Barnett, S. "Finding Answers to Persistent Problems," paper presented at the Seventh Annual Symposium on Justice and the Behavioral Sciences, Univ. of Alabama, Center for Correctional Psychology, 1975.
Erickson, R.; Crow, W.; Zurcher, L.; and Connett, A. *Paroled but Not Free.* New York: Behavioral Publications, 1973.
Fields, S. "Mental Health and the Melting Pot," *Innovations*, Summer 1979, pp. 2-7.
Glaser, D. *The Effectiveness of a Prison and Parole System.* New York: Bobbs-Merrill, 1969.
Lenihan, K.J. "The Financial Condition of Released Prisoners," *Crime and Delinquency*, July 1975, pp. 266-281.
Santamour, M., and West, B. *The Mentally Retarded Offender and Corrections.* Washington: National Institute of Law Enforcement and Criminal Justice, Government Printing Office, 1977.

Staples, Robert. "Race and Family Violence: The Internal Colonialism Perspective," in *Crime and Its Impact on the Black Community*, ed. Lawrence E. Gary and Lee P. Brown. Washington, D.C.: Howard Univ. Institute for Urban Affairs and Research, 1976.

U.S. Dept. of Justice, Law Enforcement Assistance Administration. *Source of Criminal Justice Statistics, 1974.* Washington: Government Printing Office, 1975.

Survey of Inmates of Local Jails, advance report. Washington: Government Printing Office, 1974.

Index of Names

Mendelsohn, H., 6
Mercer, J., 64
Merton, R.K., 12
Messinger, S.L., 44
Michael, S.T., 22
Mikulas, W.L., 121
Miller, K.S., 77
Miller, N., 12
Miller, W.B., 12
Monahan, J., 70, 71, 78
Mowrer, O.H., 12
Moynihan, D.P., 95
Myers, J.K., 24

Nacci, P.L., 48
Nagel, S., 4, 7
Nash, J.R., 71
Neale, J.M., 69
Nelson, S.D., 30
Newman, D., 163

Ohlin, L., 12
Opler, M.K., 22
Overby, A., 4
Owen, E.R., 11
Owens, C.E., 116, 147, 163, 171

Palmer, S., 101
Parker, M., 122
Parker, M.L., 51
Parsons, L., 61
Pasamanick, B., 23
Peoples, E., 61
Perls, F., 41
Pettigrew, T., 32
Pierce, R., 77
Piliavin, I., 6
Poussaint, A., 163
Prange, A.J., 23
Prettyman, E.B., Jr., 78
Pogancy, E., 27

Quay, H., 61

Reckless, W.C., 13
Redfering, D.L., 79
Redlich, F.C., 22, 78
Rennie, T.A., 22

Ridgeway, J.R., 69
Ring, K., 54
Robinson, J., 70
Rogers, C., 87
Roper, S., 119
Rosenthal, R., 65
Rothman, D., 78

Samenow, S.E., 11, 82
Samuda, R.J., 64
Santamour, M., 65, 137–139
Sattler, J.M., 130
Scacco, A., 168
Schleifer, C.B., 24
Sear, R.R., 12
See, J., 27
Seligman, M.E., 98
Sheldon, W.H., 11
Sillen, S., 23, 67
Silverman, D., 24
Simon, R.J., 25
Singer, B.D., 23, 67
Smith, A., 123
Smith, G., 70
Smith, P.N., 176
Sorrow, H.A., 78
Srole, L., 22
Stadsklev, R., 125
Staples, R., 28, 95, 142
Steadman, H.J., 25, 27, 71
Steele, J.B., 7
Stoffels, K., 72
Stone, A.A., 73
Stone, A.S., 27
Sutherland, E., 12, 104
Swan, L.A., 100
Sykes, G., 44
Szasz, T., 27, 28, 87

Taft, D., 167
Teeters, N.K., 6, 59
Terry, R., 23
Thomas, A., 23, 67
Thomas, C., 32
Thompson, C.B., 23
Thornton, J.C., 24, 90
Tracy, J., 28
Tucker, R.N., 118
Turk, A.T., 12

Index of Subjects

professionals, 112–113; training
for the black experience, 135

Not guilty by reason of insanity, 24–27

Police, 6, 109, 123
Political prisoners, 14, 15
Prisons: *See* Correctional institutions
Psychoanalytic therapy, 11, 86–87
Psychological Abstracts, 16

Race relations: and biracial groups,
118–120; and offenders, 120–121;
in simulations and gaming, 123; and
training programs, 122–123
Racial self-acceptance, 31
Rape, 72, 130
Rational emotive therapy, 88–89
Reality therapy, 89
Rehabilitation, 144

Schools: and criminal-justice programs, 107–109; and delinquency,
103–106; and similarities to prisons,
104
Sociological theories of crime, 12
Stanford prison experiment, 46–44

Testing: issues in, 63–67; and IQ, 16,
61–67, 68, 137–139; personality,
62, 65, 68; programs, 61
Therapeutic community, 91–92
Theories of crime, 9–15
Therapy: effectiveness of, 77–79; in
correctional settings, 78; racial
concerns in, 82; resistance to, 81;
socioeconomic level and, 71; types
of, 86–92

Victims of crime, 102

About the Contributors

William M. Chambers is currently a practicing psychotherapist in Flint, Michigan. Dr. Chambers previously worked as a counselor with the Albuquerque Job Corps Center for Women and has served as a chief psychologist at the Minnesota State Reformatory for Men. He was involved with both the Center for Correctional Psychology and the Center for Student Mental Health.

Michael Leon Lindsey is currently a Psy.D. candidate in the psychology program at Hahnemann Medical College and Hospital. Mr. Lindsey has worked as a staff psychologist at the North Carolina Department of Corrections, as director of a residential program for emotionally disturbed children in Kentucky, and as a part-time instructor at various academic institutions. He has conducted individual and group therapy sessions. Mr. Lindsey is a member of the National Association of Blacks in Criminal Justice and the National Association of Black Psychologists.

About the Author

Charles E. Owens is an associate professor in the Psychology Department at the University of Alabama. He was coeditor (with Jimmy Bell) of *Blacks and Criminal Justice* (LexingtonBooks, 1977), which focused on the black experience in the criminal-justice system. Dr. Owens organized and administered conferences that led to the formation of the National Association of Blacks in Criminal Justice. He has worked with inmates in the Wisconsin prison system, and he assisted in organizing and implementing the Alabama Prison Classification Project in 1976. In addition, he has conducted both individual and group therapy sessions in a variety of settings.